UNDER CONSTRUCTION

UNDER
CONSTRUCTION

**THE GENDERING OF MODERNITY,
CLASS, AND CONSUMPTION IN
THE REPUBLIC OF KOREA**

Edited by
Laurel Kendall

University of Hawai'i Press
Honolulu

07 06 05 04 03 02   6 5 4 3 2 1

Library of Congress Catologing-in-Publication Data
Under construction : the gendering of modernity, class, and consumption
in the Republic of Korea / edited by Laurel Kendall.
    p. cm.
    Includes bibliographical references and index.
    ISBN 0–8248–2407–5 (cloth : alk. paper)—ISBN 0–8248–2488–1
    (pbk. : alk. paper)
    1. Sex role—Korea, South. 2. Masculinity—Korea, South.
3. Femininity—Korea, South. 4. Social classes—Korea, South.
5. Women—Korea, South—Social conditions. I. Kendall, Laurel.

HQ1075.5.K6 U53 2002
305.3'095195—dc21   2001028121

University of Hawai'i Press books are
printed on acid-free paper and meet the
guidelines for permanence and durability
of the Council on Library Resources.

Designed by Argosy
Printed by The Maple Vail Book Manufacturing Group

Contents

Preface and Acknowledgments

This is a volume about south Korean women and men in the 1990s, about the structures that define their lives, and about how they assume agency within these definitions. It is also about how women and men, of different ages and class positions, perceive themselves and each other. It is about how these women and men "do" masculinity and femininity in Korea at century's end. The chapters by Nancy Abelmann, Cho Haejoang, Roger L. Janelli, and Dawnhee Yim were initially written for a workshop on "Gender and Social Change in Late Twentieth-Century Korea," held at Columbia University in the spring of 1995 under the sponsorship of the Center for Korean Research with the support of the Korea Foundation, which has also subsidized the preparation of this manuscript. June J. H. Lee, So-Hee Lee, and Seungsook Moon also agreed to write chapters for this volume, broadening the scope of our discussion. The original papers were subsequently revised to take account of the I.M.F. (International Monetary Fund) crisis of 1997 and its impact on Korean social life. Chungmoo Choi, Eun-Shil Kim, Seung-kyung Kim, and Eun Mee Kim also participated in the initial workshop, and their thoughts and comments contributed to this final product. Ann Wright-Parsons, Senior Scientific Assistant in the Department of Anthropology, American Museum of Natural History, assisted in preparing the manuscript for publication.

This volume would not exist if Gari K. Ledyard had not proposed the initial workshop on the grounds that it was time the Center for Korean Research "did something about women." I am grateful to Samuel Kim and the Center's support of this project through its long gestation. Three anonymous reviewers from University of Hawai'i Press gave very good advice on how to strengthen the arguments presented in this volume.

The authors use McCune-Reischauer romanization for Korean terms except where alternative spellings are conventionally used in English-language writing on Korea (e.g., Seoul, Park Chung-hee) or where authors have established their own preferred name romanization. Korean names appear in Korean order—family name first, given name second—unless the subject has a published identity in Western order. Most of the Korean-born authors in this volume, such as So-Hee Lee, use Western order for this and other English-language publications, but Cho Haejoang's family-name-first preference is respected. While this lack of consistency may be initially confusing, it is indicative of the self-conscious effort and good faith required of all who engage in binational projects and traveling feminist dialogues.

INTRODUCTION

laurel kendall

> *It can be a creative adventure for modern men to build a palace, and yet a nightmare to have to live in it.*
> Marshall Berman, *All That Is Solid Melts into Air*, 1988

The title of this book is meant to be playful. "Under Construction" evokes the language of contemporary gender theory in its assertion that masculinities and femininities are perpetually constructed and reconstructed in the busy unfolding of histories (Butler 1993; Caplan 1987; de Lauretis 1987; Ortner 1996; Scott 1986). As a pun, "Under Construction" also evokes a palpable Korean condition. Since the late 1960s, the entire south Korean urbanscape has been quite literally under construction: torn down, rebuilt, extended, elaborated, reconfigured. Anyone who has lived in Korea in these years will have encountered that condition of modernity where, in Marshall Berman's apt citation of Marx, "all that is solid melts into air" (Berman 1988). Over the last three decades, lives have been refashioned on the shifting ground of urbanization, industrialization, military authoritarianism, democratic reform, and social liberalization. In this process, class and gender identities have been "construction sites" for new definitions of home and family, work and leisure, husband and wife. Construction metaphors come readily to mind when describing these experiences. In this volume, Cho Haejoang speaks of middle class wives who created a modern lifestyle that was as coarse and hastily fabricated as the Korean economy itself, and June Lee equates the ailing bodies of white-collar men with the disastrous rush-hour collapse of Seoul's Sŏngsu Bridge as parallel symbols of a flawed modernity.

The term "modernity" is invoked in these pages as a broadly recognizable view of the world that has been rendered into many different languages and read through many different historical moments. As an ideological position, modernity implies a receptivity to social and technological innovation and a repudiation of the past, perceived as stifling and irrational tradition. The objects of these valorizations, however, are not fixed but are fluid, variable, and sometimes contradictory (Baudrillard 1987; Rofel 1994, 1999; Kendall 1996, ch. 3 for Korea). As a cultural expression and ideological stance, "modernity" may be distinguished from "modernization," the measurable material processes of industrialization, technological innovation, expanding capitalist markets, and rapid urbanization. Modernities are the cultural articulations of modernizations as self-conscious experiences and discourses, judgments, and feelings about these experiences (Felski 1995, 12–15; Berman 1988, 16–18). A voluminous literature now documents, quantifies, and analyzes the process of Korean modernization. The living of Korean modernity is subtler stuff and has received far less attention.

In Korea, no less than anywhere else, modernities are gendered innately and consequently vary with the "multiplicity of diversity of women's (and men's) relations to historical processes" (Felski 1995; Rofel 1994). The modernity of a middle class Korean housewife is not identical to her white-collar husband's modernity, her mother's or her daughter's modernity, or the modernity that impinges upon the life of a woman worker in a south Korean electronics plant. We emphasize the different ways Korean women and men "did" modernity in the 1990s and how a *specifically Korean* experience of modernity and its postmodern discontents inscribes their diverse experiences of masculinity and femininity. Generational histories, ideologies, relationships of class, structures of employment, family obligations, and the fun-house mirror of media representations frame the subjectivities of the women and men described in chapters on middle class life, office and factory work, and sexual experimentation. At the same time, contemporary Korean understandings of gender and sexuality are realized within the global reach of popular culture, heightened consumption, and portable notions of "modernity" and "middle class" that have been described in other places, both Western and not (Miller 1994; 1995). We offer one more resounding counter-example to the homogenized presentations of "third world" or "non-Western" women that have prompted deserved critiques (Grewal and Kaplan 1994; Mohanty 1988; Ong 1988). This volume is part of a decisive turn in the anthropology of gender, from its early quest for the ultimate causes of female subordination to a fine-tuned analysis of the historical, cultural, and class-based specificities of gender relations (Moore 1988; Ortner 1996; Silverblatt 1991) and the tension between gender as an ideological construct and gender as a lived experience (Moore 1994, 58).

Berman (1988) defines modernism, the artistic expression of modernity, as a particular subjective act, as "any attempt by modern men and women to become subjects as well as objects of modernity, to get a grip on the modern world and make themselves at home in it" (p. 5). Broadly speaking, this struggle to "get a grip" engages all of the subjects of this volume, from the ambitious middle class housewives of Cho's and Abelmann's chapters to their sexually rebellious daughters, described by So-Hee Lee. Engagement is found in women office workers' mild resistance to a demeaning term of address (Janelli and Yim, ch. 5), among young men who actively reject the dominant notions and practices of masculinity as epitomized by corporate life (Seungsook Moon, ch. 4), and in the disgruntled ruminations of their elders (June Lee, ch. 3). For some of the subjects of these essays, and most of the authors, the prospect of making oneself at home in the modern has dissolved into the necessity of coming to terms with toppled certainties and tarnished optimism, of living with a condition of flux and contradiction that some would describe as postmodern (Jameson 1984). Others, Berman among them, would see doubt and uncertainty as the very stuff of modernity (Berman 1988, 9–10).

With some backward glances, this volume witnesses the particular turn that south Korean society made in the 1990s. From the 1960s through the 1980s, Korean life had been marked by rapid industrialization, tight political control, public discourses of hard work and personal sacrifice in the name of national development, and a rising climate of political dissent. It was also, despite intense political frustration, a period of optimism marked by a sense that things would get better because, by all visible markers of material life, things were palpably improving. Indeed, south Korea was judged a miracle of rapid economic development, marked in the 1980s by the nation's entry into the ranks of the Newly Developed Nations and celebrated in its hosting of the 1988 Olympics. The 1990s saw a return to civilian rule, a loosening of censorship and social control, and with global economic success, the emergence of a full-blown consumer culture. The broad-based Democracy Movement that had sparked the imagination of a generation receded, a victim of its own success. The militancy of the 1980s is recollected in Cho Haejoang's and So-Hee Lee's discussions of how the politicization of Korean university campuses gave women social ideals that now seem irrelevant to their younger siblings. So-Hee Lee suggests that changes in the social mood from campus militancy in the 1980s to a 1990s youth culture preoccupied with questions of self-realization and sexuality has meant that among younger Korean women, siblings separated by even a few years engage the world through very different expectations and desires. As Cho notes in her chapter, the second-wave Korean feminism of the 1980s was also a casualty of the affluent youth culture of the 1990s.

The men and women who are the subjects of these essays simultaneously celebrate and condemn the enhanced opportunity for consumption possibilities, from luxury apartments to plastic surgery. Chapters by Nancy Abelmann and June Lee describe how members of a successful middle class deride the materialism of the present moment, mustering nostalgia for what they remember as a time of common hardship and sacrifice. Disillusionment is very much in evidence. National campaigns to foster appreciation for the overworked and underappreciated male breadwinner mask anxieties about shrinking market competition and vanishing job security (June Lee and Seungsook Moon in this volume). These discourses have become even more intense since the Korean market crash in November 1997 because business failures and massive layoffs belie a progressive teleology and the government's capitulation to conditions imposed by the International Monetary Fund (I.M.F.) is read as a national humiliation. We witness the vertigo of a society that has come to question the social costs of its own swift success, posing its critiques and frustrations in gendered imagery: the avaricious middle class housewife, the alienated and ailing middle-aged father, the sexy young wife on the make.

But how valid is a study built on an image? How real are the gendered subjects of advertisements, films, and the popular press? Does a novel about youthful sexual experimentation or a television serial about an adulterous wife tell us anything about the behavior of young Korean women? Would the novels of Jaqueline Susann inform a Korean anthropologist about American life? Readers accustomed to apprehending modernization through the hard data of statistics and broad-based surveys will probably be uncomfortable with some of the material discussed in this volume. Modernities are the cultural expressions of complex industrial societies, and as such, modernities are most widely articulated through various forms of mass media: advertisements, films, popular literature, magazines, and television programs. People respond, not always predictably and never uniformly, to what they see and hear. In south Korea today, the media is a ubiquitous presence; it cannot be ignored in any wide-ranging discussion of contemporary Korean life. The issue is not in the verifiability of, say, a sensationalized survey published in a popular magazine or a semi-autobiographical novel. Indeed, June Lee goes to great lengths in her chapter to show how the supposedly hard data on middle-aged Korean men's "world's highest mortality" was, at best, a loose reading. As in Janice Radway's (1984) canny study of the romance novel or Beth Bailey's (1988) mapping of changing American courtship patterns through a reading of women's magazines, Cho Haejoang, June Lee, So-Hee Lee, and Seungsook Moon use the products of popular culture to tell us not so much what people do, but how they understand, articulate, and argue about social practice. The following chapters provide many added examples of how media portrayals raise possibilities, stoke anxieties, and engender new lexicons of behavior. Our authors, in their different ways, show a dialogic tension between the production and public reception of media-generated gender talk.

LEGACIES THAT ENGENDER: THE CHAEBŎL AND THE MILITARY

Being "modern" (*hyŏndaejŏk*) has engaged Korean women and men for several generations. The colonial cities of early twentieth-century Korea (1910–1945), with their businesses, department stores, schools, and cinemas, introduced new social practices into the domains of work, education, and consumption (Eckert 1990, ch. 15; Robinson 1994). In this volume, Cho suggests a more insidious legacy in the "feudalistic authoritarianism" that permeated the modern efficiencies of the Japanese Empire, leaving genealogical traces in the structure of postcolonial Korean education, police, business, the military, and in the mass mobilization campaigns of the Park Chung-hee era (1961–1979). The conditions of work and domesticity that frame the lives described in these pages were even more immediately a product of the Republic of Korea's history after the Liberation in 1945. The imposed division of Korea by occupying Russian and American armies, the subsequent solidification of two hostile states through the fratricidal tragedy of the Korean War (1950–1953), and global Cold War security interests made the U.S.-supported military a major force in south Korean life. Seungsook Moon has described how the shadow of a hostile north Korea across the Demilitarized Zone provided a rationale for three decades of authoritarian rule by military men in civilian dress and allowed the influence of the military to shape vast domains of everyday experience in south Korean life (Moon 1998a, b, and in this volume).[1]

Some analysts of south Korean development emphasize the positive consequences of military mobilization, suggesting that the army prepared rural men for proletarian life, that it "taught them time orientation and subjugation to formal authority" (Koo 1990, 677). (It might also be noted that in the 1960s and 1970s, the subordination of daughters within the Korean family was deemed sufficient preparation for the discipline of the factory [S. Kim 1997].) Military service is a nearly universal passage rite for Korean men, a necessary marker of adult masculinity (Moon in this volume), and a unifying experience evoked by men who have little else in common than a nostalgic taste for certain songs and re-creations of military cuisine (Nelson 1996, 13). In "The Production and Subversion of Hegemonic Masculinity: Reconfiguring Gender Hierarchy in Contemporary South Korea," Seungsook Moon argues that universal conscription naturalizes masculine privilege. Having defended the nation from the omnipresent threat of attack by the Democratic People's Republic of Korea (north Korea), men are considered "true citizens," a status that few Korean women attain. The state bestows upon men the status of legally recognized heads of domestic units as well as granting them other privileges, including assigning them a higher starting rank in public sector employment (Moon, ch. 4). Men who passed their military service as officers are hired into some private corporations largely on the recommendation of their commanding officers (Janelli and Yim in this volume). Gender asymmetry is manifest in many domains of social practice, from the significant underrepresentation of women in all branches of government to the difficulties that women face when they apply for passports because their loyalty is more suspect than that of former soldiers (Moon 1998b, and in this volume; Soh 1991).

Many of the distinctive hierarchical and disciplined practices of Korean *chaebŏl,* the conglomerates that have dominated the Korean economic landscape for the last several decades, take the military as an unacknowledged model (Janelli with Yim 1993). While it is widely believed that military service leads to subsequent business success (Moon in this volume), and at least one published first-person account makes this link explicit, many young workers have found it disappointing that company life is so similar to that of the military (Roger Janelli, personal communication, 30 December, 1998). The term "*kunsa munhwa*" (military culture) is invoked to criticize the extension of essentially military practices into other domains of social life (ibid.).

The *chaebŏl* are the products of a dynamic alliance between capitalist interests and the state, which favored them with low-interest loans in specific industries and controlled labor unrest, allowing the *chaebŏl* to grow at phenomenal rates.[2] Not only do the *chaebŏl* employ a significant segment of all Korean labor, management, and clerical workers, but, owing to their early success, the *chaebŏl's* organizational structure was widely emulated by small and medium-sized enterprises (E. Kim 1997). The *chaebŏl* have thus had a profound influence on the gendering of work and domesticity and on the construction of new social classes. By fostering a large managerial class, the *chaebŏl* created a dominant image of clean, respectable middle class employment (Moon 1990). By requiring long working days followed by long evenings of work-related socializing, the *chaebŏl* also set the terms for a middle class lifestyle that rigidly dichotomized work from domesticity and the male salary earner from his wife and family. The consolidation of work space by the *chaebŏl* into corporate centers separated from most employees' residences by a long commute reinforces this sense of separation and compounds the difficulty of combining work with domestic tasks. Mary Brinton and her colleagues found that in Taiwan, which shares many cultural assumptions with Korea and Japan but where government policies have encouraged smaller enterprises, businesses are scattered through the landscape closer to employees' residences, and far greater numbers of married women work (Brinton, Lee, and Parish 1995). Thus, while Korea would seem to replicate Japanese middle class life (Imamura 1987; Vogel 1968), the exclusion of married women from the workplace is not an inevitable product of East Asian or "Confucian" gender assumptions but a consequence of specific economic policies that receive traditionalist rationalization after the fact.

Patterns of doing business and socializing within the *chaebŏl* (often difficult to distinguish) reinforce the notion that managerial work is a masculine activity. Accounts of *chaebŏl* life describe the critical importance of group carousing, sometimes combined with varying degrees of sex play, as a means of building solidarity among coworkers, and at the higher levels, for furthering business deals and gaining the good will of government officials (Janelli with Yim 1993; Janelli and Yim in this volume; Shin 1991; Yi 1993, 1998). One of Hei-soo Shin's (1991, 141) businessman informants summarized the strategy behind these encounters: "Drinks make all men become friends, especially when they get naked and sleep with women." With the marked expansion of the Korean economy in the late 1970s and through the 1980s, the entertainment industry grew at a phenomenal rate, fostering a distinctive style of work-related play that encouraged many white-collar men to come home only to sleep (Shin 1991; Kim 1998; Yi 1993). The wife of a middle-aged manager told June Lee (in this volume) that if, in the long years of her marriage, her husband came home before midnight and sober, she marked it on the calendar. For his part, her husband saw his work, both sober and intoxicated, as dedicated to the important task of Korean development.

Okpyo Moon finds a metaphoric equivalence between the white-collar employee and the scholar-official of dynastic times who attained his position in the world of public affairs through a series of competitive examinations and slowly advanced through a hierarchical structure (Moon 1990). She suggests that both scholarship and corporate work are perceived as "clean" endeavors, performed with pen and paper (or computer) at a great remove from the dust and fury of the marketplace. Ironically, the image holds even when this clean work involves commerce on a global scale such that the *chaebŏl* leaders have themselves failed to shed the taint of the entrepreneurial activities that built their fortunes (Eckert 1991; Janelli with Yim 1993, 99). This equation of the corporate employee and the scholar-official makes a public virtue of corporate life, a perception fostered within the *chaebŏl* by daily practices and rhetoric that underscore the important patriotic mission of the enterprise (Janelli with Yim 1993, 111). Men like Park-sangmunim, the middle-aged manager who is the subject of June Lee's chapter, describe themselves as having sacrificed their particularistic involvement in family life "for the sake of the nation." The white-collar men interviewed by Eunhee Kim Yi (1993, 1998) speak of time spent with wife and family as "an indulgence."

Korean government directives explicitly define a woman's primary responsibility as facilitating her husband's work "in society" (Moon 1998a), a principle internalized by many housewives (Yi 1993). Seungsook Moon (in this volume) holds that this ubiquitous view—men do (and are entitled to do) the critical work of society—is the basis of contemporary Korean patriarchy, the legal and emotional privileging of husbands over wives. But from the perspective of the middle class Korean household, these are patriarchies without patriarchs. According to Cho Haejoang (in this volume), women create and perpetuate middle class Korean culture. The rigid spatial gendering of work and domesticity vests wives with basic responsibilities for consumption, investment, education, and the range of activities that Hanna Papanek describes as "status reproduction work" (Kim 1992, 1993; Moon 1990; Papanek 1979; Yi 1993). Nancy Abelmann's recent work suggests that class positions are by no means fixed with marriage, but are continuously negotiated through the ambitions of married women, the investments they make, and the educations and marriages they secure for their children (Abelmann 1997a, b, and in this volume). The role of the middle class wife as family manager is at least tacitly acknowledged by the *chaebŏl*, who routinely dispense wages not into their employees' pockets, but into family bank accounts (Janelli and Yim 1996). Given the social demands placed on white-collar men, and the necessity of maintaining face through generous hospitality, this arrangement also encourages thrift while allowing a colleague to blame his penny-pinching wife for his slender allowance of pocket money with all stereotypes preserved intact.

DOING "PUBLIC" AND "DOMESTIC" IN KOREA

Some observers of the middle class Korean family have posited a continuity with the domestic life of the old *yangban* nobility where women managed the inner quarters (*nae*) while men performed acts of propriety and distinction in the "outside" (*woe*) realm (Lett 1998, 209; Moon 1990; Yi 1993). Such a conflation permits members of Korea's new middle class to see themselves as modern-day *yangban* vested with a reassuring sense of cultural continuity and a "traditional" rationalization for gender asymmetry. This appeal to the past elides important distinctions between older familial arrangements and contemporary middle class life. Superficially, past and present genderings of *nae* and *woe* would seem to replicate Michelle Zimbalist Rosaldo's early notion that the distinction between public and private (or domestic) realms is the root cause of women's subordination to men (Rosaldo 1974). A purported universal principle, transmitted through a distinctive Korean custom, "explains" the seeming inevitability of gender discrimination in the late twentieth century. But this is simplistic. A number of gender scholars, including Rosaldo in her later work, have argued against clear and absolute generalizations. They emphasize the variability of relationships among women and between women and men in different cultural milieus, and underscore the private realm as a place where many significant things transpire. Of particular importance to our discussion, they stress the historical contingency of any conceptualization of public and private space (Nicholson 1986, Rosaldo 1980). Anthropologist Sylvia Junko Yanagisako (1987) has shown how a seemingly commonsensical distinction between public and private may obscure significant distinctions in the meaning imparted to space and labor, even within the history of a single society or group over the space of a single generation.

In Korea today, masculine endeavors in the corporate world are deemed the work "of society" for which women offer domestic support. In dynastic times, the public personas of scholar-officials were never void of family and lineage identification, and the fruits of public accomplishment were returned to family and kin in a currency of officially meted honor or disgrace. Public identities were embedded in families and the domestic realm was accountable to the state (Ko et. al. n.d.). Moreover, most men, even most *yangban* men, were not scholar-officials. Their primary identities were derived from webs of extended kinship and their significant "work" was carried out within family agrarian enterprises.

Traditionalist models also conflate outside and inside, as an organizing principle of gendered domestic space in *yangban* homes, with the distinction between productive work and domestic consumption, a spatial dichotomization that is commonly (Sacks 1974; Zaretsky 1976) though not inevitably (de Grazia 1996b, 152) associated with nascent capitalism. In Korea, this analogy of past and present is false. The gendering of productive labor as male and consumption as female did not exist in the agrarian economy of premodern Korea. While men literally worked outside the house wall, they labored within the frame of a domestic enterprise that also included the women who worked behind the wall. Male corporate employees work outside in a more fundamental *economic* and *social* sense than did their grandfathers who labored in their family's owned or rented fields. Their grandmothers, who labored in seclusion, clothed the entire household in handwoven cloth, maintained kitchen gardens, and processed virtually all of the family's foodstuffs (Kendall and Peterson 1983; Sorensen 1988, 133–141). While Confucian ideology and social practice denigrated women, women were never regarded as innately unproductive. The energy and industriousness of a potential daughter-in-law was a critical factor in rural matchmaking into the second half of the present century (Kendall 1996, ch.4)

If, on the one hand, the Korean middle class household makes a fundamental contrast with its own antecedents, Korean spheres of work and home also are invested with very different ideological content than were their counterparts in early capitalist Europe and America. Contemporary Korean valuing of society, as a realm of selfless national endeavor, over the home, a place governed by the particularistic ambitions and materialist concerns of women (Moon 1998b; Yi 1993), contrasts with the nineteenth-century Euro-American sentimentalization of the domestic realm as a repository of purity and goodness, a refuge from the worldliness of the marketplace (Cott 1977). Writing of late nineteenth- and early twentieth-century Sweden, Frykman and Lofgren describe how a middle class man, "in the secluded privacy and intimacy of the home, surrounded by his nearest and dearest, . . . was able to behave in a more relaxed fashion, showing emotions that were taboo in the public sphere" (Frykman and Lofgren 1990 [1983], 135; Douglas 1977, 48). As evidenced in the chapters by Abelmann, June Lee, and Moon, the nuclear households of the Korean middle class do not carry this same ideological and emotional weight. The larger, noncoresidential family is the ideological locus of loyalty, and non-sexual intimacies have been, until recently, most frequently shared among members of the same gender (Cho in this volume).

If the Victorian "angel in the home" was an icon of purity and civiliz-ing influence, protected from the sordid world of commerce, in contempo-rary Korea it is quite the reverse. Middle class women are perceived as immersed in the fury of the marketplace, dealing with the hands-on prag-matics of stocks, high-interest loans, and real estate, and sometimes besting their husbands' paychecks (Cho in this volume; Cho and Koo 1983; Kim 1992, 1993).[3] Okpyo Moon suggests that middle class Korean men would be uncomfortable with the "unclean" activities of investment and equates masculine reticence with the delicacy of the *yangban* men of old whose hands should not touch cash (Moon 1990). Matchmaking, as a means of asserting and advancing class position, also is appropriately dominated by women who risk rebuffs and enter into excruciating negotiations over the wedding gifts, activities that would be damaging to a masculine sense of face (Kendall 1996, ch. 5). Wives readily become scapegoats for the zeitgeist when the public mood turns against the perceived excesses of middle class life (ibid., 216–220). Seung-kyung Kim reports how officials accused dur-ing the anticorruption campaigns of Kim Young-sam's administration pleaded innocent by virtue of ignorance, claiming that it was their wives who managed the family finances (Kim 1997, 182 fn. 7). More generally, middle class wives have been the targets of criticism directed against such social ills as excessive consumption and dubious real estate transactions (Abelmann in this volume; Nelson 1996, 187). Such criticisms have been so internalized that in some quarters, avaricious housewives even have been blamed for bringing on the I.M.F. crisis itself, an assessment that overlooks dealings in the masculine world of government, banks, and international currency trades. Writing from the perspective of a concerned social critic, Cho Haejoang (in this volume) offers her own unlovely portrait of a gen-eration of ambitious middle class wives.

THE MIDDLE CLASS AT MIDDLE AGE: HUSBANDS AND WIVES

Nancy Abelmann's chapter, "Women, Mobility, and Desire: Narrating Class and Gender in South Korea," permits one of these women to speak for her-self. For Abelmann, middle class women's narratives of success and failure define class identities as a "shifting frontier," which they push back through their own efforts. Their stories, she suggests, are "not metanarratives of class but the very stuff of it." The subject of her essay, So-yŏn's Mother, admits to having made her family what it is today—comfortably upper middle class—through her own entrepreneurial spirit, shrewd investments, and the energetic crafting of a lifestyle that evidences distinction. Neither her father, immobilized by the trauma of refugee life, nor her successful banker husband matched her in ability and ambition. Her transgenerational perspective foreshadows the three-generation archetypes described in Cho's chapter. So-yŏn's Mother looks backward to her docile mother and her father's robust primary wife, two self-sacrificing women who together sustained the family in their refugee existence. Her own carefully nurtured daughter's cautious approach to life falls short of the splendid ambitions that So-yŏn's Mother had once entertained on her behalf. As an undercurrent of her self-justifying narration, So-yŏn's Mother acknowledges the faint odor of immorality that wafts over her investments, the sense that making money and spending it are dirty activities.

In "Discourses of Illness, Meanings of Modernity: A Gendered Construction of Sŏnginbyŏng," June J. H. Lee provides the complement to the stereotypically ambitious middle class woman by describing the complaints and disorders of a middle-aged white-collar man. Park-sangmunim's life, like that of So-yŏn's Mother, is comprehensible only within the particular gendering of public and domestic space among the Korean middle class. As is typical of successful company managers, Park-sangmunim has been an absent patriarch, spending long hours at the company and more long hours socializing with his coworkers. Lee suggests that for her primary informant, as for many Korean men, this ideal of middle class accomplishment has gone sour. Beset by ills that are a consequence of overwork and socially mandated drinking, Park-sangmunim is alienated from his wife and children. His wife's impatience with the requirements of his special ulcer diet is of a piece with the black humor attributed to middle-aged women who resent the special needs of aging husbands and are allegedly desirous of early widowhoods (Cho in this volume). With the revelation that middle-aged Korean males hold the world's highest mortality rate for their age group, the media initiated a wide-ranging discussion of sŏnginbyŏng, (adult diseases) associated in popular medical discourse with overworked white-collar men. Through this idiom, Park-sangmunim contemplates his ulcer, his troubled relationship with his family, the early death of a friend, and uncomfortable thoughts regarding Korea's hasty modernity; ineptly constructed buildings and bridges collapse, even as the aging male body commits its own acts of betrayal.

Moon (in this volume) describes an outpouring of popular literature sympathetic to the complaints of middle-aged men and highly critical of their mercenary spouses. This material is of a piece with the *sŏnginbyŏng* discourses described in June Lee's chapter, fueling a national campaign to appreciate the male breadwinner. Both authors are keenly aware that stereotypical portrayals of unsympathetic wives and ungrateful children elide more fundamental sources of male discontent, whose roots are to be found in the basic structure of work and family expectations, and in the human costs of economic rationalization as off-shoring and an economic downturn belie prior promises of job security. Moon suggests, as a hopeful sign, that many young men are rejecting corporate employment and that members of a nascent men's movement are attempting to sustain meaningful participation in family life. Park-sangmunim notes, with a trace of envy, that his junior colleges are now better able to resist compulsory after-hours drinking, acts of resistance also evidenced in the trading company studied by Janelli and Yim. By the late 1980s, company policy required that all lights be turned out at 7 P.M. to encourage workers to depart (Janelli with Yim 1993, 231–232).

JOBS WITHOUT CAREERS

In "Gender Construction in the Offices of a South Korean Conglomerate," Roger L. Janelli and Dawnhee Yim describe how the gendering of roles within the workplace tends to naturalize male privilege for the large numbers of Korean women and men who experience office life via the *chaebŏl*. Clerical work is the fastest-growing occupation for Korean women (Koo 1990, 673) but pink-collar employees are expected to leave their jobs before the age of thirty. This brief season of employment is shaped by hierarchical relations within the office. Male employees, as college graduates, enter corporate life at a higher rank than do female employees, who are graduates of two-year professional colleges. With more years of education as well as military service behind them, even new male employees are older than most of the women with whom they work. Because female office workers usually are not promoted beyond the lowest rank, a woman who stays employed eventually will find herself taking orders from a male superior who is her junior in age as well as in corporate experience (even newly-hired women routinely take orders from male superiors who have less corporate experience than they do). Janelli and Yim suggest that this incongruity between age and authority is why most women meet company expectations and quit by their late twenties, whether married or not. Perceived as temporary and easily replaced, women are consequently less valued than male employees, whose superiors attempt to nurture harmony and solidarity by encouraging common dining and after-hours activities. Male privilege is further naturalized by differences in class and education (usually a function of class). The men are graduates of top universities; the women are graduates of a growing number of vocational high schools and, as Cho relates (in this volume), they are often selected on the basis of their physical attractiveness. Janelli and Yim end their essay with the observation that in recent years, a small number of women have been hired for the managerial track, owing to a decline in the quality of male applicants in the corporate hiring pool. By the late 1980s, many young men were questioning the formerly idealized life of the company employee and "voting with their feet" (Janelli with Yim 1993, 155). It is ironic that male disillusionment with the corporate lifestyle, as noted in the chapters by Moon and June Lee, has given some women this very narrow opening to masculine privilege. It remains to be seen whether these women ultimately will subvert the naturalization of masculine privilege in the office or will succumb to it. As Janelli and Yim also note, their numbers are very small and recently hired women were an obvious target of the massive layoffs that followed the I.M.F. crisis.

While Janelli and Yim describe women's office work as a condition of subordination, the women factory workers who are the subjects of Seung-kyung Kim's published ethnography (1997) saw it as enviable employment. Even the term "*Missŭ*" (Miss), which the women office workers find demeaning, would be preferable to the crude terms of address women factory workers routinely endure. In a society where perceptions of status and virtue are linked, factory women are considered coarse and sexually promiscuous. Like office workers, the factory women regard their work as a temporary life phase rather than as a badge of class or personal identity. Like women office workers, they aspire to middle class marriages, but they also know that they are far less likely to have them. The ranks of Korean women workers are now diminished by off-shoring, the fickleness of multinational factories, and the growth of service sector jobs. Even so, Kim's ethnography is a striking example of how work experience led a generation of south Korean factory women to imagine alternative notions of womanhood by exposing them to movement politics, new modes of consumption, new notions of sexual attraction, and new dreams of class mobility. Following Kim, and the work of Janelli and Yim in this volume, other south Korean workplaces might profitably be considered as sites for the construction of gendered identities.

The authors of the last two chapters, So-Hee Lee and Cho Haejoang, are members of the Seoul-based Alternative Culture Group (Ttohanaŭi Munhwa). Their writing is part of an effort to rethink Korean feminism. Founded in the early 1980s, Alternative Culture brings feminist ideas to a broad public through a journal and publication series, educational and theatrical events, and an alternative summer camp for children. Members range from social scientists to literary figures. In the politically charged 1980s, the group was sometimes criticized by more radical and grassroots women's organizations for the privileged professional orientation of its membership. Alternative Culture survived many of its critics and continued through the politically more quiescent 1990s into the new millennium. Even so, members express concern that issues of gender equality do not spark the imagination of a younger generation of students and have been deemed irrelevant by many older women. As socially engaged scholars seeking a more effective connection, Cho and Lee confront the issue of subjectivity: Why do different cohorts of women do what they do and think what they think?

Following Foucault (1980–1987, 212), they use the term "subjectivity" to indicate a condition whereby personal agency is both constituted and constrained by prior power relations, some of them global in scope, and is realized through social practice.[4] Abelmann's portrait of So-yŏn's Mother and Lee's portrayal of Park-sangmunim are similar evocations of subjective selves as agents, but not free agents. In both Western and Korean feminist writing, subjectivity (*chuch'esŏng*) is emphatically not the culture-bound notion of the individual, an atomized exemplar of free will whose appearance was once taken as sign and symptom of modernity.

EMBODIED CONSUMPTION: BEAUTY AND SEXUALITY

In "The Concept of Female Sexuality in Korean Popular Culture," So-Hee Lee analyzes several recent works of literature, film, and a television drama, all of which provoked popular and sometimes heated responses. Even as Lee prepared her chapter, the Korean television audience was riveted to a serial drama describing the love affair of a married professional woman. For Western women who became sexually aware in the late 1960s and who recall the thin line between "liberation" and "exploitation," the aspirations of young Korean women might seem hopelessly naive, even self-indulgent, but this would be a superficial reading given the hegemonic notions of feminine identity these young women confront. While the chapters by Lee and Cho both describe how the promise of sexual attractiveness has become a marketable commodity in late twentieth-century Korea, Lee makes a compelling case for the radical import of body awareness and sexual experimentation as openings to new forms of feminine consciousness, new ways of thinking and seeing oneself as a woman. Similar arguments have been made for the role of consumerism in crafting new feminine identities in other times and places. Such a case has been made for the use of cosmetics in early twentieth-century North America (Peiss 1996), the bobbed hair and bare legs of the 1920s Japanese "modern girl" (*modan gäru*) (Silverberg 1991), and the market-driven femininity of women in post-Mao China (Yang 1999).

In "Living with Conflicting Subjectivities: Mother, Motherly Wife, and Sexy Woman in the Transition from Colonial-Modern to Postmodern," Cho Haejoang brings themes from several chapters together in a panorama of gendered Korean modernity. As an anthropologist whose writing includes both painstakingly researched ethnography and provocative works of social criticism, Cho's position within Korean society is somewhat analogous to that of the late Margaret Mead for a North American readership. She does not flinch from summing up the state of things with bold strokes. In this chapter, Cho presents ideal-type portraits of three generations of middle class women whose adult experiences span Korea's blink-of-an-eye transformation from an agricultural to a successful urban industrial society. Strong, self-reliant "mothers" of the immediate postcolonial and post-Korean War period struggled in threadbare times to educate sons who would grow up to be the managers, professionals, and technocrats of Korea's new middle class. "Wives," who married these men in the 1960s and 1970s, crafted a new middle class culture. Competitive consumers, aggressive investors, indifferent to their often-absent husbands, ambitious on behalf of their children's education and marriages, these women have become the butt of social critique and satire, even as the self-sacrificing mothers of the previous generation are romanticized. "Daughters," who have known only a prosperous and comfortable Korea, define themselves within a consumer-oriented society that bombards them with commoditized visions of a new femininity, telling them to be attractive, sexy, and compliant. As a social critic and activist, and as a professor taking the pulse of a new generation, Cho asks how Korean feminists might bridge their own generational perspectives and come to terms with the unprecedented desires of younger women. She offers a grim postscript, noting that in the wake of the I.M.F. crisis, any vision of a cohesive community of women has become even more elusive, as poor women struggle to survive, middle class housewives to hold on, and professional women to succeed against even greater odds.

The sexy young women on college campuses, the married but emphatically unmatronly "missy" types, and fanciful portrayals of these women in all manner of contemporary Korean advertisements and popular culture suggest a familiar metaphoric link between selling and seduction, between consumption and the satisfaction of lust (Felski 1995; Ross 1992; Williamson 1986).[5] In the Protestant West, this imagery played on older notions of the marketplace as a realm of "worldliness," equated with carnal sin (Cott 1977; Felski 1995; Miller 1987). In Korea, consumption discourses also have a long history as moral discourses (Deuchler 1992, 245; 1996), but criticisms of lavish display had nothing to do with sexuality. The moral disapprobation surrounding getting and spending comes from a general disdain for craving, appetite, and naked ambition. These emotions get in the way of Buddhist salvation and defy Confucian injunctions to practice balance and moderation in one's daily life. In late twentieth-century Korea these excesses have been personified in the unlovely stereotype of the upwardly mobile middle class matron.[6] Women are faulted for pursuing the particularistic interests of their households when excessive consumption is perceived as being counter to the national interest. The perceived patriotic limitations of women are thus confirmed. The sexualized marketplace is a relatively new phenomenon in Korea, a response to the loosening of censorship in the late 1980s, the depoliticization of Korean youth culture in the 1990s, and the tug of the global marketplace.

The ambivalence evident in Cho's, Kim's, and So-Hee Lee's grappling with contemporary, market-driven female subjectivities recalls a debate in current writing about consumption. Where some see an all-embracing market as obliterating human creativity and will (Debord 1983; Williamson 1986), others celebrate consumption as an act of identity construction, an emancipation from older moralities and older class identities (Miller 1987, 209; Miller 1994, 76; Peiss 1996). Like their Euro-American counterparts of more than a century ago (Cott 1977; Douglas 1977; Ross 1992; Williams 1982), the middle class housewives of Cho's and Abelmann's essays have used their newly democratized access to luxury goods to fashion the lifestyle of a broad new social class, deploying washing machines, pianos, and real estate as validations of membership. Seung-kyung Kim (1997) has described how women factory workers used clothing and cosmetics to counter the coarse image of female laborers and amass dowry goods toward the promise of middle class married lives.

Recognizing an irreconcilable and ultimately stultifying debate over the potentially manipulative and potentially liberating attributes of consumption, Victoria de Grazia has suggested that it is far more fruitful to examine how the category "women" is reconfigured in and by these processes (de

Grazia 1996a). This has been one of our tasks in *Under Construction*. Our authors suggest that consumption influences gender not only as an instrument of class mobility but also as a means of articulating profound generational contrasts and new sexualities, the micro-stuff of history.

The image of a married but decidely unmatronly "missy" promenading through a shopping mall in her short leather skirt contrasts with the image of the young woman factory worker, coarsened and sexualized by her experience of the shop floor (Kim 1997) as illustrations of how gendered identities are realized through bodily performance (Butler 1993; Robertson 1992; Williams 1989). The range of material presented in this volume amply demonstrates that even within a single society, embodied experiences of gender and modernity are numerous and varied: the eating disorders and sexual exploits of adolescents, the aerobics classes of affluent middle-aged women, the plastic surgery and diet that might be prerequisite to office employment. Gendered bodily experiences are not exclusively sexual and are by no means restricted to women (Bock 1989; Flax 1987). Park-sangmunim's encounters with *sŏnginbyŏng* suggest that we have a great deal to learn from the embodied experiences of Korean men. We might consider, for example, the masculine bodily disciplines of military life, the workplace, and after-hours entertainment.

CONCLUSION

This introduction began with Berman's invocation of modernity as that condition where "all that is solid melts into air." We might now wonder whether "modernity" is itself melting, as the postmoderns suggest. It is not just that Korea exhibits a condition of nonfixity, of gendered constructs in motion with changing politics, emergent classes, new commodities, new ways of talking about and experiencing sexuality, generational conflicts, and economic adjustments. In all of this, Korea hardly would be unique. Our broad examination of south Korean society also shakes the fixity of our own constructs. The chapters in this volume evoke a familiar scholarly language of "gender," "class," "consumption," and "embodiment," terms originally coined to describe a Euro-American experience. The experiences of Korean women and men reconfigure this lexicon in subtle ways to account for a different history and circumstance, and by doing so they subvert a seemingly familiar teleology. This has always been the promise of gender studies, not only to open and shake the categories of "masculine" and "feminine" across and within societies, but also to cast in sharp relief the social and sexual premises within which these same masculinities and femininities are realized (Moore 1988; Ross and Rapp 1983; Scott 1986).

NOTES

I am grateful to Nancy Abelmann, Seungsook Moon, Roger Janelli, and Dawnhee Yim for their careful reading of this essay. I alone am responsible for its shortcomings.

1. From Park Chung-hee's coup d'état in 1961 until the election of Kim Young Sam in 1991, south Korea's presidents were former career military men. Kim Dae Jung, elected in 1997, is the first president to have run against, rather than from within, the ruling party.

2. For a concise description of the *chaebŏl's* relationship to the south Korean state and how it has changed over time, see Eun Mee Kim's (1997) *Big Business, Strong State: Collusion and Conflict in South Korean Development, 1960–1990.*

3. There is also a more literal equation of women with the marketplace. Outside the middle class, Korean markets are full of women traders who are not averse to bargaining and importuning customers, activities that would bruise male dignity (Chung 1977; Moon 1979).

4. I am grateful to So-Hee Lee and Eun Shil Kim for their thoughts on the subject of "subjectivity."

5. This theme is most deliciously explicit in Zola's late nineteenth-century novel of a French department store, *The Ladies' Paradise*, a work that has been revisited by students of consumption even as it is read by marketing experts (Zola 1992 [1882]).

6. Foreign goods are regarded as particularly detrimental to the national well being, an abiding moral stance that has become more vehement in the current climate of economic crisis. Laura Nelson (1996) suggests that moral ambivalence surrounding consumption was also built into the particular contradictory policies of Korean development, ideologically committed to self-reliance but practically export-oriented and dependent on certain critical imported goods.

REFERENCES

Abelmann, Nancy. 1997a. Narrating selfhood and personality in south Korea: Women and social mobility. *American Ethnologist* 24(4):786–812.

———. 1997b. Women's class mobility and identities in south Korea: A gendered, transnational, narrative approach. *Journal of Asian Studies* 56(2):398–420.

Bailey, Beth L. 1998. *From Front Porch to Back Seat: Courtship in Twentieth-Century America.* Baltimore: Johns Hopkins University Press.

Baudrillard, Jean. 1987. Modernity. Canadian Journal of Political and Social Theory. *Revue Canadiene de théorie politique et sociale* 11(3):63–72.

Berman, Marshall. 1988. *All That Is Solid Melts into Air: The Experience of Modernity.* London: Verso.

Bock, Gesela. 1989. Women's history and gender history: Aspects of an international debate. *Gender and History* 1(1):7–29.

Brinton, Mary C., Yean-Ju Lee, and William L. Parish. 1995. Married women's employment in rapidly industrializing societies: Examples from East Asia. *American Journal of Sociology* 100(5):1099–1130.

Butler, Judith. 1993. *Bodies That Matter: On the Discursive Limits of "Sex."* New York: Routledge.

Caplan, Pat. 1987. *The Cultural Construction of Sexuality.* New York: Routledge.

Cho, Uhn, and Hagen Koo. 1983. Economic development and women's work in a newly industrializing country. *Development and Change* 14:515–521.

Chung, Cha-Whan. 1977. Change and continuity in an urbanizing society: Family and kinship in urban Korea. Ph.D. diss. University of Hawai'i.

Cott, Nancy F. 1977. *The Bonds of Womanhood: "Woman's Sphere" in New England, 1780–1835.* New Haven: Yale University Press.

de Grazia, Victoria. 1996a. Introduction. In *The Sex of Things: Gender and Consumption in Historical Perspective.* V. de Grazia, with E. Furlough, eds. pp. 1–10. Berkeley: University of California Press.

———. 1996b. Establishing the modern consumer household. In *The Sex of Things: Gender and Consumption in Historical Perspective.* V. de Grazia, with E. Furlough, eds. pp. 151–161. Berkeley: University of California Press.

de Lauretis, Teresa. 1987. *Technologies of Gender.* Bloomington: Indiana University Press.

Debord, Guy. 1983. *Society of the Spectacle.* Detroit: Black and Red.

Deuchler, Martina. 1992. *The Confucian Transformation of Korea.* Cambridge, Mass.: Council on East Asian Studies, Harvard University.

———. 1996. Propagating female virtues in Chosŏn Korea. "Women in Confucian Cultures in Pre-modern China, Korea, and Japan," conference held at University of California San Diego, Calif., June 28–July 1, 1996.

Douglas, Ann. 1977. *The Feminization of American Culture.* New York: Doubleday.

Eckert, Carter J., et al. 1990. *Korea Old and New: A History.* Seoul: Ilchokak for the Korea Institute, Harvard University.

Eckert, Carter J. 1991. *Offspring of Empire: The Koch'ang Kims and the Colonial Origins of Korean Capitalism 1876–1945.* Seattle: University of Washington Press.

Felski, Rita. 1995. *The Gender of Modernity.* Cambridge, Mass.: Harvard University Press.

Flax, Jane. 1987. Postmodernism and gender relations in feminist theory. *Signs: Journal of Women in Culture and Society* 12(4):621–643.

Foucault, Michel. 1980–1987. *The History of Sexuality.* R. Hurley, trans. 3 vols. New York: Vintage Press.

Frykman, Jonas, and Ovar Lofgren. 1990 [1983]. *Culture Builders: A Historical Anthropology of Middle-Class Life.* A. Crozier, trans. New Brunswick: Rutgers University Press.

Grewal, Inderpal, and Caren Kaplan. 1994. Introduction: Transnational feminist practices and questions of postmodernity. In *Scattered Hegemonies: Postmodernity and Transnational Feminist Practices,* I. Grewal and C. Kaplan, eds. pp. 1–36. Minneapolis: University of Minnesota Press.

Imamura, Ann E. 1987. *Urban Japanese Housewives: At Home in the Community.* Honolulu: University of Hawai'i Press.

Jameson, Fredrick. 1984. Postmodernism, or the cultural logic of late capitalism. *New Left Review* 146 (Sept./Oct.):53–92.

Janelli, Roger L., and Dawnhee Yim Janelli. 1996. Gender and household economy among Seoul's new middle class. Paper presented at the conference on "Seoul: Past, Present, and Future," CNRS/EHESS/Université Paris, 1996.

Janelli, Roger L., with Dawnhee Yim. 1993. *Making Capitalism: The Social and Cultural Construction of a South Korean Conglomerate.* Stanford, Calif.: Stanford University Press.

Kendall, Laurel. 1996. *Getting Married in Korea: Of Gender, Morality, and Modernity.* Berkeley: University of California Press.

Kendall, Laurel, and Mark Peterson. 1983. "Traditional Korean women": A reconsideration. In *Korean Women: A View from the Inner Room.* L. Kendall and M. Peterson, eds. pp. 5–21. New Haven: East Rock Press.

Kim, Elaine H. 1998. Men's talk: A Korean-American view of south Korean constructions of women, gender, and masculinity. In *Dangerous Women: Gender and Korean Nationalism.* E. H. Kim and Chungmoo Choi, eds. pp. 67–117. New York: Routledge.

Kim, Eun Mee. 1997. *Big Business, Strong State: Collusion and Conflict in South Korean Development, 1960–1990.* Albany: State University of New York Press.

Kim, Myong-hye. 1992. Late industrializaton and women's work in urban south Korea: An ethnographic study of upper-middle-class families. *City and Society.* Vol. 6. pp. 156–172.

———. 1993. Transformation of family ideology in upper-middle class families in urban south Korea. *Ethnology* 32(1):69–85.

Kim, Seung-kyung. 1997. *Class Struggle or Family Struggle: The Lives of Women Factory Workers in South Korea.* Cambridge: Cambridge University Press.

Ko, Dorothy, JaHyun Haboush, and Joan Piggot. (n.d.). Introduction. In *Women and Confucian Cultures in Premodern China, Korea, and Japan*. D. Ko, J. Haboush, and J. Piggot, eds. Unpublished manuscript.

Koo, Hagan. 1990. From farm to factory. *American Sociological Review* 55(October):669–681.

Lett, Denise Potrzeba. 1998. In *Pursuit of Status: The Making of South Korea's 'New' Urban Middle Class*. Cambridge, Mass.: Harvard University Asia Center.

Miller, Daniel. 1987. *Material Culture and Mass Consumption*. Oxford: Basil Blackwell.

———. 1994. *Modernity: An Ethnographic Approach: Dualism and Mass Consumption in Trinidad*. Oxford: Berg.

Miller, Daniel, ed. 1995. *Worlds Apart: Modernity Through the Prism of the Local*. New York: Routledge.

Mohanty, Chandra. 1988. Under western eyes: Feminist scholarship and colonial discourses. *Feminist Review* 30:61–88.

Moon, Jee Yoo Madrigal. 1979. *The Role of Women in Korean Society with Emphasis on the Economic System*. Palo Alto, Calif.: R. and E. Research Associates Inc.

Moon, Okpyo. 1990. Urban middle class wives in contemporary Korea: Their roles, responsibilities, and dilemma. *Korea Journal* 30(11):30–43.

Moon, Seungsook. 1998a. Begetting the nation: The androcentric discourse of national history and tradition in south Korea. In *Dangerous Women: Gender and Korean Nationalism*. E. H. Kim and C. C. Choi, eds. pp. 33–66. New York: Routledge.

———. 1998b. Gender, militarization, and universal male conscription in south Korea. In *The Women and War Reader*. L. A. Lorentzen and J. Turpin, eds. pp. 90–100. New York: New York University Press.

Moore, Henrietta L. 1988. *Feminism and Anthropology*. Minneapolis: University of Minnesota Press.

———. 1994. *A Passion for Difference: Essays in Anthropology and Gender*. Bloomington and Indianapolis: Indiana University Press.

Nelson, Laura Catherine. 1996. Measured excess: Gender, status, and consumer nationalism in south Korea. Ph.D. dissertation, Stanford University.

Nicholson, Linda J. 1986. *Gender and History: The Limits of Social Theory in the Age of the Family*. New York: Columbia University Press.

Ong, Aihwa. 1988. Colonialism and modernity: Feminist representations of women in non-western societies. *Inscriptions* 3(4):79–93.

Ortner, Sherry B. 1996. *Making Gender: The Politics and Erotics of Culture*. Boston: Beacon Press.

Papanek, Hanna. 1979. Family status production work: The "work" and "non-work" of women. *Signs* 4(4):775–781.

Peiss, Kathy. 1996. Making up, making over: Cosmetics, consumer culture, and women's identity. In *The Sex of Things: Gender and Consumption in Historical Perspective.* V. de Grazia with E. Furlough, eds. pp. 311–336. Berkeley: University of California Press.

Radway, Janice A. 1984. *Reading the Romance.* Chapel Hill and London: The University of North Carolina Press.

Robertson, Jennifer. 1992. Doing and undoing "female" and "male" in Japan: The takarazuka review. In *Japanese Social Organization.* T. S. Lebra, ed. pp. 79–107. Honolulu: University of Hawai'i Press.

Robinson, Michael. 1994. Mass media and popular culture in 1930s Korea: Cultural control, identity, and colonial hegemony. In *Korean Studies: New Pacific Currents.* D. S. Suh, ed. pp. 59–82. Honolulu: Center for Korean Studies, University of Hawai'i.

Rofel, Lisa. 1994. Liberation nostalgia and a yearning for modernity. In *Engendering China: Women, Culture, and the State.* C. Gilmartin, Gail Hershatter, Lisa Rofel, and Tyrene White, eds. pp. 226–249. Cambridge, Mass.: Harvard University Press.

———. 1999. *Other Modernities, Gendered Yearnings in China After Socialism.* Berkeley: University of California Press.

Rosaldo, Michelle Zimbalist. 1974. Women, culture, and society: A theoretical overview. In *Women, Culture, and Society.* M. Z. Rosaldo and L. Lamphere, eds. pp. 17–42. Stanford, Calif.: Stanford University Press.

———. 1980. The use and abuse of anthropology: Reflections on feminism and cross-cultural understanding. *Signs* 5(3):389–417.

Ross, Ellen, and Rayna Rapp. 1983. Sex and society: A research note from social history and anthropology. In *Powers of Desire: The Politics of Sexuality.* A. Snitow, C. Stansell, and S. Thompson, eds. pp. 51–73. New York: Monthly Review Press.

Ross, Kristin. 1992. Introduction: Shopping. In *The Ladies' Paradise* by Emile Zola. pp. v–xxiii. Berkeley: University of California Press.

Sacks, Karen. 1974. Engels revisited: Women, the organization of production. In *Women, Culture, and Society.* M. Z. Rozaldo and L. Lamphere, eds. pp. 207–222. Stanford, Calif.: Stanford University Press.

Scott, Joan. 1986. Gender: A useful category for historical analysis. *The American Historical Review* 91(5):1053–1075.

Shin, Hei-soo. 1991. Sexual services and economic development: The political economy of the entertainment industry and south Korean development. Ph.D. dissertation. Rutgers University.

Silverberg, Miriam. 1991. The modern girl as militant. In *Recreating Japanese Women, 1600–1945.* G. Bernstein, ed. pp. 239–266. Berkeley: University of California Press.

Silverblatt, Irene. 1991. Interpreting women in states: New feminist ethnohistories. In *Gender at the Crossroads of Knowledge: Feminist Anthropology in the Postmodern Era*. M. di Leonardo, ed. pp. 140–171. Berkeley: University of California Press.

Soh, Chung-Hee. 1991. *The Chosen Women in Korean Politics: An Anthropological Study*. New York: Praeger.

Sorensen, Clark. 1988. *Over the Mountains Are Mountains: Korean Peasant Households and Their Adaptations to Rapid Industrialization*. Seattle: University of Washington Press.

Vogel, Ezra F. 1968. *Japan's New Middle Class: The Salary Man and His Family in a Tokyo Suburb*. Berkeley: University of California Press.

Williams, Linda. 1989. *Hard Core: Power, Pleasure, and the Frenzy of the Visible*. Berkeley: University of California Press.

Williams, Rosalind H. 1982. *Dream Worlds: Mass Consumption in Late Nineteenth-Century France*. Berkeley: University of California Press.

Williamson, Judith. 1986. *Consuming Passions: The Dynamics of Popular Culture*. London: Marion Boyars.

Yanagisako, Sylvia Junko. 1987. Mixed metaphors: Native and anthropological models of gender and kinship domains. In *Gender and Kinship: Essays Toward a Unified Analysis*. J. Collier and S. J. Yanagisako, eds. pp. 86–118. Stanford, Calif.: Stanford University Press.

Yang, Mayfair Mei-hui. 1999. Spaces of Their Own: Women's Public Sphere in Transnational China. Public Worlds Series. Minneapolis: University of Minnesota Press.

Yi, Eunhee Kim. 1993. From gentry to the middle class: The transformation of family, community, and gender in Korea. Ph.D. dissertation, University of Chicago
———. 1998. "The home is a place to rest": Constructing the meaning of work, family and gender in the Korean middle class. *Korea Journal* 38(2):168–213.

Zaretsky, E. 1976. *Capitalism, The Family and Personal Life*. New York: Harper and Row.

Zola, Emile. 1992 [1882]. *The Ladies' Paradise* (with an introduction by Kristin Ross). Berkeley: University of California Press.

2 WOMEN, MOBILITY, AND DESIRE: NARRATING CLASS AND GENDER IN SOUTH KOREA

nancy abelmann

In this chapter, I explore tensions in women's personal narratives on class and social mobility. These narratives are both reflective and constitutive of south Korean popular and political discourses on contemporary history and social justice. I explore them in relation to a discursive contest over the relative openness or closedness of south Korean society.

The belief in open mobility reflects a democratic ideology that celebrates the equal opportunity of every individual to succeed with the requisite hard work (Sewell 1985, 234). An extension of this ideology of opportunity is a tendency to attribute people's variable social mobility fates to individual characteristics and to the microdynamics of the nuclear family—to interiorize or personalize larger social forces. As class theorist Rosemary Crompton (1993, 7) notes, the sense of equality of opportunity is a "powerful justification of inequality." In the case of south Korea, the domains of interiorization—that is, nuclear family dynamics, personality, and gender characteristics—are largely assigned to women. Furthermore, the individual attributes or proclivities that are seen as hindering or promoting social mobility are engendered—that is, coded as either male or female. Hence class—mobility and distinction—often is collapsed into or articulated through narratives on individual attributes and gender. On the other hand, there is a competing sense in south Korea that society is quite closed, that there are barriers of opportunity for people who lack particular class capital. Such class capital includes family status, educational background, personal connections, and, of course, economic leeway.

Women's narratives both reflect and produce the social tension between small stories about individuals and nuclear families and larger class narratives about cultural, symbolic, or ideological capital. Women's narratives of social

25

mobility engage the competing narratives of open and closed society and, as such, contribute to a national "contest" over the justice of south Korean contemporary history, a contest that examines the losers and victors over an era of tumultuous social, political, and economic change. We can think, then, of the competing discourses of mobility within which people narrate their *own* lives and the social transformation of post-war south Korea.[1] This chapter's focus on social mobility and gender represents a perspective on class beyond its predominant sociological life as a classification of men's productive labor. As Rayna Rapp (1982, 171) notes, "'Class' isn't a static place that individuals inhabit. Under advanced capitalism, there are shifting frontiers that separate poverty, stable wage-earning, affluent salaries, and inherited wealth. The frontiers may be crossed by individuals, and in either direction. That is, both upward and downward mobility are real processes." It is through these real processes of social mobility that people experience class distinctions and fashion their class identifications.

I begin this chapter by taking up the idiomatic and ideological contest over social mobility in south Korea. I then review the ways in which I employ the term "gender" as both a social and narrative construct. Finally I explore the play between mobility and gender in the narratives of one middle-aged south Korean woman whom I call So-yŏn's Mother. This case is part of a larger interview project on middle-aged women and social mobility in south Korea. In keeping with early innovations in urban anthropology (Bott 1957), my field research, although centered in Seoul, did not focus on any bounded community such as a neighborhood or apartment complex. Rather, I conducted in-depth multiple interviews of a small group of women in their late fifties across the class spectrum. I selected this genera-tion because they came of age during years of great economic and social transformation, and yet are still young enough to continue to participate actively in class and status reproduction today. Choosing a small number of interviewees and opting for numerous interviews, I am committed to what Abu-Lughod (1991, 150) calls "ethnographies of the particular"; she explains, "the effects of extralocal and long-term processes are manifested only locally and specifically, produced in the actions of individuals living their particular lives, inscribed in their bodies and their words."

My interviews draw on personal narratives but do not employ tradi-tional life-history methods. Rather, they are strategic life stories (Ginsburg 1989; Kendall 1988) with a particular focus on women's social mobility: narratives centered on their own lives and those of their siblings, and their close same-generation kin and siblings-in-law. I use the interview device not only to explore how particular families have distributed themselves across south Korea's class spectrum and Seoul's class geography, but more importantly to focus attention on the narratives through which people understand this distribution.

COMPETING NARRATIVES OF SOUTH KOREAN SOCIAL MOBILITY

There is a fundamental tension in south Korea between narratives, often official, that suggest society's openness—the idea that by the dint of hard work, any farmer's son (daughters have figured much less prominently in this construct), for example, can make it to Seoul National University, the apex of achievement—and people's sense that structural barriers thwart their own mobility chances.[2] Personal mobility narratives employ both logics. So-yŏn's Mother, for example, said, "If you want to develop (*palchŏn*) or move up, the most important thing is to ride the era (*sidae*) well. . . . Your happiness depends on whether or not you can move well in that historical moment, don't you agree?" But she then added: "You have to be blessed with good parents, and a good husband, and good children as well."

In the following section, I introduce south Korean society's contemporary melodramatic sensibility in order to begin an exploration of the process of interiorization that accompanies the belief in openness, and I discuss the concern for social rectitude and justice that undergirds the sense of society as somehow closed.

MOBILITY AND MELODRAMA

In thinking about the personalization or interiorization—the ways in which comparative mobility fates are mapped on individuals and families—that accompanies conviction about open social mobility, and about social dramas of good and evil, I draw on the largely Western-centered literature on the rise of melodrama as a uniquely modern aesthetic. The literature on the history of the melodramatic "imagination," as coined by literary scholar Peter Brooks (1976), explores the rise of melodrama through dramatic convention (Grimstead 1968), literary works (Watt 1957), film (DeLauretis 1984; Gledhill 1987; Modleski 1982) and most recently television, particularly soap operas (Modleski 1982). A melodramatic sensibility is pronounced in south Korea's various media and in popular and political narratives.

In the first sense of melodrama, as a modern performative and narrative aesthetic, the literature surveys the ways in which social and ideological conflicts are collapsed into the domestic setting, quintessentially the bourgeois family (Elsaesser 1987, 46). Christine Gledhill (1987, 16–17) describes how melodrama replaced the "tragic hero fixed in social hierarchy" with the "individual" of the "democratic bourgeois family." What emerges then are families in which "the characters are each other's sole referents" (Elsaesser 1987, 55–56) and whose "unhappiness . . . can only be solved by the family" (Modleski 1982, 90). In this vein, women's personal narratives turn on sophisticated folk narratives about the family's psychological matrix as a key to the variable fates of family members.

Elements of south Korean recent history nourish these idiomatic conventions. Reinforcing south Korea's modern sensibility is a familism that has roots in Confucian social structure (Chang 1991) and that has been intensified by the enormous social dislocation of the twentieth century. Cho Haejoang (n.d., 25) refers to Korea's "system of refuge": People have retreated into the family for survival. In her chapter in this book, Cho elaborates gendered aspects of this system of refuge in which, under Korea's "colonial modernity," men are emasculated, a predominant colonial and postcolonial literary theme (Em 1995), and women become the masters/mistresses of refuge. Hence Cho writes of her sense of "a grand conspiracy being reproduced by conservative, inflexible, and extremely self-defensive men and their super-adaptive women." The links between economic and social dislocation and matrifocalization have been widely documented in a variety of cultural and historical settings (Stack 1974; Elder 1974).[3] In this way, family cohorts make up a bounded universe that allows or thwarts an individual's life chances against the vicissitudes of fantastic social transformation. Correspondingly, women—who are largely assigned the private domain and the emotional universe—are the central agents in the production and maintenance of class culture.

The second sense in which a melodramatic sensibility is germane to contemporary south Korea is in terms of grand public narratives of good and evil, heroes and villains. The predominant narratives of south Korean modernity—nationalism and national development—have been proclaimed in highly melodramatic hues; this is equally true for state-drawn tyrannies of the public weal that outline the sacrifices that should be made for the state and for counter-hegemonic social visions (Abelmann 1996). As the grand narratives and actions of the public weal and oppositional nationalisms are designated the male province, women's domestic domain—Cho's sites of refuge—is rendered at odds with the public good. The domestic domain is considered the source of excesses of the familism, individualism, and consumption (Nelson 1994) that thwart development's necessary thrift and sacrifice on the one hand, or the necessary communitarian and ascetic impulse of oppositional politics on the other.

SOUTH KOREA AS AN OPEN SOCIETY—"WE WERE ALL POOR TOGETHER"

The discourse of open mobility turns on a number of calculations. The first factor contributing to the sensibility of openness is south Korea's rapid structural change: the growth of an industrial sector and the fantastic rural exodus in the 1960s and 1970s. Over the last thirty years, south Koreans also have experienced remarkable advances in their general standard of living, including diet, health, and material well being. South Korean emigrants who visit the country after some hiatus are awestruck at the seemingly universal upward social mobility and prosperity of the population. So-called structural change, which in south Korea's case refers to radical rates of urbanization and industrialization and profound restructuring of the labor market, make it complicated to assess objective and subjective indicators of individual mobility (Crompton 1993, 63). Sociologists factor out such structural change by looking at the relative chances that members of a particular social/occupational group have of attaining particular social stations, but enormous rates of structural change inflate people's perceptions of the equity of relative chances (Goldthorpe 1980). As Glen Elder (1974, 296) notes in *Children of the Great Depression*, in the case of post-war American prosperity, it was structural factors that brought about the boom, but "the important question is how it was (and is still being) interpreted, especially by parents and their children." These structural circumstances engender the feeling that "we were all poor together," a frequent refrain in many of my interviews. Divergent from this celebration of mobility, however, is a widespread public and popular nostalgia for the communality of shared poverty, of times before the onslaught of capitalism and individualism. The idea of an era of shared struggle has also been publicly promoted by the developmentalist state's calibration of its own economic achievements. Additionally, these material strides have been measured against the widely touted poverty and deprivation of south Korea's antipodal other, north Korea (Grinker 1998).

The second factor that contributes to narratives and sensibilities of openness is the Korean War. The war's real dislocations (some of them permanent)—downward mobility, devastation, and the redistribution of wealth brought about by the relatively successful land reform[4]—have contributed to the sense of a shared and equal post–Korean War starting point. Although the devastation was enormous, the costs were by no means equally incurred. In a similar vein, Elder (1974, 47) notes that because the American Depression was not shared to the extent that many people imagine, the sense of deprivation of those who did suffer is all the more acute.

Third, the sense of open mobility is reinforced because the rapidly waning rural sector today, although stratified in its own right, is relatively poor and homogenous. It is thus easy to mistakenly project today's rural sector on the highly stratified situation of the past when most wealth was landed, and rural inequities were the enormous divides between landowner and tenant, and between tenant and slave. This narrative propels the idea that people left a homogeneously poor rural sector on the strength of their own migrant grit and determination. This historical narrative of openness is further reinforced by a particular image of rural and premodern Korea as somehow less stratified or egalitarian (Chang 1991). This imagery had a vital life during the 1970s and 1980s in the community of dissent that was interested in indigenous sources of alternative social arrangements (see Abelmann 1996); likewise, into the 1990s there has been a growing, although politically less charged, interest in indigenous Korean popular cultural roots and social life as an alternative to Western consumer capitalism. Here, the rural village is figured as an egalitarian haven in contradistinction to the ills and excesses of advanced capitalism in contemporary urban south Korea.

The sense of openness is also produced by south Korea's official rhetoric about meritocratic institutions, particularly education. Education is centralized such that standardized national exams *in theory* give every boy and girl an equal chance to realize his or her dreams. Interestingly, during some of the state's most authoritarian moments when political and ideological capital held their greatest sway, the state nourished this fiction with micropolicies that ensured a meritocracy. In the early 1980s, for example, President Chun Doo Hwan instituted stringent controls on the home tutoring in which college students were employed by the rich to help prepare their children for college entrance examinations. In fact educational openness has long been mediated by outright graft and a myriad of extracurricular and even in-school preparatory activities that money can buy and symbolic capital can enhance (Cho 1995).

Collectively these narratives or myths of open mobility efface a number of historical and contemporary realities. They obscure the incredibly heterogeneous experience of rural exodus—the huge discrepancies between the exit of the children of rich landlords and those of poor tenants, farm hands, or servants. These stories also obscure the various ways in which class capital—economic, cultural, educational, and social—was transferable in south Korea's cities despite various dislocations, including the Korean War. For women, in particular, these stories ignore the reality that even beyond the contingencies of marriage, class and social standing were transferable to some extent.[5] Finally, these sensibilities leave little room for the urban poverty and squalor that resulted from the rural exodus, the large numbers of people who were long excluded—as some still are today—from any real advances in their standard of living.

SOUTH KOREA AS A CLOSED SOCIETY—"WHY HAVEN'T MY ATTRIBUTES TAKEN ME FURTHER?"

Competing narratives and sensibilities recognize south Korean inequality and the barriers to mobility. First, there has long been a pervasive sense in south Korea that social standing is in part political; that positions, goods, and services were procured through contacts and the right backing. So it was that the 1993 mandated assets disclosures of politicians and government officials became a national spectator sport which vindicated the widespread, if hushed, sense that political favor meant enormous financial gains. Engineered by the newly elected president, Kim Young Sam, this disclosure required all elected officials and high-level bureaucrats to detail their assets in order to expose those who had curried illicit favor or consumed to excess. Critical here was the community of dissent in south Korea—the forces and movements that contested the state and the ruling elites—that spoke out about the myriad ways in which south Korean society was closed, and pointed to the continued reign of colonial-period collaborating elites and to the mechanics of how privilege and power had conspired to reproduce themselves.

Also critical to the sense of a more closed society is the gradual emergence, particularly in the late 1980s, of the visible culture and consumption patterns of the rich, which was epitomized by the lavish residential and consumer enclaves south of the Han River. The Apkujŏng-dong Hyundai apartment complex, for instance, is infamous for its nouveau-riche lifestyles and profligate spoiled children, and more generally, for the trappings of a cosmopolitan elite whose lifestyles and cultural orientations are far removed from the "folk." Also associated with this relatively recently settled area is a sense of the insider knowledge, tip-offs, graft, and connections through which land, housing, and opportunities were procured. In part, this subculture was able to emerge because of the political achievements of the 1980s and 1990s, which have transformed public discourse, political practice, social sensibility, and personal identity (Abelmann 1996). These political transformations, which allowed for the public expression of conspicuous consumption, in conjunction with the economic boom of the 1980s, created visible enclaves. This is not to say that there were not fantastically wealthy people before, but the various relaxations of the late 1980s and 1990s catapulted the lives of the rich into the public eye and popular imagination. All of this, of course, has taken new turns recently in the aftermath of the I.M.F. crisis.

The sense of open mobility has also been thwarted by the role of land ownership in many south Koreans' social ascendances. With rapid GNP growth came soaring land and housing costs that gave rise to a nouveau-riche class fattened by wise or fortuitous land and real estate investments. It has become increasingly evident that the unpropertied majority has been excluded from the remarkable real estate boom of the 1980s and 1990s. These phenomena contributed to a sense of extreme political inequities; the assets disclosures, for example, confirmed what most suspected: that the housing and real estate boom rode the waves of insider knowledge, tip-offs, and friends in high places. Also, as land and housing ownership became barriers to relative wealth such that the returns of even a stellar income were dwarfed by the benefits of owning the right patch of land south of the Han River, public confidence in open social mobility with the requisite educational capital faltered.

The perception that social mobility is closed has led to a pervasive sensibility that is entirely at odds with the aforementioned sense that "we were all poor together": "Why haven't I gone further?" or "Why haven't my attributes (education, upbringing, intelligence, etc.) taken me further?" This sensibility has produced a collective frustration, a pervasive dissatisfaction about one's lot in life in the face of social injustice. The various waves of emigrants also can be seen in this context, as individuals who seek to extend their horizons beyond their thwarted potential at home (Abelmann and Lie 1995).

In my interviews with women, a tension emerges from this mobility contest between an interiorization of social mobility fates (the sense that they are authored by the individual) and the idea that they are structurally determined (that their efforts have not taken them far enough). Before turning to this contest as it emerges in the stories of So-yŏn's Mother, I review the usage of "gender" and "class" in this chapter.

THINKING ABOUT GENDER AND CLASS

I consider gender in three ways. First, I am concerned with gender in its common use to refer to men and women. Here, I am interested in the particular roles that women play in the daily production of status and in the inter- and intragenerational (re)production of class. This perspective emerges from an important feminist literature that underscores the limitations of focusing on the productive labor (formal employment) of men to the exclusion of the domestic and status-making labor of women (Abbott and Sapsford 1987, 150). In Korea past and present, women and the performance of engendered attributes have been essential to the expression of class (Cho, 1998; Deuchler 1977; Haboush 1991; Janelli and Janelli 1982; Yi 1993). Further, women's social, economic, and familial activities are integral to class expression and reproduction. Women largely take charge of the aesthetic dimensions of life, such as the personal adornment and etiquette of family members or home decoration, and of those institutions central to intergenerational class reproduction, education, and marriage (Cho 1995; Kim 1993; Kendall 1996; Moon 1990). As Bourdieu (1984) and others insist, class is enacted both through social relations and through noneconomic symbolic and cultural capital.

That women's labor in status reproduction—beyond the workplace—is central to the production of social standing, is critical to an understanding of both class and work. In the case of patrilineal societies such as south Korea, we need to think beyond received narratives in which women's entire class fates are sealed by marriage and the occupational status of their husbands. Certainly, women's marriage arrangements and choices are affected by their class background, but so too are their fates beyond marriage, through the ongoing real effects of their own class capital, including their personal resources, employment experience, and the contributions of their natal family members. A growing critical literature on women and class underscores both the material and ideational aspects of women's often different experiences from their husbands. The vast literature on intergenerational mobility that focuses on men, for example, ignores the fact that women too make intergenerational comparisons between their fathers and husbands (Elder 1974, 57).

It is particularly relevant that in recent decades women in south Korea have played key roles in the amassing of unearned income, one of the primary avenues of families' class mobility, including land and real estate investment (Nelson 1994). In fact, in the aforementioned assets disclosure, women were centrally implicated. Often it was the wives of politicians and upper-level bureaucrats who were captured hiding their faces from the camera as they were arrested. Indeed, many of the trouble spots, such as the illegal ownership of property or land (see Han 1993), machinations over college entrance, the excesses of consumption (particularly automobiles), and the extreme instrumentalities of marriage arrangements, are loosely assigned to, or associated with, women. As Smith-Rosenberg (1986, 34) points out, women are frequently scapegoated for the social and relational aspects of capitalism. Similarly, Rayna Rapp suggests (1982, 183) that women are the very ground on which the contradictions of capitalism are enacted: "Women have structurally been put in the position of representing contradictions between autonomy and dependence, between love and money, in relations of families to capitalism."

Second, I take up gender in terms of the ways in which class itself—its sensibilities, expression, aesthetics, and attributes—is engendered, that is, coded as somehow "male" or "female." This perspective follows widespread trends in feminism and the anthropology of gender that argue that we must consider not only men and women but the ways in which power and discourses are engendered (Scott 1988). In her discussion of masculinity and femininity in the eighteenth- to early ninteenth-century formation of the middle class in Birmingham, Catherine Hall (1992, 95) argues that the development of class itself is gendered. Sherry Ortner (1991, 171) suggests that mobility narratives in the contemporary United States are often entirely silent on class: "[They] shift the domain of discourse to arenas that are taken to be locked into individuals—gender, race. . . ." As K. Drotner (1994, 10) points out, "gender fundamentally serves to define and delimit the process of modernity." The expression of gender is coded as modern or antimodern. In the case of south Korea, patriarchy itself, a system of gender relations as well as a psychosocial complex, articulates with modernity. Although patriarchy has been widely considered antimodern, much of south Korea's political and institutional life has reproduced the practices and discourses of patriarchy.[6] Class hierarchies are inextricably bound with gender relations through the culture of families. Furthermore, these broad public narratives are constantly producing subjectivities for women, that is, delineating the contours of their gender and national identities (Cho n.d.).

Third, building on class and other subjectivities as gendered, I consider that the rhetorics of class mobility—why one or another person does or does not "make it" in society—are gendered. Social constructs of maleness and femaleness or masculinity and femininity are central in the interiorization or personalization of social mobility, promised, achieved, or thwarted.

The people who emerged in many of my interviews are men and women who quite flexibly are described by male and female traits, that is, menlike women and men, and womenlike men and women. This is not to suggest that a gendered idiom of personal attributes necessarily refers to flexible or fluid gender identities. Rather, it suggests that the idiom of personal character or personality is frequently articulated through the engendering of women's particular family structure and culture. Although there is no clear identification of either gender itself with the wherewithal or achievement of social mobility, many people attribute a constellation of gendered traits to successful mobility. These traits are gendered not only for being male or female per se, but also for being produced in the crucible of particular gender relations.

My interviews reveal considerable reflection on the social production and reproduction of maleness and femaleness; women narrate the social and psychological circumstances that produce gendered traits, traits that in turn engender particular life trajectories. In this context patriarchy is itself narrated as a particular social-psychological matrix that produces particular family dynamics and individual personalities or proclivities.

In the case of south Korean social mobility narratives and idioms, I have found particular associations between gendered personal attributes and social mobility inclinations. Femininity, for example, is often seen as mitigating against interested behaviors of class mobility and distinction. In this way, women are presented with impossible situations in which they are to be at once the performers and producers of cultural capital and again somehow isolated from these very instrumentalities. Under patriarchal capitalism women are thus ironically barred from productive relations, are assigned social reproduction, and are stripped of material desire. Carolyn Steedman (1986), in her brilliant working-class memoir, *Landscape for a Good Woman: A Story of Two Lives*, argues that material desire has been expunged from men's popular and academic narratives on working-class consciousness and experience. She sets out to tell a "social story" that makes room for the aching material desire of her childhood, a desire signified by her mother's longing for a "new look" skirt: " . . . by allowing . . . envy entry into political understanding, the proper struggles of people in a state of dispossession to gain their inheritance might be seen not as sordid and mindless greed for the things of the marketplace, but attempts to alter a world that has produced in them unfulfilled desire" (1986). In the case of south Korea, there are particular configurations of gender and class norms that surface in media and personal narratives: "interested" women driven by material desire who appear evil if rich and heroic if poor; effete men who are rendered merely incapable if poor and civilized if rich; feminine women who are pathetic or ill-fated if poor and cultured if rich, and so on. Attributes, however, are not scattered randomly across the class spectrum. Rather, class positions are associated with particular attributes; it is these stereotypes that make up the daily life sensibilities of class distinction and prejudice. Nonetheless, because of south Korea's enormous and rapid social dislocations, these interpretive and evaluative frameworks are flexible, allowing both for multiple interpretations and constant recalculation.

A SOCIAL MOBILITY STORY

I now turn to one woman's stories, which illustrate the play between narratives of gender, class, structural determinants, and individual attributes. The tensions in So-yŏn's Mother's narrative are many: between the myths of open mobility and the realities of limited social opportunities, between femininity and material desire, and between individual desire and social morality. These tensions are produced particularly in the narrative conventions of storytelling in the play between human agency, social causality, and inevitability.[7]

So-yŏn's Mother—An Introduction

The granddaughter of an eldest son and the oldest child of a second son, So-yŏn's Mother spent her early childhood in Kaesŏng, in what is now north Korea, cuddled in the accoutrements of privilege, including western things such as wool and hand-knit sweaters. Her great-grandfather had been poor, and while her grandfather had managed to amass riches, he was unschooled. Refugee poverty, however, followed this early fortune. Her own mother married her father ignorant of the "big mother" (*k'ŭnŏmŏnim*), her father's barren first wife. In Inch'ŏn, where they originally settled, and later in Seoul, her father never worked a day, while the big mother sold wares and her own mother kept house. Amid much shifting ground, the bedrock of all her tales is the steadfast friendship and true love of these mothers: the "manlike" big mother who "had she been born a man would have been a match for Chŏng Chu-yŏng [Hyundai Corporation's founder]," and her real mother, a "womanlike woman among women." Early on, the big mother told her mother, "This is our fate (*inyŏn*) so let's try to make something out of this household."

So-yŏn's Mother defied her family's advice, leaving Inch'ŏn for high school in Seoul and eventually almost single-handedly supported the nuclear family with her excellent bank job. She worked for six years at this job, which she was lucky to procure "like plucking a star from the heavens." She found this job thanks to her paternal grandfather's contacts, which she calls her "true advantage": "My grandfather lived as a *chaebŏl* (capitalist)." In Seoul, her life circled around fantastically wealthy émigré kin, the families of her grandfather's younger siblings (her grandparents never made it to the south), who seemed to have carried their wealth and prestige successfully across the armistice line, at least in the short run. In comparing the fates of relatives, So-yŏn's Mother stretches her stories far along kinship lines, to as far as second cousins, the daughter of her paternal grandfather's youngest sister, and nonbiological kin, the children of her father-in-law's second wife, and as close as her own siblings, a younger brother and two younger sisters.

So-yŏn's Mother married a banker: "On account of my grandfather I could marry a good man." Her reflections on her bank job and her husband, however, are not entirely uniform; it was the job that prevented her from attending college: "I hated my grandfather for not letting me go to college." She also has considerable ambivalence about her husband. Her mother-in-law, who had tormented her in the early years of her marriage, had herself been effectively abandoned early in her own marriage when her husband took a second wife. His family hailed from the still-discriminated-against Chŏlla provinces in south Korea's southwest; So-yŏn's Mother's husband's recent promotion to the very high ranks of a prominent bank would have been, So-yŏn's Mother suggests, unthinkable before the reforms of President Kim Young Sam. Extraordinarily capable and a womanizer, her husband always has kept his earnings to himself, contributing only lump sums to the family economy at critical points for the purchase of property and domiciles.

So-yŏn's Mother professed that she made the family what it is today: upper-middle class, able to educate the children well, able to decorate their home with the works of Korean artists and trappings from their two-year stay in England, and able to marry off So-yŏn with a large and lavish wedding. So-yŏn's Mother often spoke about the details of her home decor: A Swiss chalet–motif brocade purchased in Europe trims the walls of the home, several hand-carved statues of Jesus are placed in prominent places, and Korean antique items, including brass rice and soup bowls, are displayed about the home. So-yŏn's Mother does not dress in the stereotypical garb of a woman of her standing: She eschews makeup and designer-brand clothing, and stands out for having let her hair go gray, a decision inspired by her time abroad. She told me about the day she dressed herself up in the sapphires that So-yŏn had received from her in-laws prior to the wedding: "My whole life, I have never worn real jewelry, but when I went out in just plain slacks and a plaid shirt, and dressed it up in that jewelry, I could see that it was different—it really did something for this gray hair and these wrinkles."

In listening to So-yŏn's Mother, I realized that the lives against which she narrated her life, figuring its transgressions and calibrating her agency, are not merely those of her siblings or school chums but also include imagined lives. Thinking of her own second and third cousins who emigrated, for example, So-yŏn's Mother often mused on how things might have been had she, too, left Korea: "When I went to England [several years ago] I felt very grateful. I felt that my ancestors had done well by me so that I could go and see England, and I thought that if I had gone then [after high school] that I could have really done something there. When I practiced golf alone there [in England] I used to think about that again and again. And when I saw the white [transparent] glass of the school [the university where she took English classes] that was all I could think about." So-yŏn's Mother spoke of unfortunate people like herself who were left behind in Korea (i.e., who didn't emigrate).

It is in this sense that Arjun Appadurai (1991, 197–199) writes about the "genealogies of cosmopolitanism" along which people "imagine" other life possibilities. He reminds us that we live in the midst not only of immediate or far-flung personal networks, but also in the panoply of mediated lives and a myriad of imagined life trajectories. I am interested in the networks of people, again real and imagined, against which people reckon their own social standing or class fate. For south Korean women's lives, this means considering the Hollywood melodramas that nurtured their adolescences, the Christian testimonials that answered to their middle-aged angsts, the stories of emigration to America that stimulated their dreams (see Abelmann and Lie 1995), or the media portrayal of lives in north Korea that stretched their ideological imagination, to name a few.

BIG AND LITTLE STORIES: AGENCY VERSUS INEVITABILITY

The narrative conventions of So-yŏn's Mother's storytelling allow her to make a number of points. These points seem to be made in response to a silent interlocutor who praises, questions, or challenges aspects of her life. A frequent refrain in So-yŏn's Mother's stories is wonder at a number of decisions she made and actions she took that affected her personal, and later her family's, social mobility. Psychologist and narrative theorist Jerome Bruner suggests that "the 'feel' of agency in our lives is what is most likely to undergo exaggeration in the remembering" (1990, 5). Prominent here is her sense that "my friends [under the circumstances] could never have done as well." This self-wonderment at other moments is circumscribed by a sense of the inevitability of her course of action, both as a product of small forces—her family—and of grand matters—twentieth-century Korea. These tensions emerge in her stories and conversations.

While many of her stories underscore her agency, particularly in the achievement of her personal and familial mobility, So-yŏn's Mother is also extremely self-conscious and sometimes critical of ways in which she transgresses social norms. Bruner (1990, 18) suggests that autobiography is a form of apologia: "an arrangement of oneself against a set of normative standards." Certainly "agency" and "apologia" are not incompatible narrative conventions as people tell their lives. In the case of So-yŏn's Mother's life, her moments of greatest agency are at once reckonings with personal transgressions of social and, in particular, gender norms. It is precisely her reflections on transgression that reveal social patterns far beyond individual idiosyncrasy. In this regard Bruner notes (1991, 72) that much of self-making through storytelling is about "a violation of the folk-psychologically canonical that is itself canonical." It is precisely such "canonical" violations that reveal the fault lines of social contests and the ways in which individuals are caught up in them. Particularly fascinating, for example, is So-yŏn's Mother's reckoning of her own tales of personal mobility against her strong sense of a public good that in part precludes such individual action; she thus narrates against the stereotype in which she is so easily subsumed.

A central tension in her stories is that between her romantic nostalgia for her postrefugee poverty in south Korea and her celebration of her current prosperity. In this regard, So-yŏn's Mother particularly regreted that it was only in recent years that she had come to recognize the "fortune" of her post-war impoverished childhood years. Her nostalgia for poverty is primarily narrated through the relationship between her two mothers and the kindness of her incapacitated father. She explained that, at the time, she wasn't enlightened or thankful, but that she heard over and over from former neighbors "that I had lived amidst so much love, that my parents were like saints, that my mothers didn't fight. . . ." She often spoke of the home-made *mandu* (dumplings) that her mothers made, and of how those *mandu* were the envy of all of her childhood friends. She also spoke frequently of the moral superiority of the poor today, epitomized by the stories she hears from her Catholic priest about the generosity of the poor in contrast to the stinginess of the rich, who won't even give the priest a cigarette. Her reconstructed past is complicated, however, because her attachment to her childhood poverty is intertwined with her memories of the virtues of her extended family in north Korea before fleeing: "In my grandmother's era it was all of us together." In this context, she waxed nostalgic about the reach of her extended family, of the dozens of families that were cuddled in its economic embrace.

In this way, two very distinct elements of So-yŏn's Mother's past are integrated in a single nostalgia: the patriarchal trappings of the landholding elite *and* the communalism of poverty. This sort of slippage, however, is not at all anomalous in personal narratives or public discourse. Indeed, in south Korea today we find both a neo-Confucian resurgence, not unlike the family-values Christian Right in the United States, and a populist nostalgia for premodern indigenous communitarianism. Although these nostalgias are born in entirely different political and ideological crucibles, they can coexist as they do in the narratives of So-yŏn's Mother.

Engendering "Desire": So-yŏn's Mother's Family Cohort

Much of So-yŏn's Mother's discussions centered on key individuals in her life, including her father, her two mothers, one of her younger sisters, and finally her daughter, So-yŏn. If anything gave her the unerring resolve to move to Seoul and aspire to social mobility in her early days, it was her father's "lack of ability." A *yangban* member of a noble lineage and landlord's son, he wanted to feast on the delicacies of the old days, but rattled on about his disdain for money, had no business acumen, and never succeeded in bringing in any money. Furthermore, because So-yŏn's Mother was his first-born, arriving after the barren hiatus of his first marriage, he spoiled her. Repeatedly So-yŏn's Mother turned her palms to the sky, bouncing them upward to refer to this precious treatment. As a child in both Kaesŏng and Inch'ŏn, she was protected from gender discrimination, pampered, adored, and even addressed in honorific language. It was this pampering, she insisted, that ill-prepared her for the ways of the world. So-yŏn's Mother discussed how, in the painful early years of her marriage, she came to realize her own ignorance of patriarchy:

> Once I put a "question mark" [in English] to my husband: "Can't men and women be the same?" He said, "No," and explained that women must bolster their men, but I didn't agree. When I was in school I thought that men and women were the same, but at my place of work what a difference [was accorded them]. . . . and oh, after marriage I realized it more. My family [*chip*]

was wrong: Love is a good thing, but theirs was too much. You need to suffer [*kosaeng*] some. [After marriage] I had no energy [*kiun*], no sense of being alive [*saengdonggam*].

So-yŏn's Mother recalled her earliest brush with overt gender discrimination, her observations of a woman at the hands of a mother-in-law whom she encountered when they took shelter with a former tenant during the Korean War. She was shocked by the mother-in-law's harsh treatment—for example, that it was the mother-in-law who measured out the rice each meal, an indication of the mother-in-law's ongoing control of the household economy: "We were rich. We didn't know anything about that sort of behavior." Here, the relaxation of patriarchy is interestingly a marker of class privilege. Accompanying this relaxation, however, was her father's inability to assume the role of family provider, a lack that she abhorred.

Her father's lack of ability (*munŭng*) is among her frequent narrative refrains: "I was very unsatisfied [*pulman*]. He did things for other people, but never brought in any money. I was 'no comment' [in English] about it. He was *munŭng* so when I was in middle school I just came up to Seoul. It was my will [*ttŭt*], mine alone." Her decision to go to Seoul is one of the key ways in which she measured her agency in the sense that Bruner describes. Of the pathetic figure her father cut in her mind as a child, she said, "When it rained he came to school with an umbrella. I was so embarrassed. It would have been one thing if it was a good umbrella, but he would come in old clothes and with an old umbrella. Other children were met by their maids. I was ashamed and escaped to Seoul. I hated even looking at my father."[8] Later, faced with a hard marriage, she decided to be satisfied with what she could achieve from her own efforts: "I never even thought about whether my husband would succeed [*ch'ulse*]; I decided that it was my own efforts that would determine how I lived. I have thought about my life that way since I was a child."

In her husband, who pursued her at the workplace, she attests that she found the male qualities so lacking in her own father: "If they [men] have a goal they just go after it. . . . He is the sort who keeps his 'style' [in English] wherever he goes. He would live well in any nook and cranny of the globe." So-yŏn, in turn, "because she didn't want my life [*insaeng*]," opted for a dentist, a dull and quiet fellow, rejecting a promising lawyer whom she suspected of being a womanizer (like her father) and an aggressive social climber. In her chapter, Cho Haejoang writes of south Korea's "three generations of women who flatly refuse to live like their mothers," suggesting that such intergenerational conflict is itself a product of south

Korea's enormous social dislocation and of the way in which key cultural transformations have been mapped on women.

If her father, as a weak figure, inspired the *yoksim* (desire, drive, or greed) which propelled So-yŏn's Mother to Seoul and social mobility, over the years she has arrived at a very different perspective on her father. She understands now that, as the son of a *yangban*, her father had no interest in laboring. Again and again So-yŏn's Mother spoke about her conceptions of labor. Although she thinks of herself as having labored for her family's upward social mobility, she reflects formal Confucian ideologies in her conviction that labor is somehow base. In her discussions, she thus meanders between competing and necessarily gendered senses of optimal work lives. Beyond her father's *yangban* upbringing, she explains that his basic composition or heart and his upbringing made him *munŭng*.[9] Not only So-yŏn's Mother, but also the wealthy relatives in Seoul, have come to understand her father: "In those days some relatives used to ask me why my father didn't work, but now as they get older, they understand why it was that he couldn't go off and do hard labor." As for her natal family's early poverty in the south, So-yŏn's Mother figures that timing played a large part; her family were latecomers. Luck was also a factor: Her family sold a home they had owned in Seoul. "If only we hadn't sold it. . . ." she said.

As for her relatives, who had lived in the wealthy neighborhood of Hyoja-dong, to her great surprise, but not delight, many of them are struggling today. Some of their offspring have met tragic fates, one even his death in an American prison. Stressing the precarious fates of the once-rich, she said to me on another occasion: "The people [who work] at the Tongdaemun Market [one of the largest indoor-outdoor markets in Seoul] are not to be taken lightly; they are all from the north, and there are both *yangban* [rural elite] and *sangnom* [commoners] among their ranks."

So-yŏn's Mother's portrayal of her two mothers also reveals various reckonings with the past. There are times when she refers to both of them as "mother" because her real mother "in her heart gave my younger brother and me to the big mother." The big mother had the " 'style' [in English] of a male-type" and, she explains, "was both father and mother to me." Later, when So-yŏn's Mother was struggling with small children and an inattentive, noncontributing husband, the big mother helped her to run a boarding house, which launched the capital that So-yŏn's Mother has extended through frequent moves and the purchase of stocks and real estate over some forty years: "It was almost as if she was our maid. Because of her infertility she slaved in gratitude [for being able to join in the joy of having a family and children, and for not having been sent back to her natal family]." At another point, she explains: "She [big mother] worked 'till she sweat blood [*p'inanŭn nodong*]; it wasn't as if she was really making money like a man. So honest and hardworking, fit to be among Buddhas; I felt really sorry for her. How good she was!" So-yŏn's Mother attests that most women who began where she did have not come as far, even half as far, but that she owes her own success to her father's *munŭng* and her big mother's help.

If she praises the big mother, she also finds hers a tragic life: "Life is really about ups and downs. The worst thing is if in the end, as in the case of my [big] mother, you end up alone with no money. My [big] mother could have lived so well if she had just gone off on her own and worked, but instead she sacrificed herself and didn't make money on her own. If she had, she would have been better off than any of us." So-yŏn's Mother cried as she recalled the big mother's final departure from the house, the only option at the time because the big mother was going senile and prone to rising and screaming out all night long: "When she walked down the garden steps for the last time, she chuckled as she sang, 'When will my feet touch these stairs again?'" Still, in spite of all her praise, So-yŏn's Mother always carries a piece of paper in her pocketbook on which she lists the good *and* the bad attributes of her big mother. In the "bad" column are her obsessive stinginess and her "calculating, ambitious nature."[10]

So-yŏn's Mother is full of remorse for not understanding her biological mother better while she was alive and for only beginning to empathize with her in her own later years, after her mother's death. For a long time, she could not understand why her mother only did the housework (*sallim*) while the big mother went out and brought in money. Her own mother had seemed stupid (*pabo*) to her. Now she thinks of her mother with great sadness as "a true woman, a kind small bespectacled woman, the prototypical kind Korean woman." She was good at knitting and cooking, and she was pretty; "if only she [we] could have been rich." So-yŏn's Mother contrasts her own style with her mother's: "My basic composition isn't the sort that lays on the charm [for men] (*aegyorŭl purinda*), but my mother had more of that than I do. . . . To men, I can seem cold and indifferent. Men see young pretty girls in their midst, but come home to their wives who wear shabby clothes. . . ." She also mentions her "lack of charm" in relation to her difficulties at the hands of her mother-in-law and her philandering husband, suggesting that she was ill-prepared to win their favor. So-yŏn, in turn, often complains to her mother that she shouldn't speak so badly of men and marriage, making it impossible for her to enjoy her newlywed years. In the context of the three generations of women that Cho sketches (in this volume), So-yŏn's Mother seems betwixt and between the norms of both the grandmother's generation's active and aggressive ways, embodied in her big mother, and the wifely ways she finds in her own mother. Even this one woman's stories make clear that Cho's generational portraits are normative and narrative tropes through and against which women's lives are crafted.

So-yŏn's Mother had thought of her mother as unsociable and not adept at the ways of the world, but she saw things differently when, in her later years, her mother became active in the church. She realized that all along her mother had possessed considerable social abilities (*sahoesŏng*) "but that they had never surfaced because all she did was cater to my father who, after all, what with two wives and all, was somewhat conservative. I feel truly sorry for my mother, a woman having to live with another woman, and sacrificing everything for the children! If I think about it, I feel completely crazy. Once, when we were doing some health insurance paper work, we discovered that she [her mother] wasn't even recorded properly in the register, listed merely in the manner a boarder would be. . . . It's unthinkable, something that by today's standards just couldn't be, a life like hers!" It is to this mother that she also credits her drive (*yoksim*); just witnessing her mother's life gave her desire: "That she came from a rich family and still ended up like that gave me *yoksim*."

I conclude this vignette with So-yŏn's Mother's reflections on one of her younger sisters, a banker who married poorly and struggles to support her family on her own wages, and with her dreams for So-yŏn, her only daughter. The sister told So-yŏn's Mother frankly that she was determined not to make money in the same way that she had—"working [stocks and real estate speculation]." The sister preferred "to live cleanly, bringing in a salary." "But that was before her marriage. Now she looks at me differently," So-yŏn's Mother explains, because "she didn't understand the reality of our country." About being a woman banker So-yŏn's Mother is blunt: "When you really think about it, my sister really has been doing labor [*nodong*] her whole life; she has had to labor to make money. It isn't as if what I have done is so bad. And now she doesn't live well [her husband goes through all the money]. . . . If women go out in society [as with her sister] it isn't as if they really can make money." Thinking about her own years of running a boarding house, So-yŏn's Mother says, "As a woman, it was the only way to live." Yet she understands that her sister also did what she did in response to the *munŭng* of their father. Framed under a piece of glass beneath the mirror of So-yŏn's Mother's vanity chest in her bedroom is a photo of herself, her two sisters, and her sister-in-law. Once she glanced at the photo and remarked, "It is only women here, all women whose husbands have not helped them." Over the many months when I was interviewing So-yŏn's Mother, her husband was away on an out-of-town bank assignment, and I often felt that hers was in many ways the home of a woman who had labored alone.

So-yŏn's Mother crafted her daughter's prospects in keeping with her understanding that "women themselves can't do things freely [*chayuropta*] the way men can," and that women need to have some sort of special skill or talent "in order to get recognition." She explains, "The way our society is . . . men's work is a grand thing [*taedan hada*] while women's work is but a matter of course [*tangyŏn hada*]. That isn't what I think, but women's everyday work is the same, and if only once something isn't just right—the rice is bad, for example—men protest. And on top of that, you live under the gaze of your mother-in-law. And you have to agree with her no matter what. If she says an apple is rotten and you taste it and find it isn't, you still have to declare the apple rotten. No matter how far from reality you have strayed, there are no two ways about it."

So-yŏn's Mother set her sights on a piano for So-yŏn, a quintessential symbol of Western modernity, femininity, and status. Instead of kindergarten, So-yŏn went to piano lessons: "I made piano something that had to be done, like going to school or the hospital." As it turns out, after attending a prestigious arts school and almost entering Seoul National University's music department, So-yŏn prepared anew for college and became a dentist. There is a long and large story about why So-yŏn turned to dentistry, a tale about graft in which So-yŏn and her mother decided against the payoffs that were required for admission at that time. That story was but one of a number that illustrated So-yŏn's Mother's profound disappointment in the ways of south Korea and its elite establishments, even as she aspired to these for her children's future. Nonetheless, in dental school "It was So-yŏn's musical talent that people noticed. Even her professors asked, 'Why did someone like you come to pull teeth?'" So-yŏn was very popular in dental school, and was proposed to many times: "The most important thing was that she could sing and play the piano. Men want a woman with those sorts of skills." So-yŏn's Mother was particularly proud that four suitors had traveled all the way to England to court So-yŏn. I remarked that I wasn't surprised because of So-yŏn's intelligence, kindness, and beauty. So-yŏn's Mother insisted, however, that it was not those attributes but her piano and voice that had been the draw. Beyond womanly virtues, So-yŏn's Mother also spoke of the potential earning power of piano playing in south Korea. She stressed the permanence of these skills against the vicissitudes of educational capital.

Over the course of our discussions, So-yŏn's Mother expressed a range of thoughts about the promise of educational capital and work experience.

She explained that although it used to be the case that any landowning farmer could expect a profitable return for selling his paddy to educate his children, "things are not so clear today." On the one hand, she told me about a friend of her son who tried to make his way in the world through odd jobs and "real experience" and who had eventually concluded that "education is the only way." On the other hand, her eldest son eventually procured an excellent job in spite of weak educational credentials. "It would be best if all God-given jobs were respected in this society," she said, but she worried about the realities of various career paths for her children. Perhaps the most sensitive feature of her own life story is her lack of a college degree, something which, to this day, she has never formally communicated to her own children. Indeed it was only months after our meetings that she broke the silence with regard to her post–high school education. During the years of her bank job, she had thought to enroll in college classes in the evening, but because she was assigned to a branch office, the commute would have been too difficult. "If only I had spoken up and asked to be transferred to the main office." At one point she came to know professors at a newly opened university who could have arranged things for her there, but she declined because she did not think that such a degree would ever amount to anything. The university has become solid and reputable today and she regrets her youthful decision. Over the course of our interviews, it was never entirely clear what So-yŏn's Mother believes a college degree would have afforded her, but certainly she ponders what might-have-been. Over the last few years, her husband earned a doctorate and she mused how wonderful it would have been if she too could have earned a Ph.D.

Sometimes So-yŏn's Mother regrets that So-yŏn has become a laborer of sorts—doing the technical work of dentistry—but she is relieved at the stable, if dull, life that her daughter's profession and marriage provide. She is, though, it seems, still satisfied by her daughter's past potential for upward mobility by the grace of piano lessons.

Public Melodramas

Each time I arrived at So-yŏn's Mother's house, she began, as she had the week before, with rhetorical queries: "Korea isn't heading in a good direction, is it?" or "This society is on the path to ruin, isn't it?" or "The moral fiber of this society is being destroyed, don't you find?" Again and again she lamented the twists and turns of social hierarchy:

> Nowadays, all people do is move from apartment to apartment, and again from apartment to apartment and on and on, so that they can make money. Children

these days don't move because their father has been transferred but because their parents are trying to make money from buying and selling. These days, people have no fear of money, and you can no longer become rich just from hard work and a good salary. . . . People don't want to get rich by working, but by real estate. And then others are jealous of them, so nobody is happy. People who used to be nothing are getting fat. The smart people need to be rich, but that doesn't happen. We need to create a new class of people who will work hard for the country. . . . It is hard for men to achieve a better society because of their own desire and because of their wives who share in that desire. It is as if the wives of bank managers become bank managers themselves.

Regarding her own frequent moves, not unlike those of the people she chided, So-yŏn's Mother said, "one has to keep up with the tempo. . . . but I wouldn't really call what I've done investment, I've just moved a lot." The once-wealthy Hyoja-dong relatives did not keep up and consequently fell into the middle class. "They live okay, but not as good as me."

So-yŏn's Mother's social mobility story is stitched from the complexity of south Korea's modern history. What emerges is not a linear narrative but one that winds among the articulations of class, social circumstances, opportunities, and gender. So-yŏn's Mother's stories about her own and So-yŏn's life chances are played out between personal attributes, educational capital, and social-political barriers. They straddle the narratives on openness and closedness with which I began this chapter.

The tensions in So-yŏn's Mother's stories reveal the discursive struggles and contemporary transformations reviewed in this chapter's earlier discussions. Although she spent her entire adult life laboring under patriarchal inequities, she criticizes women who are caught up in the desire for material things that ruins society. On the one hand, she reared her daughter to play the piano and to attract a prosperous and promising man with her feminine virtues; on the other hand, she is relieved by So-yŏn's marital decision and resigned to the fact that due to the patriarchal nature of her father, So-yŏn did not choose materialism and masculine ambition. Similarly, although So-yŏn's Mother once trusted in musical accomplishment as her ticket to well being, So-yŏn's personal musical path was blocked by powerful social and economic barriers. So-yŏn's Mother's own successful upward mobility meanders through gendered attributes, child rearing, class capital, and historical circumstances: the rejection of her father's *munŭng*; the pain of watching her confined mother; the inspiration and the direct help of the big mother; the remnants of her father's former wealth in the shape of her otherwise unthinkable employment at the bank; her lack of a college degree, which left her no option but labor; Korea's division, which separated her family from its former wealth; and so on. Indeed, her stories traverse the competing narratives of south Korea's contemporary history and inequality.

Her narratives are variously gendered. There are simple gender attributions, such as in the discussion of her manlike big mother and womanlike mother, who together she referred to as "like a couple" (*pubu*). In sometimes oblique references to shared conventions of patriarchy, she often notes transgressions, as in the style of her own upbringing: her elevation as a girl that was out of keeping with conceptions of how things are or ought to be done, and of her own inability to be flirtatious. Here too we can think of her father's *yangban* upbringing and its gendered attributes, an effeteness spoken through *munŭng* and negated through her choice of a manlike husband whose firm resolve and singleness of purpose in his courting style made it seem "a waste to leave him for another woman to snatch up." "If only," she mused, "I could be like him, never wasting a morning moping about or suffering a sick spell." At many points, she stressed the importance of physical health for attaining one's desires, and she bemoaned her own failing health and often delicate condition. In her view, it is her husband's very ambition, that has made him think lightly of her, "regarding her as laughable." Here So-yŏn's Mother refered both to her own drab housewifely attire and to her educational failings. So-yŏn, in turn, chose a dull match: "terribly thin and pale and too doting for a man." *Yoksim*, synecdoche for the desire or pursuit of upward mobility, is alternatively gendered: male as an attribute of her successful husband, but female and demonized for women unable to succeed in the public domain.

Interestingly, she considers all the work of the women in her universe to be menial labor, from her mother's housework to her big mother's market days, her own management of a large and successful boarding house, her sister's high-level job at a prestigious bank, and even her daughter's highly skilled work as a dentist with a degree from one of the country's most respected programs. Only piano playing, a luxury that she was never afforded and that she went to great pains to provide for her daughter, is somehow both feminine and distant from toil. Class is also about gender as she describes her childhood where, in times of prosperity, patriarchy was relaxed and her mother, the picture of gentility and femininity, could flourish.

CONCLUSION

I have demonstrated how women's mobility narratives can be taken as part of a larger inquiry into contemporary historical reckoning in south

Korea. This reckoning of social mobility, rife with contest and in constant flux, is nothing short of a full-fledged debate on social, moral, and political justice and visions for south Korea. Personal and mediated narratives take up dissensions at the heart of this debate, including contests over equality of opportunity, legacies of social structure, gender relations, and economic distribution. The discursive contest itself is gendered. Women are both positioned and take up particular positions in narrating class. Women straddle, in their lives and narratives, conflicting relations to desire for material things. Femininity is marked as a noncapitalist domain, even as women are assigned crucial roles of class expression and reproduction. In the narratives of So-yŏn's Mother we have seen how women both reproduce and contest received stories and histories. Furthermore, women both participate in and contest the personalization of class. In popular and political convention they long for the triumph of, and comment in detail on, gendered personal attributes, but they also call critical attention to received political and patriarchal structures and to historical continuities that diminish the potential of personal agency or the effects of personal proclivity.

Through one woman's story of social mobility, we can observe the central contests of contemporary south Korea, contests over nothing short of social and historical reality. In her introduction to this volume, Laurel Kendall writes of "getting a grip," of the ways in which Koreans grapple with the vertigo of Korean (post)modernity, with the flux and contradictions of their lives. Of course, So-yŏn's Mother's story—the story, after all, of one woman—cannot offer a final word on the contests I have outlined here or the contradictions of her times. What I suggest is that these are the contests that constitute the fabric, the vertigo, of contemporary lives. Thus we find in her narratives the interiorization of large processes onto the family and even personality, while at the same time we can observe the ways in which she draws on the most public of narratives. Throughout this chapter, I have insisted that the central narratives and sensibilities of contemporary south Korea are gendered; indeed this is the conviction of this volume. Furthermore, we cannot think about class other than through gender and narrative. Gendered narratives are not just metanarratives on class but the very stuff of it. We cannot talk about class as it is lived in its profound social distances and distinctions, without paying attention to the social discourses through which and against which it is narrated. Class, then, is in part lived through gendered trajectories of mobility and engendered narratives that chart, comment on, and contest that mobility.

NOTES

I would like to extend my thanks to Laurel Kendall for organizing the conference "Gender and Social Change in Late Twentieth-Century Korea" and for providing excellent and extensive editorial comments and suggestions on this paper. I am also grateful for the helpful comments and criticisms of all of the conference participants. Additionally, I would like to thank the friends and colleagues who kindly read this manuscript—John Lie, Patricia Sandler, Ann Saphir, and Karen Winter-Nelson. Finally, I am indebted to the research assistance of Hae-Young Jo, Hyun Hee Kim, Soo-Jung Lee, So Jin Park, and Jesook Song.

1. Writing about a post-Tiananmen Chinese soap opera, anthropologist Lisa Rofel (1995, 307) discusses a parallel contest, "an ambivalence about whether the Wang family dilemmas were personal or historical."

2. See Abelmann 1997b for further discussion of social mobility in south Korea.

3. In his study of the children of the American Depression, for example, Glen Elder (1974, 88) found that deprivation was the greatest predictor of the intensification of the mother's role.

4. Although the south Korean land reform had its own limitations and lacunae, its redistributive efficacy was significant.

5. Although the common sense view of the extremes of patrilineage and patriarchy suggests that women sever material ties from their natal families upon marriage, it is certainly the case today, as well as in the past (Kendall 1985), that marriage does not present impermeable boundaries for the flow of patrilineal class resources to daughters (both tangible and intangible).

6. See Janelli and Yim 1993 for an important discussion of the pitfalls and limits of thinking about the continuities of patriarchy from the premodern to the contemporary era.

7. For further discussion of these themes see Abelmann 1997a.

8. Glen Elder (1974, 93) notes that in the case of Depression-era deprivation in the United States, there was a high incidence of social distance and conflict between daughters and fathers.

9. At the time of our interviews, spring 1993, Kwinam [precious boy], the male protagonist of the soap opera *Adŭl kwa ttal* (Son and Daughter), had become the media synecdoche of a male victim of the extreme privilege of patriarchy as the first born. He was a man with no gumption, a man many people explained as having a deadened spirit (*ki*) (See Yi 1993 for a discussion of *ki* and child rearing).

10. Discussing the Depression-era cohort of the United States, Elder (1974, 112) found that over time, women developed considerable resentment of their mothers precisely because of their extreme indebtedness and resultant feelings of obligation.

References

Abbott, Pamela, and Roger Sapsford. 1987. *Women and Social Class*. New York: Tavistock Publications.

Abelmann, Nancy. 1996. *Echoes of the Past, Epics of Dissent: A South Korean Social Movement*. Berkeley: University of California Press.

———. 1997a. Narrating selfhood and personality in south Korea: Women and social mobility. *American Ethnologist* 24.4:786–812.

———. 1997b. Women's class mobility and identities in south Korea: A gendered, transgenerational, narrative approach. *Journal of Asian Studies* 56.2:398–420.

Abelmann, Nancy, and John Lie. 1995. *Blue Dreams: Korean Americans and the Los Angeles Riots*. Cambridge, Mass.: Harvard University Press.

Abu-Lughod, Lila. 1991. Writing against culture. In *Recapturing Anthropology*. Richard G. Fox, ed. pp. 137–162. Santa Fe: School of American Research Press.

Appadurai, Arjun. 1991. Global ethnoscapes: Notes for a transnational anthropology. In *Recapturing Anthropology*. Richard G. Fox, ed. pp. 191–210. Santa Fe: School of American Research Press.

Bott, Elizabeth. 1957. *Family and Social Network: Roles, Norms, and External Relationships in Ordinary Urban Families*. New York: The Free Press.

Bourdieu, Pierre. 1984. *Distinction: A Social Critique of the Judgement of Taste*. London: Routledge and Kegan Paul.

Brooks, Peter. 1976. *The Melodramatic Imagination: Balzac, Henry James, Melodrama, and the Mode of Excess*. New Haven, Conn.: Yale University Press.

Bruner, Jerome. 1990. The 'remembered' self. Manuscript presented at the Mellon Conference on the Remembered Self. Emory University, Atlanta, Georgia, January 24–26:1–30.

———. 1991. Self-making and world-making. *Journal of Aesthetic Education* 25.1:67–78.

Chang, Yunshik. 1991. The personalist ethic and the market in Korea. *Comparative Studies in Society and History* 33:106–129.

Cho Haejoang. 1995. Children in the examination war in south Korea: A cultural analysis. In *Children and the Politics of Culture*. Sharon Stephens, ed. pp. 141–168. Princeton, N.J.: Princeton University Press.

———. 1998. Male dominance and mother power: The two sides of Confucian patriarchy in Korea. In *Confucianism and the Family*. Walter H. Slote and George A. DeVos, eds. pp. 187–207. New York: State University of New York Press.

———. N.d. Mothers, heroes and restless children: Two stories and an introduction. In *Male Frames, Female Pictures: A Post-colonial Critique of South Korean Society*. idem, ed Forthcoming.

Crompton, Rosemary. 1993. *Class and Stratification: An Introduction to Current Debates*. Cambridge: Polity Press.

DeLauretis, Teresa. 1984. *Alice Doesn't: Feminism, Semiotics, Cinema.* Bloomington: Indiana University Press.

Deuchler, Martina. 1977. The tradition: Women during the Yi dynasty. In *Virtues in Conflict: Tradition and the Korean Woman Today.* Sandra Mattielli, ed. pp. 1–48. Seoul: Korea Branch of the Royal Asiatic Society.

Drotner, Kirsten. 1994. Cross-over culture and cultural identities. Paper presented at the nineteenth IAMCR conference, Seoul, Republic of Korea.

Elder, Glen H. Jr. 1974. *Children of the Great Depression: Social Change in Life Experiences.* Chicago: University of Chicago Press.

Elsaesser, Thomas. 1987. Tales of sound and fury: Observations on the family melodrama. In *Studies in Melodrama and the Woman's Film.* Christine Gledhill, ed. pp. 43–69. London: British Film Institute.

Em, Henry H. 1995. Yi Sang's 'Wings' read as an anti-colonial allegory. *Muae* 1: 105–111.

Ginsburg, Faye. 1989. *Contested Lives: The Abortion Debate in an American Community.* Berkeley: University of California Press.

Gledhill, Christine. 1987. The melodramatic field: An investigation. In *Studies in Melodrama and the Woman's Film.* idem, ed. pp. 5–39. London: British Film Institute.

Goldthorpe, John H., in collaboration with Catriona Llewellyn and Clive Payne. 1980. *Social Mobility and Class Structure in Modern Britain.* Oxford: Clarendon Press.

Grimstead, David. 1968. *Melodrama Unveiled: American Theatre and Culture, 1800–1850.* Chicago: University of Chicago Press.

Grinker, Richard Roy. 1998. *Korea and Its Futures: Unification and the Unfinished War.* New York: St. Martin's Press.

Haboush, JaHyun Kim. 1991. The Confucianization of Korean society. In *The East Asian Region: Confucian Heritage and Its Modern Adaptation.* Gilbert Rozman, ed. pp. 84–110. Princeton, N.J.: Princeton University Press.

Hall, Catherine. 1992. *White, Male and Middle Class: Explorations in Feminism and History.* New York: Routledge.

Han, Do-Hyun. 1993. Capitalist landownership and state policy in 1989–1990 in South Korea. *The Korea Journal of Population and Development,* December.

Janelli, Roger L., and Dawnhee Yim Janelli. 1982. *Ancestor Worship and Korean Society.* Stanford, Calif.: Stanford University Press.

Janelli, Roger L., with Dawnhee Yim Janelli. 1993. *Making Capitalism: The Social and Cultural Construction of a South Korean Conglomerate.* Stanford, Calif.: Stanford University Press.

Kendall, Laurel. 1985. *Shamans, Housewives, and Other Restless Spirits: Women in Korean Ritual Life.* Honolulu, University of Hawai'i Press.

————. 1988. *The Life and Hard Times of a Korean Shaman: Of Tales and the Telling of Tales*. Honolulu: University of Hawai'i Press.

————. 1996. *Getting Married in Korea: Of Gender, Morality, and Modernity*. Berkeley: University of California Press.

Kim, Myung-Hye. 1993. Transformation of family ideology in upper-middle-class families in urban south Korea. *Ethnology* 32:69–83.

Modleski, Tania. 1982. *Loving with a Vengeance: Mass-Produced Fantasies for Women*. Hamden, Conn.: Archon Books.

Moon, Okpyo. 1990. Urban middle class wives in contemporary Korea: Their roles, responsibilities and dilemma. *Korea Journal* 30:30–43

Nelson, Laura. 1994. Gender, nation, and the politics of consumption in south Korea. Manuscript presented at the Conference on Women in South Korea. University of British Columbia.

Ortner, Sherry B. 1991. Reading America: Preliminary notes on class and culture. In *Recapturing Anthropology*. Richard G. Fox, ed. pp. 163–190. Santa Fe: School of American Research Press.

Rapp, Rayna. 1982. Family and class in contemporary America: Notes toward an understanding of ideology. In *Rethinking the Family: Some Feminist Questions*. Barnie Thorne and Marilyn Yalom, eds. pp. 49–70. New York: Longman.

Rofel, Lisa. 1995. The melodrama of national identity in post-Tiananmen Square. In *To Be Continued . . . . : Soap Operas Around the World*. Robert C. Allen, ed. pp. 301–320. New York: Routledge.

Scott, Joan. 1988. *Gender and the Politics of History*. New York: Columbia University Press.

Sewell, William H., Jr. 1985. *Structure and Mobility: The Men and Women of Marseille, 1820–1870*. Cambridge: Cambridge University Press.

Smith-Rosenberg, Carol. 1986. Writing history: Language, class, and gender. In *Feminist Studies/Cultural Studies*. Teresa de Lauretis, ed. Bloomington: Indiana University Press.

Stack, Carol. 1974. *All Our Kin: Strategies for Survival in a Black Community*. New York: Harper Row.

Steedman, Carolyn. 1986. *Landscape for a Good Woman: A Story of Two Lives*. London: Virago.

Watt, Ian. 1957. *The Rise of the Novel: Studies in Defoe, Richardson and Fielding*. Berkeley: University of California Press.

Yi, Eunhee Kim. 1993. From gentry to the middle class: The transformation of family, community, and gender in Korea. Ph.D. dissertation, University of Chicago.

3

DISCOURSES OF ILLNESS, MEANINGS OF MODERNITY: A GENDERED CONSTRUCTION OF SŎNGINBYŎNG

june j. h. lee

From my field diary, October 21, 1994:

I was sitting in a taxi cab in the center of Seoul's Kangnam District, south of the Han River. It was a rainy afternoon and I wasn't prepared for the rain. What a stupid idea! Taking a cab on a Friday afternoon in a humongous city where you can expect rush hour traffic virtually 24 hours a day. Even more stupid was making an unforgivably naive decision to do fieldwork among Seoul's privileged, affluent, and world-media savvy middle class families, and most particularly on their middle-aged[1] male heads. Preoccupied with the frustratingly slow progress of my fieldwork, I was looking out at the rain and at the busy streets of Kangnam through the window of the almost motion-less cab when an unexpectedly shrill and panicky voice from the radio announced that the Sŏngsu Bridge over the Han River had just collapsed. A bus full of schoolgirls had been on the bridge at the time, and they were all presumed dead. I felt a sudden pang of alarm for Park-sangmunim,[2] thus far my only "key informant." He crosses the bridge every morning to go to his office from his apartment in the Kangnam District.

Anxious to hear from him, I spent that whole afternoon in front of the TV, hypnotized by the live report from the bridge, the rescue, the repeated remorse over this "man-made calamity." Could Park-sangmunim (and consequently my research project) be a victim of Korea's excessive haste to build a modern[3] nation?

Finally, late in the evening, I got a call from Park-sangmunim. "I'm all right," he said. When I asked his whereabouts at the moment of the disaster, he answered in a dazed voice, "I was in my car. The car in front of mine fell off the bridge." After a silent second, he added "I was just one car away from death."

During this interesting year of fieldwork in Seoul (from mid-1994 to mid-1995), there were other, bigger accidents in Korea. After the bridge collapse, there were two gas explosions, one in the center of Seoul in December 1994 and the other in the city of Taegu in April 1995. Additionally, right after I left Seoul, in late May 1995, a department store in a particularly wealthy area of the prosperous Kangnam District collapsed, again making world headlines. Hundreds died, more were injured, and the whole nation was deeply hurt. This was a blow to Korea's newfound pride as a wealthy creditor nation. These accidents were readily characterized by the media as "manmade calamities" attributed to rushed and consequently "unreliable construction" (*pusilgongsa*) which were quite common during Korea's frenzied pursuit of rapid economic growth. This pathological obsession with speed was diagnosed as "the Korean disease" and the rampant "side effects" of the nation's hasty modernization now came under full-scale media scrutiny.

In earlier decades, scholarly works and literary writings had highlighted modernization's undesirable effects on Korean life, but by the 1990s this social critique had permeated the language of ordinary people. In popular discourses, the weariness and disillusionment of middle-aged men like Parksangmunim was read as a sign of the exhaustion of Korea's modernization project. In this chapter, I analyze several cultural texts that articulate critical and critically gendered understandings of what was once hailed as Korea's grand social transformation. Discontent with modernization, already widespread in the first half of the 1990s, was amplified after the nation submitted to the economic regulations imposed by the I.M.F. in late 1997.

By "cultural texts," I mean published national statistics and their interpretation, articles from major daily newspapers and magazines, and presentations in audio, visual, and print media. In and through these texts, the ailing middle-aged Korean man is canonized as the altruistic victim of prevailing chronic diseases. These diseases, locally labeled as "adults' diseases" (*sŏnginbyŏng*), are also commonly referred to as "illnesses of modernization" (*hyŏndaebyŏng*), because the men who suffer from them are portrayed as having worked themselves sick in creating Korea's rapid economic success. In *sŏnginbyŏng* narratives, men are defined through their work, and it is their work that makes them ill. Modern Korean masculinity is intrinsically perceived through and embodied in the particularly local effects of industrialization-cum-modernization.

In accordance with current literary criticism, I do not view narratives as unmediated reflections of experience, or just "a story of what happened." The stories presented in cultural texts are selective formulations of reality; they represent a highly idealized means of engaging personal and public circumstances. Conversely, illness narratives themselves are mediated and modified by human experience. Here, as elsewhere (Lee 1998), I am concerned with how middle-aged Korean men make and unmake the connection between their own experience and the media representations, statistics, and other textual productions on health and illness. In this discussion, I emphasize the narrative's regulative and constituting effects within institutionalized systems for the production of knowledge and the exercise of power and social control (Bové 1995). I describe how illness narratives featuring middle-aged Korean men articulate with social and economic forces to produce images of social reality that have come to be held in common across a broad national community in Korea, and as such have provoked commentary on experiences that are simultaneously national and intimate. As a demonstration of this dynamic process, I offer the midlife reflections of a white-collar man. Park-sangmunim's personal narratives, as they reflect the anxieties of other middle-aged Korean men in similar circumstances, have much in common with the popular representations of this group in media portrayals of *sŏnginbyŏng*. They are, at the same time, his own distinctively personal dialogues with popular understandings of *sŏnginbyŏng* as he comes to terms with his own life.

MODERNIZATION QUESTIONED

Unlike the dramatic collapse of bridges and buildings, *sŏnginbyŏng* presents a more direct, intimate, and day-to-day source of anxiety for many Seoulites. The term *sŏnginbyŏng* generally covers hypertension, diabetes, diseases of the heart, liver, and stomach, chronic bronchitis, and various cancers. Although these diseases are not restricted to adults, they are particularly prevalent in middle life. *Sŏnginbyŏng* narratives, like the rampant "Korean disease," have risen with Korea's accelerated economic growth. Sporadic discussions about *sŏnginbyŏng* appeared throughout the 1980s, but they were muted relative to the swell of concern expressed in the 1990s. The timing is significant. As Foucaultian studies have taught us, only some biological givens, and among them only certain illnesses, become culturally meaningful (Lock 1993). As I illustrate in the following pages, *sŏnginbyŏng* became an abiding concern when a particular group of Korean men were associated with this illness at a particular historic pass. But first I provide the context for such body politics by examining discourses on the changing Korean family and the national economic crisis as two aspects of the complicated social changes that Koreans experienced in the 1990s.

Sŏnginbyŏng narratives strongly articulate existing and widely accepted moral criticisms of changing domestic relationships, namely family nucleation. The argument is as follows: With the disintegration of the traditional extended family, the modern nuclear family fails to maintain such Confucian virtues as familial solidarity, filial piety, and self-sacrifice, and thereby ruptures the possibility of harmonious and stable support among family members. This moral discourse was uncritically accepted and effectively deployed in the policy debates of the early 1990s that concerned both population and public welfare. Not only did the policy makers fail to identify the actual sites of family welfare problems—an aging rural population, single-parent families, the urban poor—but they used familist ideology to justify the government's continuing low-level welfare expenditure (Chang 1997a). Korea's first civilian government in thirty years thus failed to initiate a long-awaited transition from economic growth–oriented state intervention to social welfare–oriented state intervention. Instead, the new Kim Young Sam administration focused on family support as the means and objective of its welfare policy (Chung 1991, cited in Chang 1997b). Ultimately, "family welfare" meant that Korean wives, as mothers and daughters-in-law, had a state-defined responsibility to take care of children, the elderly, the disabled, and other dependents. To this end, the elite neo-Confucian tradition once again was mobilized as Korea's legitimate cultural heritage and given new emphasis in public education (Cho 1998).

In *sŏnginbyŏng* narratives, the root causes of the illness are also sought in relation to the purported collapse of the traditional family, and particularly in the assumed-to-be problematic relationship between midlife husbands and wives (see Cho in this volume). Specifically, *sŏnginbyŏng* narratives dictate a causal relationship between "the collapse of the traditional family" and the male family head's ill health. This alleged link is made when, for the first time in recent history, the interest of these white-collar Korean men is divorced from that of their employers, the family-owned large Korean conglomerates or *chaebŏl*.

From the early 1990s, Korea's competitive advantage in the world market suffered a precipitous decline. Factors that had propelled Korea's remarkable economic growth during the 1970s and 1980s—the fortuitous combination of low-wage, high-quality labor and cheap foreign capital under favorable conditions for international trade—diminished in the face of local wage hikes and increased price competition overseas. Corporations were (and still are) in dire need of structural reform, coincidentally phrased as a "[bodily] constitutional improvement." They responded by implementing labor control and intensifying the rationalization of production (Park

1997). These reforms are seen generally as enabling the slow-footed giant conglomerate's traditionally conservative and consensus-driven management to become more agile, more aggressive, and, most importantly, more adaptable in the furiously changing international business arena. For the first time in modern Korean history, the corporate white-collar worker came to be viewed as part of the problem.

Corporate downsizing became the defining reality of the workplace in Korea in the 1990s. Dubbed locally as "weight-reducing management," "employment clearance," and most ominously as "getting rid of the dead weight" (*kunsalppaegi*), downsizing shook the white-collar class's fundamental assumption that loyalty and longevity were sure paths to advancement. In the late 1980s, one heard intermittent neighborhood rumors about senior managers who were passed over for promotion in favor of their junior colleagues or even dismissed by their companies. Slowly but relentlessly this trend accelerated through the early 1990s, and by mid-1995 these once-infrequent occurrences had achieved the status of a mass phenomenon.

The "neck-tie squad" of white-collar salary workers lacked the blue-collar workers' militant unions to support them in their worsening plight, but they did have an ally in the sympathetic media. Since the mid-1990s, incessant media attention has been lavished on "the white-collar blues," "the end of the salary man era," and the "middle-aged men's crisis." Television and print media ran features devoted to the problems middle-aged white-collar men faced as a consequence of white-collar restructuring. In these portrayals, male self-pity is unremittingly generated in the saga of the "forgotten hero of economic growth" and is replayed again and again. These programs, in concert with a series of nostalgic television dramas, public exhibitions, and novels of the "remembering the hard times" genre generate a climate of male longing for things past. Exuberant energy, manly spirit, and paternal authority are seen as things that the white-collar men of Korea lost in their battle to build a modern metropolitan nation. In this context, accounts of the faltering health of middle-aged Korean men drew an enormous amount of attention.

THE "WORLD'S HIGHEST MORTALITY" OF MIDDLE-AGED KOREAN MEN

Four Out Of Ten Koreans' Health Is In Danger! Those in their forties and fifties are the least healthy. Men are generally less healthy than women at all ages (*Han'guk Ilbo* 9 September 1995).

According to Professor H[4] from the Seoul National University School of Medicine, *sŏnginbyŏng* attack *those adults who are at the prime of their working careers* and cause not only *the loss of productivity* but also unnecessary medical expense. Hence it is *the most serious medical problem of the nation* (*Naeoekyŏngje Sinmun* 28 April 1995) (emphasis added).

Since 1990, mortality- and morbidity-related public health statistics have received serious media attention in south Korea. In the past, the figures that had been central not only to official Korean discourses on modernization, but also to everyday conversations, were those related to GNP, fertility, or the amount of exports. When Korea was striving to achieve statistical indicators of "development" or "progress," mortality and morbidity statistics were not a part of the discussion. This changed decisively when, on February 23, 1990, a new statistical report on Korean mortality was released by the National Bureau of Statistics (NBS), a branch office under the Economic Planning Board. This report consisted of a series of life tables made for the years 1983, 1985, 1987, and 1989. According to the media-quoted government announcement, the smallest mortality decline over this period was for men in their forties (to be precise, men between the ages of 45 and 49). Furthermore, the mortality rate of these men was higher than that of Korean women at the same age and higher than the mortality rates for Japanese, Canadian, French, and Taiwanese men in the same age bracket. The major causes of death for these Korean men were various kinds of cancers, liver diseases, cerebrovascular diseases, and accidents. On the day the report was released, the high mortality of Korean middle-aged men was featured in nearly every Korean evening newspaper and TV news program. The appalling qualifier, "world's highest," was derived from the statistical assertion that "middle-aged Korean men's mortality was the highest among the 47 nations who regularly report their mortality rates to the World Health Organization" (*Han'guk Ilbo* 25 February 1990).

In fact, several medical professionals with whom I have discussed this matter expressed strong doubts about the validity of this comparison with the other forty-six countries. At least one professional publication cited the unreliability of Korean mortality data, asserting that it cannot be reliably compared with mortality data from "advanced nations (*sŏnjin'guk*) who are capable of analyzing mortality well" (Suh 1990, 21). Because the mortality rate reported at the year of death is very low among Koreans (less than 8 percent) the reliability of the mortality rate for any given year is questionable (Kim 1993). In general, mortality measures have a very limited applicability for the comparison of health status differentials among various populations, owing to the fact that the data on which the mortality rates are based is very often incomplete and inaccurate. Unlike fertility data, which are easy to gather and relatively accurate, mortality data are subject to a much greater possibility of misinformation and distortion (Hansluwka 1987; Phillips 1991).

The Korean media ignored all such qualifications in constructing their "world's highest mortality" stories. Quoted uncritically in most subsequent popular texts, the vulnerability of Korean middle-aged men swiftly became an item of common knowledge among Seoulites. Moreover, while the report referred to men who were between the ages of 45 and 49 between 1985 and 1989, the press glossed over this point and attributed the rate to men who were in their forties as of 1990. In fact, the news was soon transformed from a cohort of age 45 to 49 into *all* men in their forties or even all men of "middle age" (*chungnyŏn*). The actual victims of the high mortality rate are buried deeply in these statistical and textual constructions. In the popular imagination, the age of 40 has become a threshold of the deadly mortality rate for all men. Moreover, media hyperbole about the unusually high male mortality rate completely overshadows other aspects of the population's health.

While the media focused on mortality rates, morbidity data more accurately indicate the state of an industrialized nation's health. According to Phillips (1991, 399), as epidemiological transition progresses, "chronic or degenerative diseases increase in importance [and] they may be associated with considerable amounts of ill-health, restricted activities, and need for health and social care." Highly frequent, disabling, but nonfatal diseases such as rheumatism and arthritis are much more intractable but are not reflected in mortality data to any significant degree. Therefore, Korean men's high mortality does not necessarily mean that middle-aged men are the nation's most afflicted members. On the contrary, according to the 1992 National Health Survey, women in their forties actually showed higher morbidity rates than did men of the same age (Korea Institute for Health and Social Affairs 1993, 24). Both acute and chronic morbidity were higher in women than in men from age 30 on, increasing markedly from age 40 (370 − 257 = 113 per 1,000) (see Table 3.1). In diseases of both the musculoskeletal system and of the cardiovascular system, women over the age of 30 show higher morbidity rates than men, with diseases of the musculoskeletal system even more pronounced in women from the age of 50 on (see Table 3.2). By this measure, middle-aged women need equal, if not more, resources for their health and general well being. However, as I unequivocally demonstrate in the following pages, Korean popular medical discourses entirely digest middle-aged Korean women into the production of the male-dominant sick role.

Table 3.1 Acute* and Chronic Morbidity per 1,000**

	ACUTE MORBIDITY		CHRONIC MORBIDITY	
AGE	MALE	FEMALE	MALE	FEMALE
0–4	526	545	30	22
5–9	269	257	48	36
10–19	126	136	63	59
20–29	125	153	110	97
30–39	130	208	158	201
40–49	130	200	257	370
50–59	145	208	395	555
60+	127	172	522	636

*Acute morbidity is based on the answers to questions such as "Have you experienced any illnesses over the past fifteen days that are not chronic conditions?" and "Have you had any accidents and/or poisonings over the past fifteen days?"
**This table is a combination of two tables, Table 3-2 and Table 3-3 from the *National Health Survey, Purple Volume* (KHASA 1993, pp. 19, 23).

Table 3.2 Rate for Three Major Chronic Diseases per 1,000*

MAJOR CHRONIC DISEASES	AGE**							
	30s		40s		50s		60+	
	M	F	M	F	M	F	M	F
Musculoskeletal	27	40	63	62	127	307	201	377
Digestive	65	72	109	114	122	108	104	95
Cardiovascular	13	31	36	49	75	111	100	132

*From *1992 National Health Survey, Purple Volume*. Seoul, Korea: KHASA. p. 26.
**Those in their thirties (ages 30 to 39), forties (ages 40 to 49), fifties (ages 50 to 59), and sixties (ages 60 and up).

THE BODY ABOVE ALL BODIES: MIDDLE CLASS, MIDDLE-AGED KOREAN MEN

Simultaneous with the media splash about the "world's highest mortality," a picture of "the suffering middle-aged white-collar man" was produced and subsequently reproduced wherever urban Koreans watched television, browsed through magazines, read books and newspapers, and perused subway posters. Indeed they were bombarded with a stunning quantity of images and information on the subject on almost an hourly basis throughout their day. It is not an exaggeration to state that this cultural trope has been a catalyst for the development of the Korean health industry, which has been growing exponentially over the past decade or so.

Initial coverage attributed the fundamental cause of Korean middle-aged male mortality to these men's "stress from living as family heads in a traditional patriarchal society." That said, the commentators avoided any concrete discussions of the features of a "patriarchal society" that might have a negative influence on the health of these men. Instead, they emphasized the historical experience of this particular generation: "These men had experienced World War II and the Korean War. They had to struggle to survive during the rapid and tumultuous social change after these wars" (*Chungang Ilbo* 23 February 1990).

One might ask why Korean women, who went through the same historical turmoil, do not show an equally high mortality rate. The answer to this question can be found in some of the newspaper articles that filled the editorials and opinion pages of major dailies in the days following the government announcement. Their unshakable assumption was that Korean men's "world's highest mortality" was due to heroic, patriotic overwork. Even though some critics chided these men for their excessive drinking and smoking, no one would dream of challenging the "historic fact" that middle-aged Korean men were the heroes of Korea's fantastic economic progress over the past several decades. Newspaper commentaries, like those that follow, thus make a direct link between the experiences of middle class males, who would have entered corporate life in the critical decades of the 1960s and 1970s, and the nation's socioeconomic history:

And what about our middle-aged [men]? . . . These Korean men *are the leaders of our age of high economic growth* against all odds, braving wind and waves. Indeed, they have lived like bulldozers. As a consequence, they must have accumulated tremendous *mental* stress while struggling through (*Chungang Ilbo* 24 February 1990) (emphasis added).

Our Society's Shadowy Self-Portrait! The Mortality of Men in their Forties Is a Problem for All of Us! Korean men in their forties deserve our sympathy. Highly developed medical technologies have not reduced the high mortality of these men. . . . The most miserable group of people on Earth are Korean men in their forties. . . . On national, societal, familial, as well as individual levels, *the most important age group is men in their forties*, but their mortality is the world's highest. This is the kind of problem one must not overlook. There is no easy solution for this. However, for the nation's continuing dynamism and for social and familial stability, we need comprehensive countermeasures against the problem. . . . *Sŏnginbyŏng* is a social problem before it is an individual's. *The problems of men in their forties are those of Korean society* (*Chungang Ilbo* 24 February 1990) (emphasis added).

These descriptions position Korean middle-aged men as the major if not the sole victims of *sŏnginbyŏng*, increasingly prevalent chronic, degenerative diseases. *Sŏnginbyŏng* is a broad and fluid illness category. In more general medical discourses, women, children, and young adults also suffer from some of the diseases commonly associated with *sŏnginbyŏng*, and physicians disagree on the precise range of diseases that qualify as *sŏnginbyŏng*; some recognize cancer as a *sŏnginbyŏng* and some do not. A very successful female pharmacist who has her own pharmacy in Seoul's Kangnam District restricted her definition of *sŏnginbyŏng* to rheumatism, arthritis, and bronchitis, the common complaints of her long-term clients. Most of my lay interviewees, however, described cancer as the most threatening of all *sŏnginbyŏng*.[5] Yet not all cancers are equally represented in the media portraits of *sŏnginbyŏng*. Not surprisingly, cancer of the liver, an organ with strong masculine associations in Korea, provides the locus for dominant visual images of *sŏnginbyŏng* (Lee, 1996b).[6]

Media representations of *sŏnginbyŏng* belie these shifting definitions with a clear and persistent message regarding the identity of the *sŏnginbyŏng* epidemic's victims. They are middle-aged, male, white-collar workers in large corporations, the *saellŏrimaen*. They are the heads of the ideal middle class family, men who had been "aggressive and competitive go-getters in their twenties and thirties" who are now "at the prime of their working careers." Their health problems are caused by the inevitable "fierce competition associated with industrialization." Their failing health, which resulted in a "loss of productivity," is deemed "the most serious medical problem of the nation." The most striking feature of these accounts is that men in positions of relative power and privilege are characterized as "weaklings" (*yakja*) in the eyes of the public, the medical community, and the media. Although the male body has been omnipresent, literally or figuratively, in all Korean social dynamics, it hardly ever has been visualized in popular imagery of any sort, let alone as a "weakling's" body. The *sŏnginbyŏng* discourses, however, have mushroomed out of the male body on which Korea's recent history of modernization is inscribed, and not every middle-aged body, but those defined as the "leaders of our age's high economic growth." The link between *sŏnginbyŏng* and successful white-collar middle-aged Korean men was made early on in the press. The following passage is representative:

> There are reasons for the high mortality rates of men in their forties. When one reaches his forties, he gets *a managerial position in the company*. This means the most work and the most responsibility in the company. He has to arrive at the office first and be the last to leave (*Chosŏn Ilbo* 24 February 1990) (emphasis added).

While ailing middle class men command media attention, Korea's middle-aged urban poor have far higher morbidity and subsequent mortality than those in other classes (Kim 1990). Of the middle-aged urban poor investigated in Kim's study 70.3 percent had one or more chronic conditions, and middle-aged urban poor women got ill more often than men in this same group. Class bias, explicit in the media portrayal of the typical *sŏnginbyŏng* sufferer, were implicit in the government report on male mortality. The report assumed a forgiving tone toward male drinking habits, which contribute to high frequency of hepatitis, liver cirrhosis, and liver cancer; it deemed this a consequence of an "unavoidable social life," the necessary after-hour socializing with fellow company men.

Though listed in the report, accidents did not draw any specific exegesis, even though the National Bureau of Statistics *1990 Annual Statistical Report on the Cause of Death* listed accidents as the second most frequent cause of death for Korean men of all ages (NBS 1990, 25).[7] "Accidents" include not only traffic accidents but also industrial hazards, which affect a great number of working class men (Seoul National University School of Medicine 1985; Ministry of Labor 1988). While legal compensation measures have been devised for victims of workplace accidents, industrial hazards have never generated anything near the popular uproar associated with the "world's highest mortality."

It could be argued that the heroes of industrialization are not only to be found in the white-collar class. In the years of rapid development, thousands of young female factory workers, mostly from rural villages, spent their youths in industrial complexes producing cheap export goods (Kim 1997). Thousands of construction workers spent years laboring under difficult conditions in the Middle East to earn much-needed dollars during the "oil shock." No matter who is the most significant in terms of contributing to the national growth, one can safely characterize all Koreans as more or less similarly driven to get out of poverty, and indeed, they succeeded in making Korea one of the newly industrialized countries (NICs) in Asia in just over a scant twenty years. Needless to say, the narrative of personal sacrifice and triumph among middle-aged Korean men often ignores the once-favorable international market conditions that made it possible. Instead, individual male ardor and attitude are emphasized.

Men at Work

While the Korean media valorize white-collar men's contribution to the "economic miracle of the Han River," they also criticize the white-collar male lifestyle as full of unhealthy practices. Heavy drinking and smoking are often cited as causes of *sŏnginbyŏng*, as in this newspaper article:

> It's a matter of how they relieve stress (and not a matter of the sources of stress). Most Korean men in their forties tend to relieve stress by drinking alcohol. They *believe* that having one quick shot [of liquor] will relieve their fatigue. But it never ends with just one glass. They tend to go on to the second round and then the third round and end up overdrinking. Once this becomes an established habit, then various *sŏnginbyŏng* are inevitable. To reduce the mortality rate of men in their forties, we should first find ways to *improve* their drinking habits (*Kungmin Ilbo* 24 February 1990) (emphasis added).

The four major explanations for the high mortality rate of middle-aged Korean men include the stress of being a modern patriarch, the stress of being a leader of the radical social transformation, smoking, and drinking (*Chungag Ilbo* 23 February 1990). The term "stress" valorizes this generation of men, whereas smoking and drinking assign individual blame. While stress and struggle are seen as necessary for the benefit of family and nation, albeit negative in their individual consequences, smoking and drinking are seen as matters of personal volition. By this logic, all middle-aged men were stressed out during the tumultuous period of social change, but only those who drank and smoked became ill and/or died.

Indeed, all of the white-collar men I interviewed during my fieldwork agreed, some grudgingly, that most *saellŏrimaen* drink liquor as a way to relieve stress, whether work-related or not. As one of them said to me, "You get stressed because of your office work, drink to get rid of the stress, and the next morning get more stressed-out due to the hangover from the previous night's drinking." Most of my respondents also acknowledged that this is a vicious cycle grounded deep in their lifestyle.

The visual images that are associated most frequently with *sŏnginbyŏng* are middle-aged *saellŏrimaen* wearing suits and ties; wandering around bars;

drinking beer and smoking cigarettes with coworkers, business associates, or clients; and sleeping on the subway on the way home. These images are avidly reproduced in newspapers, TV dramas, commercials, and even news magazine programs dedicated to highlighting the problem of *sŏnginbyŏng*. This profile of the victims of the "world's highest mortality" as middle-aged, white-collar workers whose achievements are praiseworthy but whose drinking habits are pathetic is placed firmly at the center of *sŏnginbyŏng* discourses. Dismissive of the social pressures that may have forced these men into the literally sickening practices of drinking, the *Kungmin Ilbo* article seems to suggest that, despite an enormous workload, one can find ways to avoid the habit of drinking and thereby avoid actually developing a chronic disease.

None of the *saellŏrimaen* I interviewed failed to point out that drinking is not just a way of relieving stress but also a context for the after-hours socializing that more or less comes with the territory if one is a *saellŏrimaen* (Janelli with Yim 1993). This assumption may be generation-bound. The enactment of such a blurred concept of work and play brings about sharply divided opinions among the different generations of white-collar men who now inhabit most corporate offices. According to the results of my questionnaire survey among white-collar workers (Lee 1998), those in their forties or older seem to be more tolerant of after-hours socializing and drinking than those in their late twenties. Drinking, once considered the lubricant of *saellŏrimaen* life, or at least necessary for harmony and esprit de corps among the workers, is now criticized by younger *saellŏrimaen* as the most unproductive of office practices. But while younger men resist drinking and challenge its social significance, it is still practiced by middle-aged men who consider drinking with business associates and superiors a part of their job.[8] As one of the *saellŏrimaen* I interviewed said to me, "The name of the game is how long one endures the omnipresent stress."

THE PATHOLOGY OF THE MODERN KOREAN FAMILY

We have seen how statistics and media commentary are deployed to establish the "fact" that white-collar male illness is inextricable from the culture of Korean industrialization in a broad, historical sense. So defined, the ill health of these men is not linked to specific features of work structure and company policies, and hence these cultural texts do not deploy *sŏnginbyŏng* discourses as a demand for change in industrial structure and practices. Instead, they assign a critical healing role to the home. "This [high] mortality [of Korean men] sends a message to their families. For one thing, reduce the amount of pressure on these men. . . . If the members of the household could just be more understanding. . . ."(*Han'guk Ilbo* 25 February 1990).

The gap between rhetoric and reality looms large. As noted throughout this volume, the middle class lifestyle fosters a deep sense of distance between white-collar men and their own families. These men were rapidly absorbed into the public arena of work where Korean society allots both opportunities and resources for individual achievement and self-worth. In addition, Korean men were further estranged from their families by authoritarian office practices and the emphasis on after-hours activities.[9]

The diminished presence of the father was aptly caught in a kindergarten teacher's description of children's family portraits. The children drew their fathers as either sleeping, watching TV, or reading newspapers and in much smaller proportions than their mothers, who assume an active presence in their daily lives (*Tonga Ilbo* 3 February 1997). In a recent survey, middle and high school students ranked the father last person on a list of those with whom they would discuss problems, after mother, friends, and siblings. The men's sense of estrangement amplifies when they try to return home and re-establish their role as disciplinarian fathers and respectable husbands. In some cases, this return of the father was forced by layoffs as a consequence of the corporate restructuring of Korean companies.

Sǒnginbyǒng narratives do not regard the predicaments of middle-aged couples as a consequence of how the separate spheres of their lives have been structured. Instead, these cultural texts give lopsided attention to the men's familial plight, simultaneously portraying their wives as indifferent to or unaffected by a husband's hardship. The father, already exposed to a toxic environment at work, suffers from what are assumed to be more profound emotional afflictions generated by his lack of paternal authority at home:

> The forty-somethings are weary. . . . The forty-something family heads attempt to release their stress at home, but their families make them all the more stressed. Above all, the attitude of children and wives toward these men seems to be changing. In the past, unconditional respect for family heads seems to have been guaranteed. These days, however, it appears that [the family] finds fault with a man's not so impressive outward success. Whenever hearing about "so-and-so's father" or the "man next door" [from one's children and wife] one cannot help but feel hurt [by the implied unfavorable comparison]. These things impair what little pride these moderately successful men can muster ("A Diary of a Family Head," *Tonga Ilbo* 7 March 1993).

Whatever the relationship of these pitiful characterizations to the lived reality of many middle-aged Korean men, they have come to constitute an all-pervasive model narrative generating social knowledge that excludes certain other events, objects, and persons. While the celebrated story of Korean industrialization is a staple in the reworking of male identity at midlife, *sŏnginbyŏng* narratives simultaneously mount a critique against contemporary femininity. For example, the popular novelist Yi Munyŏl's novel *Choice* (*Sŏnt'aek*) idealizes the life of a traditional Korean woman of noble background in contrast to the apparently liberated but lost generation of modern Korean women. While the lady of the past embodies all possible virtues of Korean womanhood as a mother, wife, and daughter-in-law, her present-day counterparts are described as confused and misled by the changes brought about by modernization-cum-westernization. The novel ignited a heated debate among Korean feminists. *Father* (*Abŏji*), another best-seller in which a cancer-stricken father reconciles with his alienated wife and daughter, is an even more blunt attempt to redefine femininity (Lee 1997; Moon in this volume).

But these are stories. How do real lives articulate with them? In this media-generated atmosphere of middle-aged discontent, I carried out my interviews with a middle-aged Korean corporate man I call "Park-sangmunim." His personal observations should not be read as either the product of an unambiguously rational and self-conscious recounting of his own way of life, or as an automatic acquiescence to the values, beliefs, and systems of meaning that have been articulated by particular social interests. I offer Park-sangmunim's personal story because it reflects the ways in which he actively attempts to organize his own experience in a culturally conventional fashion.

PARK-SANGMUNIM'S REFLECTIONS

Park-sangmunim, a successful but stressed-out assistant executive officer, developed an ulcer about ten years ago, due either to his surreal effort to "get ahead" and support his family or to his surreptitious drinking. His ulcer forced him to quit drinking and adapt to a bland diet. For more than twenty years, Park-sangmunim hardly ever had eaten dinner at home except on holidays. "If he came home before midnight," Mrs. Park said, "I marked it on the calendar. On maybe only a handful of days a year, he came home before midnight sober. TV and the telephone seem to have kept our marriage together so far." She added this with a hint of a sarcastic sigh, meaning she either watched television or talked on the phone while waiting for her husband all those years. Blushing, Park-sangmunim disagreed, "Children and church have kept you occupied in my absence, wouldn't you say?"

Mrs. Park is unhappy about her husband's recurring stomach problems. "I didn't make you work late and drink. I want to be liberated from kitchen work." Now in her late forties, Mrs. Park deplores the fact that she has to worry about what and how to cook for her husband because of the unusual diet prescribed by his doctor. "His guts are so sensitive. Just one meal with some spicy food and his tummy starts aching." Much to Mrs. Park's chagrin, Park-sangmunim still drinks occasionally, but his drinking practices have changed over time. Park-sangmunim recalls that when he was a rookie, his superiors always initiated after-hours drinking, but these days, his drinking buddies are not recruited from among his subordinates. With a wry smile, he conceded forcedly that it is better to distinguish between work and "personal life" (*sasaenghual*); he claims to have missed the latter when he was young. Park-sangmunim admits that more often than not, his drinking still is part of his work, but he usually drinks with business partners and superiors.

Park-sangmunim denies the possibility of death-from-overwork. Although there have been cases where companies have been forced to compensate survivors for a man's "death-from-overwork" (*kuarosa*), these suits did not involve white-collar men. In fact, allegations of death-from-overwork are typically dismissed as instances of the victim's lack of moderation.[10] In Park-sangmunim's words, "Who in the world can be so stupid as to work until they kill themselves? We all have to drink, but not all of us die. Individual indolence and family problems on top of the stress from work and so on, and yeah, these days people say one's constitution determines the kinds of diseases one is prone to. That could be another factor. It's a murky business. One can't tell what triggered someone's death." Just as the concept of "stress" is institutionalized, so too is Park-sangmunim's deep-seated belief in the active agency of an individual.

It was the death of one of Park-sangmunim's friends that originally prompted Park-sangmunim to talk with me about *sŏnginbyŏng*. Over the year of my fieldwork, Park-sangmunim often referred to this death in our conversations, yet each time with slightly different interpretations regarding the cause of death. This childhood friend had worked as a journalist for a newspaper company in Taegu, the third-largest city in Korea, and was known among his circle of friends for his successful career and happy family life. Due to the geographic distance and different occupational tracks that this friend and Park-sangmunim persued, they had lost contact with each other years before his friend's sudden death. Because this was the first death among their cohort, most of the dead man's friends gathered at the funeral. At the funeral and afterward, there was a lot of speculation among them about the cause of his death.

Biomedically, the friend, a chain smoker, died of a heart attack, but the death happened at his office. Since he was known to be a workaholic, his coworkers talked speculatively about death-from-overwork. At the time of his death, he was working madly to meet the deadline for his newspaper column, "or something," said Park-sangmunim, who does not remember clearly. At the funeral, friends who were closer to the deceased than Park-sangmunim said the friend's perfectionist personality killed him. The friend had been a compulsive overachiever and at the time of death, he had launched his own publishing company, which he planned to join on his retirement. He was working harder than ever, trying to avoid any complaints from his current employer. "Type A personality was the killer, wasn't it?" was one of Park-sangmunim's interpretations at one time. Much later, Park-sangmunim heard that the real cause of his friend's death was neither overwork nor his personality. Rather, the death was due to his worry and disappointment over his son, who had failed a college entrance exam and was supposed to study for the second attempt in Seoul.[11] The boy had disappeared, leaving a note behind that asked his father not to search for him. The friend's subsequent trip to Seoul put him behind schedule at work at the time of his death. Other friends of the deceased also confided to Park-sangmunim that the real reason behind the new publishing company was that the deceased friend had not looked forward to staying at home after retirement because of the never-ending battle between his wife and his 79-year-old mother. "Now [even though] I can see the big picture, it still is not clear to me because my situation is not much better than this friend's, but I am still alive and well," continues the inquiring mind of Park-sangmunim, hardly daunted by the revealing truths about his friend's death.

Park-sangmunim has not had a family life that was any easier than that of his deceased friend. His male identity as a father and a husband is acutely contested as he now attempts to resume the roles that he neglected during his younger years as a white-collar worker. For years, the strained relationship between Park-sangmunim's mother and his wife was the overriding concern in his family life. Now, with his mother deceased, what remains of these turbulent days is his distant relationship with his wife. To Park-sangmunim, this is much less problematic than his relationship with his son, a high school junior who does not have good study habits. "I suppose I am pretty knowledgeable about society, history, and all that. But I don't understand my own son's behavior. The way his mind works. A totally different species. He does-n't seem to have the same drive that made me study and work hard. I don't expect him to support me in my old age, but at least I hope we can com-municate with each other. I fear that this is going to be too much to expect." Park-sangmunim's situation has many parallels with the sympa-thetic media portrayals of the dilemmas of middle-aged Korean men, the men who see themselves as having endured the stress of work on behalf of wives and children but who now find themselves in estranged relationships that are an additional source of stress.

But if stress is institutionalized both at home and at work, and recog-nized as potentially lethal, stress is still not inevitable according to Park-sangmunim, the insurmountable optimist. He will not abandon the vision of a rationalized and continually rationalizing society. "These days, the work hours are shorter and efficiency is the prime concern of the work place [not the number of hours worked]. There is no longer pressure to stay on after hours. Promotion is going to be based more on one's capability than on how well one gets along with superiors and coworkers. At home, one can have more time to spend with his family. One can be a family man [while being a *saellŏrimaen* at the same time]."

Why was all of this impossible for him? Park-sangmunim does not seem to have a ready answer, although he is highly conscious of answers provided in the media. "We are the sandwich generation, as they say. We were born into an extended family but now live in a nuclear family. Most of us are sons of farmers but we are white-collar workers. With all these dizzying changes, we were busy just keeping up with the world out there. Family was simply supposed to follow [our initiatives] and support [us]. Now we find ourselves surrounded by everything modern, but we still think in old-fashioned ways (*kusik*). For example, look at the computer. How fast it can help you work! It does a lot of different things at once, without the bother of meeting people. But we still like person-to-person interaction. Without it, I just feel odd. Really, we are the sandwich genera-tion. Modernization started with us but it is not quite done yet." So goes Park-sangmunim's diagnosis of his generation's modernization as "an incomplete project" (Habermas 1987).

Park-sangmunim at fifty, having spent his younger years working as a typical "worker bee of industrialization," now frequents *posint'ang* (dog-meat soup) houses for lunch. He says he feels much better after a bowl of *posin-t'ang* and a short nap in his office, which, he says, has recently become his favorite cure for the previous day's late night work. *Posint'ang*, a kind of folk medicine, is also called "*yang*-restoring soup" (*poyangt'ang*), soup that restores the vitality of the male principle. *Posint'ang* is a potent, if old-fashioned, symbol of male identity (Janelli with Yim 1993, 186). Park-sangmunim's declining bodily strength, associated with his involvement in ruthless business activities, has to be restored by taking a warm bowl of folk-medicine food. Lately he has also become actively involved in various "school cohort meetings" (*tongch'anghoe*), such as that of his elementary school, activities that he neglected in the past. He explains his new interest in terms of friendship and the shared experience of the old life, not so much as a way of broadening his social network. Park-sangmunim has gotten to know how others lived their lives while he was completely preoccupied with his job at an export company. He considers this to be the major benefit of his involvement with these meetings. They give him perspective and keep him abreast of what is going on outside his narrow business world. What is going on turns out to be, ironically, family life. School cohort meetings are occasions where those men's common—in Park-sangmunim's case rural[12]—origins are emphasized despite the difference in their present status and wealth. The traditional, communal, and humanistic life of their common past is glorified over their modern, individual, and impersonal present.

Park-sangmunim's newly-developed food preference and routine attendance at the school cohort meetings are part and parcel of the life of those middle-aged Korean men around whom the popular discourses of *sǒnginbyǒng* have evolved. *Sǒnginbyǒng*, unpredictable and uncontrollable, constitutes a major threat to the middle-aged Korean men who once saw themselves as building a social world in which actions, rules, and meanings were to be increasingly predictable, manageable, and intelligible. Their continuing uncertainty, despite all these efforts (including bodily uncertainty under the threat of *sǒnginbyǒng*), seems to be mitigated by reassuring associations with the past.

In the premise of *sǒnginbyǒng* discourses, "the modern lifestyle is bad for you." The risk of high mortality for middle-aged, middle class Korean men like Park-sangmunim is rooted in modern institutions, large corporations, and nuclear families. For men who have built their lives around these institutions, this risk presents yet another hurdle to surmount. What it takes to overcome the hurdle, according to most *sǒnginbyǒng* discourses, is individual effort, exercise, and proper diet (Lee 1996a). According to my questionnaire survey of *saellǒrimaen*, most of them eat *posint'ang* more or less regularly. Interestingly, the survey also shows that "peace of mind" is one of the most commonly selected solutions for *sǒnginbyǒng* (Lee 1998). The soothing warmth of a bowl of *posint'ang* and the school cohort meetings may keep Park-sangmunim from becoming a high mortality statistic.

Concluding Remarks

Although disquieting in their invocation of high mortality rates, the *sŏnginbyŏng* narratives provide many middle-aged Korean men, like Park-sangmunim, with culturally shared "idioms of distress" (Nichter 1988). Their illnesses are viewed as the unforeseen consequences of their victimization as worker bees and of their sacrificial suffering as family heads; the sufferers see themselves as entitled to social recognition and individual attention. Middle-aged Korean men are no longer "the worker bees of industrialization" (*sanŏphua ŭi yŏkkun*), but their shadow is long and the memory of "the worker bee" continues, re-inscribed daily in middle class men's bodily experiences, even as the bodily experiences of women and the poor are marginalized in the construction of these same narratives.

Sŏnginbyŏng narratives are explicitly conservative. They are a response to a moment of economic downturn and a loss of optimism. At stake in the popular understanding of health as a male problem are the broadest issues of social order which some would peg to a re-imagined neo-Confucian androcentrism. The cultural texts imply that if men could only be revitalized by familial care, their enhanced productivity would revive the nation. It is no accident that these cultural texts were produced when the social movements that had come to prominence in the 1980s were under attack (Park 1997). Conservative political interests articulate modernity's discontent, assigning all manner of blame to the breakdown of the sense of traditional familial harmony. To this end, the *sŏnginbyŏng* narratives nurture new cultural sensibilities toward harmony while concealing differential access to resources and power. For the sake of the appearance of harmony, Korean women remain underprivileged.

Epilogue

Park-sangmunim once told me that for years, when he would come home from work after midnight, drunk in a taxi, he used to think that the lights on the Sŏngsu Bridge were beautiful. His wife and two children were safely sleeping in his nice, roomy apartment on the other side of the bridge. All his hard work was worthwhile. However, these days whenever he passes by the broken bridge, he says he feels a smothering sense of unease and wants to pass by the bridge as quickly as possible. Does the broken bridge remind him of something? His unredeemable nostalgic past, periodically recreated through his school cohort meetings? His lost youth? Seemingly unreachable young subordinates at work? The distance between himself and his wife and children? All those nights of drinking? His ulcer? Mortality itself?

NOTES

The original version of this chapter was presented in Honolulu at the 48th Annual Meeting of the Association for Asian Studies. I am indebted particularly to Laurel Kendall and two anonymous readers for a stimulating discussion of the early draft.

1. Middle age, or *chungnyŏn*, is not a biological concept but a cultural category. Koreans understand that the age of forty marks the beginning of one's midlife. This generally coincides with the time when a couple's last child is already well advanced in the school system and the first child is not yet married. A family head is well-established in his work and his wife is a seasoned housewife who can find time to enjoy her own pursuits. Midlife can be realized early or later, depending on an individual's age at marriage, spacing of children, speed of promotion, and so on.

2. "Park-sangmunim" is the way I addressed this middle-aged man during my interviews with him. It is in accordance with the way he is addressed in his workplace by his subordinates, and I assumed a subordinate role during the interview. It is also the way this man identifies himself most often. "*Sangmu*" is the Korean title for an assistant executive officer. "*Nim*" is an honorific ending for one's senior. "*Park*" is not his real family name.

3. Terms such as "modern," "modernity," "modernization," and, later in the text, "scientific" are necessarily locally constructed. For the sake of brevity, I omit quotation marks when using these terms.

4. In the newspaper (*Naeoekyŏngje Sinmun* 28 April 1995), the real name of the professor appeared. He is one of the leading public health professors in Korea and also the most popularly known advocate of a "balanced" and "traditional Korean" diet as the solution to various *sŏnginbyŏng*.

5. The pathology of cancer—"it grows in you without letting you know"—and its moral punitiveness—"you have done wrong to your body"—feeds the popular image of cancer as a sly and sneaky demon, the epitome of *sŏnginbyŏng* in general.

6. The overrepresentation of the liver in Koreans' popular pathologies of *sŏnginbyŏng* has a great deal to do with the nationwide publicity on the hepatitis epidemic among Korean men in the mid-1980s and the continuous increase in alcohol consumption.

7. Accidents are the number-one killer for Korean men, from their teens through their thirties, and are the second-most frequent killer for those in their forties.

8. See Moon's discussion of the young men's resistance in this volume.

9. As Kim Hyo-sŏn (1986) describes in her thesis, Korean white-collar men have lived a life in which their primary source of identity is their work. Indeed, most men in Kim's study subjugated the demands of wife and children to those of their work and coworkers. (Kim and Hŏ 1988).

10. The general dismissal of any allegation of death-from-overwork (*kuarosa*) in Korean companies is an extension of the well-recognized difference between the professed ideology of employees' welfare and actual labor-management practices (Kim 1979).

11. Because a financially rewarding career is virtually guaranteed if one graduates from one of the better universities, college entrance exams are considered the most important rite of passage in the lives of most Koreans. The Korean education system is said to be based on principles of equality. As such, a child from the most humble of families could enter the best universities, and this does in fact happen at times. However, these days a widely held view is that the children from middle- and upper-class families are more successful in the college entrance exams than are those from the lower class who also aspire to white-collar occupations and middle class lifestyles. Equal access to a promising future remains an ideal rather than a reality: To secure admission into one of the good universities one has to start with a good kindergarten, and these are quite costly. In addition, extracurricular studies or private tutoring for the college entrance exam is considered necessary since most middle- and upper-class students experience these in one form or another. Middle-aged men are said to be pressured to make extra money for this extracurricular education (Cho 1994).

12. Park-sangmunim's "home village" (*kohyang*) is part of a town now and is no longer a "tiny little remote village" as he remembers it. In his school cohort meetings, Park-sangmunim and his friends from the same village enjoy talking about what went on in the village while they were growing up. "*Kohyang* is what is left in one's heart. The physicality of it at the present is not very important. My son would not have a memory of *kohyang* like I do, since he has been a city boy from birth," said Park-sangmunim.

REFERENCES

Bové, Paul A. 1995. Discourse. In *Critical Terms for Literary Study*, 2nd ed., Frank Lentricchia and Thomas McLauglin, eds. pp. 50–65. Chicago: University of Chicago Press.

Chang, Kyungsup. 1997a. Everyday conditions of authoritarian politics: Familial form of social conflict and political control. Paper presented at the conference on Democracy and Social Contentions in South Korea, Center for Korean Studies, University of Hawai'i, December 15–16, 1997.

———. 1997b. The neo-Confucian right and family politics in south Korea: The nuclear family as an ideological construct. *Economy and Society* 26(1):22–42.

Cho, Haejoang. 1994. *Kŭlilgi wa Salmilgi 3* (Reading texts, reading everyday lives, III). Seoul: Ttohanaŭi Munhua Publishers.

———. 1998. Constructing and deconstructing "Koreanness" in the 1990s in south Korea. In *Making Majorities*. Dru Gladney, ed. pp. 73–91. Stanford, Calif.: Stanford University Press.

Chung, D. 1991. Korean family welfare policy. In *Korean Family Welfare Policy and Elderly Problem* (in Korean), Korea Family Welfare Policy Institute, ed. pp. 5–42. Seoul: Korea Family Welfare Policy Institute.

Habermas, Jurgen. 1987. *The Philosophical Discourse of Modernity*. Cambridge: Polity Press.

Hansluwka, Harold E. 1987. Measuring the health status of a population: Current state of the art. *Population Bulletin of the United Nations* 23/24:56–75.

Janelli, Roger, with Dawnhee Yim. 1993. *Making Capitalism*. Stanford, Calif.: Stanford University Press.

Kim Chung-sun. 1993. Urinara samangwŏninŭi pyŏch'ŏn'gwa hyŏnhwang (Causes of death and their changes). *Journal of Korean Medical Association* 36(3):272–284.

Kim Eun-ju. 1990. Tosiyŏngsechiyŏk chungnyŏnch'ŭng inguŭi sang-byŏngyangsanggwa pogŏnŭiryŏiyong silt'aeedaehan yŏngu (A study on the morbidity and medical facility utilization among the urban poor). *Journal of Population, Health, and Social Welfare* 10(1):83–100.

Kim Hyo-sŏn. 1986. Hoesawŏn saenghwalŭl t'onghaebon Han'guk namsŏngŭi chŏgŭnggwa sowoe (Adaptation and alienation in Korean male company life). Master's Thesis. Department of Women's Studies, Ewha Womans' University.

Kim Hyo-sŏn, and Hŏ Sun-hee. 1988. Han'guk namja: Najedo ttuigo pamedo ttuinda (Korean men: Running day and night). In *Chibae munhua Namsŏng Munhua* (Dominant culture, male culture). Ttohanaŭi munhua, ed. pp. 100–112. Seoul: Chungha.

Kim, Kyong-dong. 1979. *Man and Society in Korea's Economic Growth*. Seoul: Seoul National University Press.

Kim, Seung-kyung. 1997. *Class Struggle or Family Struggle: The Lives of Women Factory Workers in South Korea*. Cambridge: Cambridge University Press.

Korea Institute for Health and Social Affairs (KIHASA). 1993. *National Health Survey Results*. Purple volume. Seoul: KIHASA.

Lee, June J. H. 1996a. Transforming society, transforming medicine: Lay medical perceptions and self-medication among contemporary Koreans. In *Society, Health, and Disease: Transcultural Perspectives*. Janardan Subedi and Eugene B. Gallagher, eds. pp. 25–46. New Jersey: Prentice Hall.

———. 1996b. Health food as gendered commodity: Body, health, and sexuality among the middle-class Korean men: An analysis of health food. *International Journal of Politics, Culture, and Society* 10(1):73–94.

———. 1997. Litany for love and its oppositional reading: Politics of gender in Korean popular medicine. A paper presented at the conference on Democracy and Social Contentions in South Korea. The Center for Korean Studies, University of Hawai'i, December 15–16, Honolulu, Hawai'i.

———. 1998. A quest for health: food and body in illness narratives of modernization. Ph.D. diss. Department of Anthropology, University of Hawai'i, Manoa.

Lock, Margaret. 1993. *Encounters with Aging: Mythologies of Menopause in Japan and North America.* Berkeley: University of California Press.

Ministry of Labor. 1989. *Yearbook of Labor Economy, 1988.* Seoul: Ministry of Labor.

National Bureau of Statistics. 1990. *The 1990 Annual Statistical Report on the Cause of Death.* Seoul: National Bureau of Statistics.

Nichter, Mark. 1988. Idioms of distress: Alternatives in the expression of psychosocial distress: a case study from south India. *Culture, Medicine and Psychiatry* 5:379–408.

Park, Joon-Shik. 1997. Working class citizenship in post-1987 Korea. A paper presented to the conference on Democracy and Social Contentions in South Korea. Center for Korean Studies, University of Hawai'i, December 15–16, Honolulu, Hawai'i.

Park Myung-jin. 1991. Ch'ŏngsonyŏnkua saeroun midiŏ munhua: P'osŭtŭ modŏn munhuaŭi kuanjŏm (Youth and new media culture: A post-modern perspective). *Sasang* (fall):238–266.

Phillips, David R. 1991. Problems and potential of researching epidemiological transition: Examples from Southeast Asia. *Social Science and Medicine* 33:395–401. Seoul National University School of Medicine. 1985. *Han'gugŭi Sanŏpchaehae* (Industrial hazard in Korea). Seoul: Seoul National University.

Suh Chŏng-hyŏk. 1990. 40-dae namjaŭi samangwŏnin'gua taech'aek (Causes of death for men in their forties and countermeasures). Issue paper, "Let's Talk Health." pp. 20–25. Seoul: Research Institute for Health Policy.

4

THE PRODUCTION AND SUBVERSION OF HEGEMONIC MASCULINITY: RECONFIGURING GENDER HIERARCHY IN CONTEMPORARY SOUTH KOREA

seungsook moon

A decade of gender studies has demonstrated that certain notions and practices of femininity and masculinity are constitutive of the smooth working of various institutions, as well as the individual sense of self.[1] This chapter is concerned with dominant notions and practices of masculinity and resistance to them in contemporary south Korea as it has been shaped in the process of rapid industrialization over the past three decades. My focus on masculinity is a response not only to the scarcity of critical studies on the subject, but also to recent representations in the Korean mass media of the "crisis" of the household head and the "problem" of an individualistic new generation unwilling to sacrifice for the collective good.[2] While often hyperbolic and conservative in its tone, this voice unwittingly highlights what it means to be a man in contemporary Korean society in response to far-reaching structural changes wrought by economic globalization and sociopolitical democratization.

Drawing on Robert Connell's (1995) study of masculinities, I use the term "hegemonic masculinity" to refer to the dominant notions and practices of masculinity that largely are accepted by various social groups as an integral part of the seemingly natural or sensible order of things. Reflecting Gramsci's (1971) notion of hegemony, this concept illuminates complexities involved in the contemporaneous process of producing and subverting the dominant configuration of masculinity. It connotes the presence of multiple and heterogeneous notions and practices of masculinity that society promotes or suppresses in tandem with the gender hierarchy. Yet consent or acquiescence to hegemonic masculinity is never complete, because it requires the absolute suppression or expulsion of nonconforming notions and practices of masculinity—for instance, that of lower class men who cannot support their families, disabled men, gays, or transsexuals. In a rapidly changing society, such as the south Korea of the past three decades, political and economic conditions that support hegemonic masculinity have undergone significant changes that are ultimately subversive of the dominant order.

The present inquiry into the production and subversion of hegemonic masculinity consists of three parts. The first section discusses the reconfiguration of the gender hierarchy in industrializing south Korea as evidenced by new forms of women's subordination that are perniciously linked to certain improvements in their lives. In this context, women as well as men generally accept hegemonic masculinity. The second section analyzes hegemonic masculinity by focusing on three interwoven notions and practices: the role of family provider, mandatory military service, and distance from such domestic responsibilities as housework and child care as a consequence of men's status as family providers.[3] As we shall see, socioeconomic changes made it possible for some men to resist these components of hegemonic masculinity. At the same time, resistance is circumscribed by the exigencies of south Korean economic development and the peculiar condition of Korea's national division—in effect, a perpetual state of potential war. Because gender is essentially about unequal social relations, the discussion of masculinity invites the discussion of "emphasized femininity" (Connell 1987, 188), a gender typing that reduces women to domesticity and reproductive labor and thereby naturalizes women's secondary position in national politics, the economy, and the household.

RECONFIGURING GENDER HIERARCHY

For the past three decades, Korean women have made varying degrees of progress in the areas of formal education, marriage, and family life. Yet new forms of subordination accompany these improvements. While the level of women's education has increased in absolute terms or in comparison with men's education level, this gain has not been fully converted into economic independence. Rather, higher education has remained a status symbol. Women's employment has been limited to temporary and marginal positions, and women's jobs are characterized predominantly by low pay, low prestige and power, low security, paucity of opportunity for promotion, or all of the above.[4] This dreary situation gradually changed over the past decade with the revitalization of women's movements and their successful lobbying for reform of the equal employment law.[5] However, the 1997

Asian economic crisis set back this progress by making women employees the first fired and last hired.[6]

While marriage has become more a matter of individual choice than in the past, it has largely remained patrilocal and continues to be regarded as a means of sustaining the institution of patrilineal descent (Kendall 1996, ch. 2). The wife/daughter-in-law is still expected to deliver a son for her husband's family, even though she does not reside in the in-law's household.[7] Women's movements have attempted to alter this situation by reforming family law, which has supported patrilineage and posed a significant institutional barrier to gender equality. Pre-1989 family law perpetuated the system of household mastership inheritance (*hojusangsok chedo*), which required the transfer of household mastership from the father to the eldest son after the former's death. The revised law maintains the order of succession based on primogeniture under the succession of the household mastership (*hoju sŭnggye*) although it has eliminated the household master's financial responsibility for family members and his legal authority over them (Kim, Chu-su 1990).

Although women have fewer children, and electric appliances and ready-made food have reduced the amount of housework, childcare and housework have remained women's primary responsibilities. A 1987 study of urban full-time housewives showed that daily housework consumed 8.5 hours, a reduction from a previous study, but this change was accompanied by an increase in childcare responsibility (KWDI 1991, 166–177).[8] In other words, while more and more women can afford to use household appliances to reduce housework, they tend to be more intensely involved in their children's formal and informal education than ever before. Moreover, a wife's paid employment does not induce her husband's participation in any of these domestic tasks (KWDI 1991, 166–167; KWDI 1985, 150–152).

Women's participation in national politics has been minimal for the past three decades of compressed industrialization and in the recent transition to civilian rule. In 1990, women held less than 1.5 percent of positions in central governmental committees and major ministries.[9] As recently as 1999, after several years of civilian rule, the extremely low representation of women in those strategic positions was little improved (KWDI 1999, 368–369). Similarly, women legislators have remained, on average, 2 percent of the total members of the National Assembly for the decades of rapid socioeconomic change (KWDI 1995, 292–297; Soh 1991). In the 1996 parliamentary election, this rate increased slightly to 3 percent (KWDI 1999, 356). In the military, women represented 0.3 percent or 2,100 soldiers in a total standing army of 650,000 as of 2000. All women soldiers are either commissioned or noncommissioned officers who are not involved in actual combat (*Yŏsŏng sinmun* 16 June 1996). The political and military realms that have dominated recent Korean history remain in the men's universe.

Accounts of contemporary gender hierarchy in south Korea, by both feminists and nonfeminists, tend to attribute gender inequality to the persistence of Korea's Confucian tradition. Although not entirely inaccurate, this explanation fails to investigate why the Confucian tradition persists and how "tradition" itself is constructed. It assumes that tradition persists automatically or that it tenaciously refuses to go away. The ahistorical nature of this view equates tradition with a set of essential values and practices that withstand the material changes taking place in society.[10] This static view of tradition elides the fact that worldwide, industrialization has historically been a gendered processes of social transformation in and by which hierarchical gender relations are introduced or reconstructed in many social settings.[11]

In order to go beyond this static and somewhat simplistic account of gender hierarchy in contemporary Korean society, we need to examine the specific practices through which it has persisted. Moreover, we need to understand that the persistence of gender hierarchy does not mean the mere reproduction of an old form but its recomposition in the process of industrialization. In south Korea, the production of hegemonic masculinity has contributed to this reconfiguration of gender hierarchy within a local context of militarization and compressed industrialization.

THE PRODUCTION AND SUBVERSION OF HEGEMONIC MASCULINITY IN SOUTH KOREA

"Masculinity" refers to more than a socially constructed set of personality traits that are to be observed in an individual man's behavior. Connell articulates it thus:

> "Masculinity" to the extent the term can be briefly defined at all, is simultaneously a *place* in gender relations, the *practices* through which men and women engage that place in gender, and the *effects* of these practices in bodily experience, personality and culture (Connell 1995, 71) (emphasis added).

This conceptualization of masculinity emphasizes its fundamentally unstable construction, open to potential and actual contestation and negotiation. That is, masculinity is not a fixed or pregiven identity but a position (or a place) in gender relations that is produced and maintained through culturally specific and continuous practices, such as certain ways of acting, dressing, or speaking. This implies that an empirical woman can occupy the position of masculinity in gender relations, although not as often as an empirical man does. Heterosexual men would occupy this position with full societal acknowledgment and encouragement and, therefore, more often and more easily than any other social group. At the same time, this definition of masculinity captures the depth and pervasiveness of certain practices of masculinity in shaping social processes that range from the individual's experience of his or her body to the working of various institutions.

Connell's definition, however, does not address the explicit link between masculinity and the male body that society promotes and normalizes. Without this link, we simply can replace the term "masculinity" with "femininity" in the definition quoted previously. While this interchangeability exposes the arbitrariness of gender binarism by uncoupling the distinction between femininity and masculinity in relation to biologized bodies, it is not conducive to the discussion of gender hierarchy as an issue of social justice. In this regard his earlier definition of gender is more useful. Connell states:

> ["Gender" refers to] practices organized in terms of, or in relation to, the reproductive division of people into male and female. . . . It should immediately be clear that this does not demand an overriding social dichotomy. Gender practice might be organized in terms of three, or twenty, social categories. Indeed our society recognizes a fair variety—girls, old men, lesbians, husbands, and so on. It should also be clear why a dichotomy of women and men is likely to be an important part of any gender order (Connell 1987, 140).

Therefore, masculinity, as a place (or a position) in gender relations, becomes meaningful and discernible only in juxtaposition to its binary opposite of femininity.

Masculinity, as a place women and men occupy through certain practices and their effects, is inevitably plural in contradiction to its singular sign because gender always interacts with other organizing principles such as class, race, and ethnicity, although the latter two are not significant factors yet in south Korea. This is to say that there are multiple notions and practices of masculinity that can be distinguished from one another by class, race, and ethnicity. Hegemonic masculinity, by definition, not only justifies (or naturalizes) men's domination of women but also induces conformity and complicity from individual men through various forms of reward and punishment. This said, let me turn to the three components of hegemonic masculinity produced in the particular context of south Korea: ability to provide for the family, military service, and distance from daily reproductive labor.

The Role of Family Provider

Since the mid-1990s, economic globalization has generated a growing number of middle-aged men who have been forced to retire in the name of corporate restructuring in order to improve competitiveness in the global market. This so-called crisis of the jobless household head has engulfed vast sectors of south Korean society since the 1997 Asian economic crisis. A record 1.762 million were unemployed by January 1999 (*The Korea Herald,* 27 February 1999). The devastating familial impact of soaring layoffs merits serious discussion as a means to their amelioration. However, the recent mass media focus on unemployed men places a central element of hegemonic masculinity under the limelight: the capacity to provide for one's family.

The ideas and practices that define men as the principal income earners of the family justify men's domestic authority and dominance in south Korean society. This masculinized practice goes hand in hand with the normative construction of women as dependent housewives or, at best, as supplementary income earners. This rigid gender division of labor is not unique to south Korea but is a crucial element of modern gender ideology in capitalist societies. As Maria Mies (1986) argues, capitalist industrialization transforms the majority of women who used to be producers into housewives whose efforts sustain and reproduce the work force, thereby freeing men for paid employment outside households. Certainly, the "housewifization" of women at a global scale does not take place everywhere in an identical manner. In south Korea, this process builds on Confucian gender ideology that functionally assigned women and men to the "inside" and "outside" of the household, respectively. The spatial divisions in the homes of the old *yangban* nobility that relegated women to interior space and men to an exterior-oriented scholars' studio are invoked to naturalize a new and very different division of labor for a broad segment of the population.

While the transformation of Confucian patriarchy into modern patriarchy is closely linked to industrialization, the modern gender ideology shapes this process of rearrangement. Initially, the modern notions of provider-husband and dependent housewife emerged in the 1930s in tandem with the appearance of the educated, urban professional man who could support his nuclear family independent of his parents' agrarian household (Kendall 1996, 100–102). However, not until the 1960s did the modern gender division of labor come to be a normative ideal. The ascendancy of the notion and practice of the provider-husband can be observed in the institution of the Korean family law that was promulgated in 1958 and enforced between 1960 and 1990. Through the regulation of kinship and inheritance of property, the law served to modernize Confucian patriarchy in two ways. First, it required the household master (*hoju*) to financially support his family in exchange for legally recognizing his authority over his family members (Kim, Chu-su 1990, 1973). Second, after the 1962 reform under Park Chung-hee's military junta, the law dictated that all married sons, except the eldest, be separated from their father's household as the legally recognized heads of independent households. The state justified this reform in light of the development of the nuclear family, which implied a discrepancy between the family provider and the legally recognized household master (S. Lee 1985, 348–349). This line of legislative action by the state indicates its attempt to modernize domestic life by designating every household master as the family provider. It also implies the popularization of the patriarchal household by legally granting every married man the headship of his household. While the largely agrarian economic structure of the early 1960s did not bolster this normative ideal, based on the separation of workplace from the household,[12] even prior to substantial industrialization, the law prefigured modern patriarchy by granting the husband authority on the basis of his role as the family provider.

By the 1980s, after two decades of industrialization, the normative gender constructs of husband-provider and housewife became firmly established.[13] A series of small-scale case studies based on interviews and surveys offer glimpses, albeit limited, of the hegemonic position of the gender norm. Even rural or urban poor women who must work for family subsistence tend to view themselves primarily as housewives. According to a 1987 study of rural families, 24.4 percent of rural wives interviewed considered themselves solely housewives. Another 33.4 percent of them described themselves primarily as housewives. While 30.7 percent responded that they were both housewives and agricultural workers, only 10.1 percent answered that they were entirely farm workers (Kim, Chu-suk 1990, 279). Similarly, a study of urban poor families in the city of Ch'ungju shows that a majority of the women considered their husbands primary providers despite the fact that other family members worked in order to maximize family income and the wife often contributed nearly half of the family income. While 55.2 percent indicated that the husband was the primary breadwinner, only 12.4 percent acknowledged the wife to be so (Kim, Mi-suk 1990, 169). These findings are not very different from an earlier study of young factory workers in Seoul, which reported that 51.5 percent of the male workers said that gender disparity in income was reasonable because a man was the provider of his family. Although lower than the male response, 38.4 percent of the female respondents offered the same answer to wage differential by gender and this was the highest percentage among their reasons (O. Lee 1982, 197).

Empirical studies of contemporary Korean families by class in the 1990s now suggest that the gender constructs of husband-provider and dependent housewife are not a perfect reflection of actual social practices, even among urban middle class families whose material conditions allow them to be the exemplars of this arrangement. On the one hand, urban middle class families do show the rigid gender division of labor in which college-educated husbands work outside the home in white-collar occupations and wives, with at least a high school education, stay home to look after children and manage the home. On the other hand, these husbands are not the sole providers. To begin with, middle class family life is often subsidized by relatively well-off parents. When a middle class couple marries, both bride and groom tend to receive significant amounts of financial support from their parents to start a new family. Occasionally, parental contributions continue beyond the initial stage of marital life. Many full-time housewives are involved in informal economic activities, which range from stock investment to tutoring (Kim, Mi-suk 1995, 178). Resembling their Japanese counterparts in their zeal for formal education, middle class south Korean parents are dedicated to sending their children to prestigious universities.[14] In this milieu wives' informal earnings have become almost a necessity in order to pay the soaring costs of cram schools and private tutoring outside of formal schooling.[15]

The role of family provider as an element of hegemonic masculinity is the material basis of men's authority as fathers and husbands. Similarly, men's earning power is a commonly accepted indicator of their manliness. Among urban middle class families, in particular, the provider-husband usually is not an active presence during the family's waking hours because his employment requires total dedication to the company. Hence, men are encouraged to consider their financial contribution as their single most important family responsibility. Failure to provide leads to a loss of respect and authority in the family and, consequently, a loss of masculinity.

Against the backdrop of this materialistic construction of masculine authority in capitalist south Korea, popular discourses on fatherhood now emphasize one's moral duty to respect the father/husband as the family head, regardless of his economic ability.[16] This type of discourse, evoking older Confucian notions of patriarchal respect, was particularly appealing to the general populace in the period of economic globalization that generated a growing number of unemployed men in their forties and fifties even prior to the 1997 economic crisis. This sentiment is captured in a recent novel, *Abŏji* (Father), by Kim Chŏng-hyŏn (1996), which was among the top-ten best-sellers for more than a year after its publication in September 1996.[17] This novel provides a sentimental portrait of a dying father/husband who is profoundly alienated from his family although he faithfully performs his duty as a provider. For years he was a dedicated government official before his doctor friend diagnosed him as having pancreatic cancer. A large portion of the novel describes the father's efforts to conceal his terminal illness from his wife and children and their inability to detect such a drastic change in him. In other words, the story focuses on the contrast between the thoughtful and self-sacrificing father, willing to embrace the devastating pain of facing death alone out of his concern for his family, and their apparent callousness in failing to notice his emotional turmoil. Although the family finally reaffirms their love for one another, this novel ironically depicts men as victims who sacrifice for their families but are left with nothing in the end. While it is certainly true that capitalism dehumanizes working men, as well as working women, the novel distorts the patriarchal nature of social arrangements in the household and the workplace by deploring the materialistic family members' indifference to and disrespect for the father. It thereby glosses over problems of gender- and generation-based inequality within as well as outside of households.

However, the unusual popularity of this novel among various segments of the population suggests a conservative type of resistance to the materialistic requirement of hegemonic masculinity. Men's own self-pity and frustration regarding the reduction of their status to that of financial provider is reflected in a collection of short stories, *When a Man Decides to Divorce*, by Kim Pong-jin (1995). The recurrent theme that underlies these stories is that men "decide to divorce" when they realize that they are demoted to mere money makers. Men come to this realization when they see that their economic performance directly affects their wives' attitudes toward them, attitudes that oscillate between ridicule and contempt on the one hand, and admiration and respect on the other. While these stories are simplistic in their treatment of divorce, and quite misogynistic, they do show the author's perception of why families fall apart, a perception shared by many men.[18]

In contrast to the expressions of conservative resistance, a potentially progressive resistance is emerging among some college-educated, middle class, white-collar workers (*wŏlgŭpchaengi* or *hoesawŏn*). They belong to a group of men who could meet the expectations of hegemonic masculinity were it not for the economic restructuring and so long as they choose to conform to the rules of the corporate world. Instead, they have begun to question their work, work environment, and their relation to their children and wives. A collection of nonfiction stories written by former or current white-collar workers—*If You Join a Company, You're Dead* (Cho and Hong 1995)—casts some light on why the workers resist the terms of their employment in business corporations. Like their conservative counterparts, they voice a recurring sense of alienation and disempowerment in their status as expendable employees of big corporations. They have become more vulnerable under the globalized corporate strategies of downsizing, off-shoring, and outsourcing in the milieu of accelerated international economic competition. Many Korean companies, especially the gigantic conglomerates where these men have been employed, now are restructuring their management and production through automation and intensification of work. Midlevel managers in their forties are among the worst casualties of this process. Because they are entitled to relatively high pay, due to their seniority, but unable to learn new technology easily, companies find it expeditious to dismiss them. Various methods are used, including nonassignment of tasks, a sudden transfer to a new job unrelated to previous job experience, a sudden transfer to a remote and unfamiliar region, or the promotion of junior workers that humiliates senior colleagues and thereby forces them to resign (Kim Chong-il 1995, 59–67).

As another indicator of white-collar workers' dissatisfaction with corporate employment in the 1990s, an ever-increasing number of white-collar workers, especially those in their thirties, quit their jobs and start small businesses of their own when they see their job security undermined by corporate restructuring (Cho and Hong 1995, 111). Yet self-employment does not undermine the masculine identity of the primary provider. Rather, it is an attempt to reinvigorate it. It remains to be seen whether this younger generation of men, disillusioned with corporate lives, will be forced to modify their relationship with their wives as a consequence of the economic change as well as women's rising awareness of gender equality. It is more likely that the wives of the self-employed men will need to exert extra effort to support their husbands' vulnerable small businesses in addition to their own paid and unpaid work. An unintended consequence of this involvement may be an increase in women's power to negotiate with their husbands.

Mandatory Military Service in a Divided Korea

Soldiering has become an element of hegemonic masculinity in south Korea in the context of the national division and the ongoing military confrontation with the North since the Korean War (1950–1953). Even without this peculiar historical situation, the intimate link between soldiering and masculinity has a long history in various types of societies. In some prestate or ancient societies, combat was not only a man's activity but also functioned to determine manliness in so far as male initiation rites involved ritualized warfare or boys' transition to adulthood required the actual experience of combat (Ehrenreich 1997, 126–128).

With the development of the military and the dynastic state, male soldiering was institutionalized by various forms of conscription. In the West, and later in other parts of the world, the rise of the modern nation-state, based on a standing army, popularized soldiering through systems of universal conscription. This allowed the incorporation of a large number of men into the systematic fighting machine for a prolonged period of time (Ralston 1990). Even in those NATO countries where women have been integrated into the military since the early 1970s, the liberal movement toward gender equality stops at the door of combat assignments, no matter how they are defined (Isaksson 1988). The consistency of the actual and symbolic link between combat and masculinity reflects the widely observed nexus between physical prowess and masculinity commonly institutionalized in the military, police, and other repressive state apparatuses worldwide.

Historically, and cross-culturally, the military has been almost exclusively a hierarchical organization of men, although soldiers may experience camaraderie among themselves. It has resisted the entry of women who are supposed to nurture and care for others. This principle of exclusion is transformed into that of marginalization once a military begins admitting women (Isaksson 1988). Women recruits are almost always assigned to noncombat positions that do not allow them to reach the top of the military hierarchy. As case studies of the U.S. military and Israeli military show, even women with professional training in specific fields often are relegated to such essentialized feminine roles as secretarial and maintenance work or nursing (Campbell 1990; Jones 1990; Yuval-Davis 1987). Gender provides an overarching organizing principle that structures hierarchically the division of labor within the military. The situation of women in the south Korean military confirms this general trend.

Despite the enduring link between soldiering and masculinity, women have been a marginal part of the Korean military since the Korean War. The precursor of the Women's Army Corps (*yŏgundan*) consisted of 491 women recruited by Kim Hyunsook, a stepdaughter of President Syngman Rhee, during the Korean War. In 1955, the Korean Army founded the Women's Military Training Center (*yŏgun hullyŏnso*) in order to create a supply of female soldiers who were trained in typing, stenography, and telecommunication. Until 1990, when the training center was upgraded and transformed into the Women's Military Academy (*yŏgun hakkyo*), all women soldiers, apart from nurses, performed clerical tasks as administrative assistants. Currently, all women soldiers are professional but noncombatant officers who graduated from the Women's Military Academy located within the Ministry of Defense compound in Seoul. Each year, the school recruits approximately fifty officer (*changgyo*) candidates among college graduates and several hundred noncommissioned officer (*hasagwan*) candidates among high school graduates. After sixteen to twenty weeks of training and education, officers are assigned to nineteen out of twenty-two branches in the army, including infantry, intelligence, engineering, military police, transportation, and logistics. (K. Pak 1998, 33; Women's Army Corps 1990; Women's Military School 1993).[19]

Women's marginal presence as administrative assistants or noncombatant professional officers affirms the persistent link between mandatory military service and combat-oriented masculinity. Men as a group have access to and control over the direct use of organized force, whereas women, even in the military, are systematically denied this avenue to power. The Women's Army Corps has attempted to ameliorate this situation. In 1995, the army corps experimented with the first woman platoon leader (*sodaejang*) assigned to the Nonsan military training camp, where almost half of new conscripts are instructed in basic military drill before they are appointed to specific branches and divisions. In a documentary film about her experiences in training new male privates,[20] she is frequently portrayed as encouraging and comforting young soldiers who are exhausted from the strenuous military drill and discipline. Interestingly, the film tries to present her feminine qualities of nurturing and caring as a positive asset for leadership. Here we can see the subversion and containment of emphasized femininity as simultaneous processes.

Does the persistent nexus between soldiering and masculinity observed in diverse historical and cultural contexts qualify military service as an element of hegemonic masculinity? Answering this question requires paying careful attention to the system of military service and its meanings in a specific context. Military service may not constitute hegemonic masculinity among the middle classes in the post-military societies of the West, where the military relies on professional soldiering equally open to women. In contrast, it may be a significant element of masculinity among the lower classes or racial minorities who are overrepresented in the military. In south Korea, military service functions to define manhood primarily because the state has considered the system of universal male conscription the desirable method to recruit high-quality soldiers necessary to protect the nation from the impending threat from the North. After numerous modifications to alleviate the burden of military service since its establishment in 1957, this system currently requires all able-bodied young men of the age of 19 and above to serve in the military for twenty-six to thirty months (Choi 1997, 99).[21] The south Korean state has attempted to strengthen its military power by creating the Homeland Reserve Force (*hyangt'o yebigun*) in 1968 and the Civil Defense Corps (*minbangwidae*) in 1975. While the Civil Defense Corps (CDC) has been eliminated, the completion of mandatory service in the standing army is followed by automatic service in the Homeland Reserve Force (HRF) until the age of 33 (Chŏng 1995, 28). During this period, men receive regular military training on a yearly basis (Kim, Chae-il 1996; Y. Yi 1996).[22]

However, the system of mandatory military service for all qualified men does not automatically establish military service as an element of hegemonic masculinity. This necessitates conscious and coordinated efforts to alter popular attitudes toward military service by making both men and women accept it as a male citizen's duty. In particular, it involved the daunting task of transforming a deeply negative view of military service that had been shaped by the Confucian tradition, the colonial legacy, and the internecine civil war. Neo-Confucianism, adopted as the state ideology by the Chosŏn Dynasty (1392–1910), was essentially a philosophy of rule by cultivated scholars. Hence, the Chosŏn court honored men of the pen over men of the sword. The lack of respect and prestige for soldiers was superseded by more active avoidance of soldiering under Japanese colonial rule because conscription by the colonial authorities meant being cannon fodder for the oppressor. The Korean War reinforced the common sense equation of military service with death, particularly because the unexpected war forced men into battle without proper training and preparation, which resulted in countless casualties. In order to supply the drastically shrinking armies, even refugees were coerced into the military (Ki 1995; Ryu 1989). The military regime of Park Chung-hee did manage to alter popular negative perceptions of military service through its aggressive conscription policy. Nevertheless, the state's effort to forge a new meaning for military service as the sacred duty of male citizens has never been entirely successful.

Even after the general populace has come to accept military service as the male citizen's duty, the potential to subvert this component of military masculinity remains.

Instrumental to the establishment of military service as a male citizen's duty was the conscription reform policy of Park Chung-hee's military regime. Imbued with the Bismarckian view of *realpolitik* that was reinforced by the vivid experience of the civil war and ongoing military confrontation with the North, Park's regime saw the building of a strong military as a task of paramount importance. Among the difficult hurdles to achieving this goal was the lack of an efficient system of conscription that could monitor the supply of conscripts. Throughout the 1960s the regime escalated punitive measures for those who evaded mandatory military service. This group of men were not only expelled from public service but also given few opportunities to pursue employment elsewhere. The regime also launched a series of campaigns to incorporate former evaders into the National Territory Construction Corps (*Kukt'ogŏnsŏldan*) as a way of compensating for their military service (Ryu 1989, 20). This heavy-handed approach was only partially successful in a social milieu that was characterized by the absence of militarized patriotism and lacked the infrastructure to control hundreds of thousands of prospective conscripts.

Inaugurated in 1970, the Office of Military Manpower has played a crucial role in administering all affairs that concern conscription. In particular, by improving techniques for conducting precise physical examinations of prospective conscripts and monitoring their overall supply and identification, the office contributed to the drastic reduction of draft evasion over time (S. Pak 1995; *Nyusmeikŏ* 1997, 31). On the other hand, the regime attempted to utilize the national network of primary, secondary, and, later, tertiary education to promote militarized patriotism against the North. In the late 1960s and the early 1970s, it established such new mandatory subjects as "anticommunism" or "defeating communism," and distributed state-approved textbooks on these subjects (Kim and Hong 1991).

Mass media collaborated with the anticommunism policy by emphasizing real and fabricated invasions or attacks from the North (Kang 1998, ch. 7–10). The north Korean threat culminated in the 1975 failed attempt to assassinate President Park by a north Korean agent, which resulted in the death of Park's highly regarded and popular wife. In conjunction with the impending threat of war in the Korean Peninsula, the changing contour of international relations in the 1970s contributed to the heightened sense of the importance of national defense among south Koreans. Popular sentiments were affected by a series of international events, including the Nixon

Doctrine, the United States' abandonment of Taiwan and its rapprochement with China, the withdrawal of the U.S. military from Vietnam, and the consequent communization of south Vietnam. This turn of domestic and international events worked in favor of establishing military service as a Korean male citizen's duty.

In the meantime, Park's regime implemented a series of initiatives to eradicate the evasion of military service.[23] The strongest measure against violators of the military service law was to deprive them of economic opportunities. Those who hired evaders were subject not only to legal punishment but also to withdrawal of various types of state approvals necessary to run a business (Ki 1995; Ryu 1989). This administrative move had both practical and symbolic consequences, which greatly contributed to the making of the popular saying "a man has to serve in the military to play a person's [man's] role" (*namjanŭn saramgusilharyŏmyŏn kune kattawayahanda*). Practically, the punitive measure prevented evaders and their collaborators from securing a livelihood. In a social milieu where men's authority is based on their earning power, unemployment symbolized the loss of their potential and actual status as family heads and threatened their sense of manliness. Consequently, the state's conscription policy brought together the two key elements of hegemonic masculinity by establishing military service as the precondition for employment.

Moreover, the state has attempted to organize the national economy around conscription as a way to motivate men.[24] By law, men gain extra points for military service when they take lower-level public service employment tests or interviews (Kim, T'ae-hong 1998). While not legally requiring it, the state has encouraged private companies to adopt this same practice when they screen job applicants.

In addition to the advantages conferred on male job applicants by virtue of their military service, it is not unusual for both public and private sector employers to consider military service as relevant job experience, entitling job entrants to a few years of seniority and higher pay. Although specific applications vary significantly from one company to another and over time, a majority of companies have offered one or more benefits based on military service (*Nyusmeikŏ* 1997, 37). No matter what the actual monetary values of these incentives are, it is difficult not to consider them privileges, as opposed to rights, in that they presuppose the utter exclusion of such social minorities as women and men whom the military deems unfit for service. The significance of military service for employment reveals a sharp discrepancy between the constitutional guarantee of a universal right to work and the systematic delegitimization of women within the Korean economy. In conjunction with other conventional practices of sexual discrimination in the labor market, the attempt to convert military service into economic benefits further undermines women's (and "unfit" men's) equal participation in the civilian workplace.

This kind of arrangement, an exchange of military service for economic or political privilege, has been observed in other social contexts in different times.[25] What is particular to the south Korean case seems to be the extensiveness and explicitness of the exchange of military service for economic privilege. This is a consequence, in part, of the national division and military confrontation with the North, a product of the exigency of economic development in the face of these conditions. The omnipresent possibility of volatile military confrontation with the North encourages south Koreans to accept universal male conscription as a necessity for national security. Yet in industrializing Korea this need for soldiers is at odds with the economic demand for workers and with the individual desire to work and improve one's situation amid a rising standard of living. One way to reduce this tension is to construct military service as a source of economic benefits.

To what extent do Korean men and women accept military service as male citizen's duty and therefore as an element of masculinity? Although it is difficult to assess the level of consent, we can glimpse it from two national surveys on public perceptions concerning military service: one conducted by the Institute for Defense Analysis in 1992 and the other by Media Research, a private polling company, commissioned by the Office of Military Manpower in 1997. Both surveys used random national samples that included diverse social groups in terms of age, gender, education level, and the area of residence—urban and rural. According to the 1992 survey, 87 percent of all respondents think that military service is beneficial for men's employment life (*sahoe saenghwal*, which connotes life in the workplace). Interestingly, more women (90.3 percent) than men (83.7 percent) answered affirmatively on this.[26] This may suggest that men who have actual military experience could develop a more critical consciousness toward it than women who are exempted categorically from it. The 1997 survey displays significant gaps between the general population and the younger generation of prospective conscripts in their attitudes toward various issues that concern military service. Over three-quarters of the general public, except the prospective conscripts, supports the continued existence of the system of mandatory service for national defense. Similarly, over three-quarters of the general population (77.7 percent) prefers that the prospective conscripts in their families serve as "resident soliders" (*hyŏnyŏk pyŏng*), as regular conscripts living in military barracks as opposed to accepting other types of supplementary or special service that do not involve full-time residence in the barracks.[27] Regarding the beneficial influence of military service on men's employment life, 80.3 percent of those surveyed, except the prospective conscripts, answered positively. Again, more women (89.3 percent) responded affirmatively to the influence of military service on men's employment life (*Pyŏngmu* 1998a). Consequently, these survey responses indicate that, despite the emergence of disagreement among the younger generation of prospective conscripts, the general public sees military service as men's duty for the country and as preparation for their role of family provider later on.

Ikumi Koyama's study (1996) of the effects of military service on south Korean men's consciousness, based on interviews of 400 men in their twenties, confirms the positive function of military service for men's employment.[28] These interviewees point out that military service teaches such attitudes as cooperation, collective orientation, and how to interact with people from various walks of life, skills that are necessary for their adaptation to organizational life in the workplace. In addition, the experience of strenuous physical training gives them confidence that they can do anything. In other words, the period of military service prepares men for employment and thereby enables them to perform the role of family provider, which is another crucial element of hegemonic masculinity. Furthermore, the physical separation from their parents, especially their mothers, and life among men of similar ages can generate the emotional distance they need for the transition to adulthood.[29]

Once forged, the link between military service and hegemonic masculinity requires continuous efforts for maintenance, partly because there is nothing natural about men serving in the military, and, as discussed previously, partly because the meaning of military service rarely has been positive in south Korea. In the absence of the historical experience of a revolutionary war in which peasants and commoners emerge as citizens through soldiering, it is difficult to motivate men to serve willingly in the military. Far from the ideological description of military service as a sacred duty, as stated by administrators, professional soldiers, politicians, and the mass media, to many men it is, at best, a necessary evil or an inevitable burden. Were it not for the presence of the hostile North, it would have been difficult to obtain acquiescence from the majority of the population. Facing the precariousness of hegemonic perceptions of the military service as men's duty, the south Korean state refashioned its conscription policy in the late 1980s against mounting popular demands for sociopolitical democratization.

Moving away from the heavy-handed punitive approach, the state promoted the friendly and service-oriented administration of conscription as a way to draw willing participation in mandatory military service from the younger generation, whose individualistic sentiments and relatively affluent upbringing predisposed them to be less tolerant of military service.[30] In response to increasing discontent with the burden of military service, the Office of Military Manpower introduced new practices to reduce the inconvenience and unpleasantness of military life, as well as to ease anxiety among conscripts and their families. For instance, conscripts are informed in advance of their draft dates, and their individual preferences are taken into consideration in order to determine these dates, if conditions permit. Individual conscripts can travel to their own military units without being dragged there as a group (Ryu 1989). The quality of barrack life for conscripts improved significantly in the 1990s. Such abusive practices as beating, depriving conscripts of meal-time, and cursing, once quite prevalent, were significantly reduced.[31] Soldiers were allowed to choose military supplies that fit their body sizes. While absolute obedience was less emphasized, individual soldiers could express their opinions (Kim, Tŏk-han 1996; Kim, Hwan-t'ae 1993). Since 1990, members of the reserve forces have been transported to their training sites by chartered buses for their convenience. Reservists, like conscripts, now also have the option of travelling independently to their military units for annual training and can be compensated for travel and meal expenses (Chŏng 1995). These minimal arrangements are designed to ensure the perception of military service as men's duty.

However, there always have been varying degrees of resistance to this "manly" duty among men for one reason or another. The evaders of the previous generation were believed to be motivated primarily by fear of death, physical hardship, and abuse (Ryu 1989, 20).[32] As these conditions have gradually improved over time, the rationale for resistance to military service seems to be tied increasingly to the practical calculation that conscripts will lose time from the pursuit of higher education and employment. As the author observed during her college years in the first half of the 1980s, this has been particularly true of students at elite universities, who see military service as a waste of the prime of life and an interruption in their career development. Given the persistant, negative perception of military service, those who are wealthy or well connected have exploited loopholes in the conscription system to alleviate the burden of regular military service or to be exempted from it altogether. Recent investigations reveal this type of irregularity. In order to understand these findings, it is necessary to delineate the contour of the complicated system of universal conscription in south Korea.

Unlike the principle of universal male conscription, for economic and military reasons few military systems in practice can ever encompass the entire body of the male population in a given national society. Moreover, the military cannot change its manpower size according to demographic fluctuations that affect the supply of prospective conscripts. Therefore, it must contrive criteria for selecting only a portion of the young male population. These criteria are always colored with varying degrees of racialized, ethnicized, and gendered assumptions about who constitutes the body of efficient and trustworthy soldiers. It is noteworthy that in the context of perceived racial and ethnic homogeneity, the Korean military has employed formal education, along with physical and psychological fitness, as salient criteria to differentiate men: those who are fit to serve, those who are not, and those who deserve lenient service or exemption. Despite several changes, especially with the demilitarization of domestic politics during the past few years, two basic categories of military service have remained essentially consistent: resident service (*hyŏnyŏk*) and supplementary/substitute service (*poch'ungyŏk/taech'ebyŏngyŏk*). The former refers to regular soldiering performed by conscripts residing in military barracks. Reflecting the increasing contestation over military service since the transition to a civilian regime in 1993, the latter consists of ever-changing categories of modified military service or substitutes for it (S. Pak 1995, 19; S. Han 1995, 21; T. Chŏng 1994).

Since military service continues to involve physical hardship and the disadvantage of being removed from civilian sectors in society, prospective conscripts and their families are extremely sensitive to the issue of equity. According to the 1993 Parliamentary Inspection of the Administration, the percentage of men judged to serve as "defense soldier" (*pangwibyŏng*, a conscript who commutes to a military unit from his own house and serves a shorter period than a regular conscript) is higher among the sons of wealthy government officers (43 percent) and employees of the Office of Military Manpower (40 percent) than the national average (27 percent). Similarly, while the percentage of military service exemption is higher among these groups, that of regular service, which involves barrack life, is higher among the poor (*Nyusmeikŏ* 1997, 29). When a numerical minority, the sons of wealthy and well-connected families, appear to receive special treatment, the issue is explosive enough to incite heated reactions and debates.[33] For instance, controversies have been periodically sparked when members of the political elite or their sons did not serve in the military.[34]

Resistance to military service from a more lofty philosophical ground has also developed since the mid-1980s. Although a very small minority, a group of conscientious objectors who "refuse to carry guns" (chipch'ong kŏbuja) has emerged as a new phenomenon (Institute for Defense Analysis 1995, 155–51). Because this category is not acknowledged by the south Korean state, these resisters have been sentenced to imprisonment for violating the military service law.[35] Throughout the 1980s, during the vibrant and militant height of the student movement, some male student activists refused to participate in military drills, which had been integrated into the university curriculum as a mandatory subject since the 1970s. They demanded the removal of compulsory drill, perceived to be an instrument of the military dictatorship. They also refused to take the annual trip to the military barracks for more extensive military training.

The end of the Cold War and the ongoing sociopolitical democratization of south Korea have had significant effects on popular perceptions of military service among the younger generation, who came of age during the 1980s and the 1990s. The 1997 national poll conducted by Media Research offers a glimpse of a trend toward the uncoupling of military service and masculinity among this younger generation of men. To almost every question asked, the group of prospective conscripts in their late teens or early twenties responded with attitudes noticeably different from those of the rest of population. For instance, more than half of them (58.0 percent) advocated the elimination of the system of mandatory military service, in comparison with only 23.3 percent of the general population. While a half of the prospective conscripts (50.0 percent) responded that military service would have positive effects on their prospects for employment, the general population showed a far more positive attitude toward the advantages of military service (80.3 percent). Similarly, less than a half of the prospective conscripts (45.7 percent) preferred regular military service in the barracks to special or supplementary service or exemption altogether whereas the general population was more supportive of regular military service (77.7 percent). Moreover, the 1997 national poll also shows that the younger and the more educated the respondent, the more critical his attitude toward military service and the less accepting of its imperative (Pyŏngmu 1998a, 1998b). In the context of a divided Korea, the older generation, which sees itself as having built contemporary Korea through enormous self-sacrifice, is deeply concerned about the "individualistic" new generation and their air of self-centeredness as reflected in these responses to military service.

ARTIFICIAL DISTANCE FROM REPRODUCTION

Separation from the daily work of social reproduction and caring labor is another element of hegemonic masculinity largely structured by the paramount role of the family provider and the related effects of military service. These responsibilities justify men's disengagement from food preparation; from cleaning and washing; from caring for the sick, the elderly, the disabled, and children; and from the business of stretching household resources in lean times. Women are supposed to do all the housework and caring services, which are indispensable but devalued.[36] Therefore, performing any of these activities is considered unmanly or emasculating.[37] As discussed previously, the military tends to segregate itself from women and the women's world of life-sustaining activities, and defines combat and killing as men's work and nurturing and caring as women's work. While these two categories of activities appear to be mutually exclusive, the military life, especially during long periods of noncombat, requires an extensive range of maintenance work for its smooth functioning. Nevertheless, reproductive labor in the daily routine of the military is overshadowed by its masculinized image as an effective fighting machine or as a patriotic institution of courageous and heroic (male) soldiers.

The link between masculinity and distance from reproduction has a historical legacy in south Korea. The Confucian scholar-official (*sŏnbi*) of the Chosŏn period (1392–1910) embodied a masculine ideal strictly separated from the life-sustaining activities of the household.[38] To be free from the drudgery of daily life, the *sŏnbi* was dedicated to studying Confucian texts in order to obtain "wisdom" with which he advised the sovereign king. Furthermore, he was not supposed to degrade himself by engaging in any form of manual labor or any economic activity. This aspect of *sŏnbi* masculinity is in sharp contrast to the hegemonic masculinity of contemporary Korea, in which the white-collar worker who embodies the middle class ideal is very much involved in business activities. Yet even in dynastic times, not every Confucian scholar was lucky enough to be a bureaucrat employed by the Chosŏn court, and not every member of the *yangban* class was sufficiently well endowed with land and slaves to sustain a leisurely existence. Industrious wives, daughters, and daughters-in-law performed innumerable tasks that enabled many a *yangban* male to sustain appearances in the public realm (Bishop 1897, 101–102, Jones 1896, 229).

In contemporary Korea, some men cannot afford to maintain artificial distance from housework, child care, and caring for the infirm, the disabled, the retarded, and the old for the simple reason that women are not available at home or are unable to perform these tasks. The dissolution of nuclear families by divorce, which is increasing, can force male involvement in reproductive activities.[39] It remains to be seen whether this kind of involuntary involvement will generate counter-hegemonic practices of masculinity.

Of greater interest is an emerging movement of individual men who are willing to subvert the practice of disengagement from reproductive activities. South Korean mass media offer glimpses of this new trend. For instance, *Yŏsŏng sinmun*, a south Korean feminist newspaper, has reported on a small but significant number of men who claim that they want to be good fathers. They involve themselves in family life, especially child rearing, and meet regularly as a group. (The groups are called *chohŭnabŏjiga toiryŏnŭn saramdŭlŭi moim* and *chanyŏ sarangŭl sich'ŏnhanŭn abŏji moim*). A young male assistant to a member of the National Assembly has been writing a regular column for this newspaper, in which he describes his experience of raising two daughters. While these appear to be positive signs, the softening of hegemonic masculinity, or the decline of domestic patriarchy, does not necessarily lead to women's empowerment.[40] It remains to be seen how the complicating of hegemonic masculinity will allow women to increase their ability to negotiate with public patriarchy in the larger society.

The emergent practice of fatherhood faces structural as well as psychological/cultural resistance. Because fathers' substantial involvement in family life demands fundamental restructuring of corporate life in south Korea, it is unlikely that this new view of fatherhood will be popularized in the near future, especially in the period of economic globalization. A case study of fatherhood based on a small group sample seems to reflect men's ambivalence toward this change. According to a study based on in-depth interviews of twenty-seven men collected by snowball sampling from various classes and generations, younger men talk about the ideal father as being family-oriented and interactive with children. However, they also express anxiety about the decline of paternal authority that accompanies this change (Han 1997).

CONCLUSION: HEGEMONIC MASCULINITY AND THE MODERNIZATION OF WOMEN'S SUBORDINATION

I have analyzed three major notions and practices of hegemonic masculinity in contemporary south Korea, as they have been shaped by capitalist industrialization and military confrontation with north Korea, to show how they have been implicated in the modernization of women's subordination. In Korean society, where economic growth has been the paramount telos of national development, economic performance has become the single most important justification for authority. For decades, military regimes claimed legitimacy on the basis of their ability to sustain intense programs of economic development.[41] In a parallel manner, south Korean men's domestic authority is legitimized by their ability to provide for their families through paid employment outside the home. This masculine role of family provider was supported by law between 1960 and 1990. The provider role relegated women to the domestic sphere despite the increase in the level of their education. As a consequence, women's paid employment outside the home is regarded as temporary, and tends to be low in both status and pay. The masculine role of the family provider has also justified men's distance from both housework and caring labor in the household. The legal and economic basis for the masculine role of family provider perpetuates a patrilineal family system that requires the married woman to provide her husband's family with a male heir.

Throughout the 1990s, the masculine role of the family provider has been subverted by economic globalization, which has undermined job security—even for middle class men—and the expectation of a rising standard of living. Moreover, the perceived need to invest in children's education has compelled wives to pursue informal economic activities. However, these challenges have not generated a dismantling of hegemonic masculinity. Rather, in a time of economic downturn in the aftermath of the 1997 Asian economic crisis, the discontent of male employees is addressed through conservative discourses that fault wives for not giving adequate emotional support to their overworked men.

Mandatory military service, as the major element of hegemonic masculinity, contributes to the modernization of women's subordination by acting as a mechanism that essentializes and naturalizes gender differences, thus reinforcing the dichotomy of the masculine provider and the feminine housewife. Because south Korea abides in an official and constant state of military confrontation with the North, soldiers are seen as performing the crucial task of protecting the nation. However, military service is not something that all men willingly and wholeheartedly embrace. It is strenuous, unpleasant, dangerous, and, more importantly, requires withdrawal from remunerative activities in a capitalist society. During the period of the Cold War and military rule, the south Korean state managed to militarize masculinity and maintain it through a combination of coercion and ideological persuasion. The end of the Cold War and contemporary south Korea's overwhelming economic superiority to north Korea have allowed a younger generation of men to begin to challenge the imperative of military service. The south Korean state must therefore offer men incentives that are strong enough for them to accept conscription. Nationalism is an important motivation, but it is insufficient without material rewards for such sacrifice.

Military service confers on men certain economic advantages, including a structure of employment that accommodates and sometimes privileges military service, and the widespread perception that military service is a valuable exercise in discipline and responsibility that prepares men for employment outside the home. In other words, there is a convergence between the different elements of hegemonic masculinity. Moreover, in the eyes of the state, men who have been incorporated into its military mechanisms are true citizens who can fight for the nation to their deaths. By this insidious logic, men are more responsible citizens than women. This gendered construction of citizenship as tied to men's martial duty opens a field of protest in the current context of south Korea's dramatic sociopolitical democratization.

NOTES

1. See Lorber (1994); Connell (1987); Mann and Crompton (1986); and Scott (1986).

2. See Yi Hyo-jae (1997) for a discussion of the recent trend to redeem unemployed fathers. See O Yŏng-hwan (1997) and Cho (in this volume) for an example of the largely conservative preoccupation with the younger generation's mentality.

3. These components of hegemonic masculinity are by no means exhaustive. For instance, I leave out heterosexual desires and practices, an adequate analysis of which is beyond the scope of this chapter.

4. The majority of women workers have been concentrated in such sectors as agriculture, manufacturing, and wholesale or retail trade, including restaurant and hotel businesses, which require neither higher education nor professional training. As recently as 1998, women represented only 5.3 percent of such high-ranking positions as legislators, senior officials, and managers (KWDI 1999, 206), despite the continuous increase in the percentage of women with higher education in the labor market. More than three-quarters of all working women are concentrated in sales and service jobs (34.9 percent), clerical positions (14.1 percent), agriculture and fishing (13.7 percent), and manual work (13.4 percent) (KWDI 1999, 208–209). Along with this general tendency, it is significant that the unemployment rate among college-educated women has been almost twice as high as that of their male counterparts since the mid-1980s (KWDI 1995, 138).

5. See Seungsook Moon (2000) for a detailed discussion of the rise of women's policy as a vehicle through which women's associations advance the interests of various groups of women.

6. According to a 1998 survey of 808 women workers, 384 unemployed women, and 52 labor unions, conducted by the Yŏsŏng Minuhoe, a grassroots feminist organization that monitors and promotes women's employment, women employees are twice as likely to get laid off as their male counterparts in the current post–economic crisis era. The practice of retirement at marriage or pregnancy is reviving rapidly (*Chosŏn Ilbo* 4 November 1998). See also special articles on women workers in the I.M.F. period in *Pyŏngdung* (1998).

7. The strong desire to have a son has resulted in a skewed sex ratio among newborns because a large number of Korean women, especially urban, young, educated, and middle class women, use prenatal sex selection tests and abort female fetuses (Pyŏn 1991). A similar practice has been observed in India (Bumiller 1990; Mies 1986) and China (Devin 1987; Hartmann 1995, ch 9). With urbanization and industrialization, children have lost their previous function as laborers and household help. Rather, they have become a major source of consumption needs, requiring extensive education and care. Advances in reproductive technology offer a problematic solution to women who want to have fewer pregnancies but feel tremendous pressure to produce a son.

8. A study in 1981 indicated that urban full-time housewives spent a total of 11.8 hours at housework each weekday and 13.4 hours each weekend day when families stayed at home (KWDI 1985, 148–149). A 1973 study had reported that urban full-time housewives spent about 8 hours a day on housework, including 2.6 hours of cooking.

9. There have been no women in the National Security Council, Government Legislative Administration Agency, Ministry of Home Affairs, Ministry of Commerce and Industry, and Ministry of Construction.

10. There is a body of literature devoted to the critical examination of the construction of tradition in colonial periods or periods of nation building. See, for example, Hobsbawm and Ranger (1983) and Lata Mani (1987). For a critical discussion of a body of Korean traditions see Kendall (1996). For a critical discussion of official nationalism that constructed Korean tradition see Moon (1998). See Janelli with Yim (1993) for a critical examination of the assumption that Korean corporate culture perpetuates preindustrial forms of social interaction.

11. For examples of studies illustrating this point see Hsiung (1996), Moghadam (1996), Gilmartin (1994), Brinton (1993), Jean Pyle (1990), Mies (1986), and Tilly and Scott (1978).

12. In the early 1960s approximately 60 percent of the population remained agrarian. See Chin-kyun Kim (1988, 83).

13. See also Elaine Kim's (1998) study, based on in-depth interviews of fifty-four married south Korean men between the ages of 24 and 69, conducted in the late 1980s. Kim also illustrates how the role of family provider is central to the men's experiences of masculinity across class and age.

14. See Brinton (1993) and Bumiller (1995) for an analytic and a descriptive discussion, respectively, of competitive education organized around the immediate goal of top universities.

15. Average monthly spending of a south Korean family for extra-school education amounts to approximately $384 for a high school student, $328 for a middle school student, and $158 for a primary school student (M. Pak 1995, 150). The exchange rate used here is $1.00 to W 885.00. These expenses are quite significant in families with two children when compared with the average monthly earnings of white-collar male workers, which are between $2,000 and $3,000.

16. Indeed, there is a gulf between the materialistic basis of masculine authority in capitalist Korea and the symbolic basis of Confucian masculinity. Patrilineage affirms a man's superiority and authority as the legitimate heir of his family line.

17. During this period, this novel was included in the lists of top best-sellers regularly printed by major newspapers and weekly magazines. For the first two or three months, it was the best-selling novel in the country.

18. Elaine Kim's (1998) study of fifty-four married south Korean men of various generations, and socioeconomic backgrounds illustrates prevalent but varying degrees of misogyny in their thinking.

19. The recent professionalization of the Women's Army Corps, simultaneous with the expansion of training to areas other than clerical tasks, has attracted a large number of female college graduates, who face a paucity of civilian employment opportunities. This has made the Women's Military Academy highly competitive. At the time of annual recruitment, it boasts a ratio of twenty or thirty applicants for each available slot (personal interviews with senior officers of the Academy in the summer of 1996).

20. This documentary film, *Yŏja sodaejang* (A Woman Platoon Leader), was produced by the Film Division of the Public Relations Office of the National Army (*Kukkun hongbo kwalliso yŏnghwabu*) in 1995.

21. Throughout this period, there have been numerous changes with respect to specific details regarding the length of military service, the minimum educational requirement, and the age limits for taking the conscription test (*chingbyŏng kŏmsa*) and receiving exemption (Cho 1996; Kang 1996; Kim, Chin-dae 1996; T. Yi 1996; Y. Yi 1996; *Pyŏngmu* 1995, 16–22).

22. The length of yearly training was reduced in 1994 from the 28-day obligation, established in 1957, to three days (Chŏng 1995, 29). This change seems to reflect the ascendancy of economic activities over nonproductive military training

during the decades of economic expansion, as well as the increasing significance of high technology in warfare.

23. The decade of the eradication campaign started with a large-scale national investigation of military service corruption involving public servants, employees of the Office of Military Service, soldiers, civilians, and prospective conscripts between December 1969 and March 1970. This was followed by localized attempts by civil servants in charge of administering conscription to identify conscription evaders. In order to sustain this campaign, the regime formed the central council and its local branches, specifically dedicated to exposing military service corruption. (Ki 1995; Ryu 1989).

24. Facing the growing trend among the younger generation of men to avoid military service, the civilian regime under Kim Young Sam legislated the Veterans Support Law in 1997 and passed its Enforcement Ordinance in August 1998. Essentially, this legislative move aims to strengthen the practice of offering specific economic incentives to conscripts. Before this, incentives were perceived as insignificant and unsystematic. See T'ae-hong Kim (1998).

25. In the ancient Greek polis, only the property-owning free male citizens were entitled to participate in politics and had a duty to fight for the defense of the polis. This close link between soldiering and political and economic privilege persists in contemporary societies. For example, the United States granted citizenship at the time of discharge to male immigrants who served in the United States military during World War II, regardless of their national origins (Kerber 1990).

26. See the Institute for Defense Analysis (1992), pages 142–108 and 142–109. These pages are intentional, as they appear in the document.

27. To deal with the excess of able-bodied young men produced by universal conscription, the south Korean government has created several convoluted categories of conscription that have no precise equivalent in English.

28. This group of men also mentions passivity and authoritarianism as negative consequences of military service.

29. The findings corroborate the role of mandatory military service as a male initiation ritual in contemporary Israel (Golan 1997; Lieblich and Perlow 1988).

30. There seems to be growing concern about this new generation's ability to tolerate military service. It is noteworthy that *Wŏlgan Chosŏn*, an influential conservative monthly magazine, published an article on how the new generation is transformed into soldiers in response to societal anxiety (Kim Tŏk-han 1996).

31. It is important to keep in mind that this positive change is relative to previous conditions in the military. According to the 1993 Parliamentary Inspection of the Administration, 139 soldiers were beaten to death between 1988 and 1993, which accounts for 6 percent of the total deaths of soldiers during the same period. (*Nyusmeikŏ* 1997, 30).

32. According to the statistics compiled by the Office of Military Manpower, the number of evaders sharply dropped from 1973 throughout the decade as a result of aggressive investigation and punishment (Ryu 1989, 20). Until the early 1980s, an absolute majority of healthy men were judged to be fit for regular military service (as opposed to supplementary military service). This trend declined until the early 1990s, when equity in military service became a controversial social issue during the presidential election in 1992 (*Nyusmeikŏ* 1997).

33. Some upper and upper-middle-class families use money and family connections to bribe government officials or pay physicians to manipulate medical records. Other families even emigrate in order to avoid their sons' military service. Some Korean immigrant women whom the author interviewed in 1996 confirmed this solution.

34. Since the end of military rule, military service has become a litmus test for candidates during elections. The most recent controversy was triggered in mid-1997 by the presidential candidate of the ruling Grand Korea Party, whose sons' military service exemptions were suspicious (*Nyusmeikŏ* 1997; *Nyuspŭlŏs* 1997). See *Wŏlgan Chosŏn* (1992) for a controversy on military service and presidential candidates in 1992.

35. This information was gained from my private interview with a senior research fellow at the Institute for Defense Analysis in early December, 1998.

36. Nancy Folbre (1991) argues that the social meaning of "unproductive housework" is an androcentric construct. By examining census occupational categories, she traces the changing meanings of housework in nineteenth-century England and America. According to this study, over the course of the nineteenth century, the meaning of housework shifted from being productive to being unproductive. This change was integral to the emergence of the industrial economy as a masculine sphere.

37. Elaine Kim's (1998) study, conducted in the late 1980s, shows this attitude among diverse groups of south Korea men.

38. In the West from the time of Plato, politics has been a prerogative of male citizens who were free from the mundane necessities performed in the household or the so-called private sphere. This deep-rooted gender difference is crystallized in the thematic dichotomy of women-nature versus men-culture (Ortner 1974). As de Beauvoir (1972) articulates, while women are confined to the immediacy of daily life, men are free to engage in "transcendental" activities in the so-called public realm. This dichotomy runs through political and social discourse in the West even into the late twentieth century (Elshtain 1981).

39. Divorce has been rising rapidly since the 1960s. In 1980 there were 5.8 divorces per 100 marriages. This ratio has increased to 11.3 in 1990 and 32.1 in 1998 (KWDI 1999, 75).

40. Barbara Ehrenreich (1995) makes a parallel assessment of the decline of patriarchy in the United States. She argues that this change harbingers not so much women's empowerment as different forms of subordination and exploitation of women.

41. For critical studies of economic developmentalism in south Korea see Janelli with Yim (1993), Cho and Hong (1995), and Han'guk sanŏpsahoe yŏn'guhoe (1991).

REFERENCES

de Beauvoir, Simone. 1972. *The Second Sex.* Harmondsworth, U.K.: Penguin.

Bishop, Isbella Bird. 1897. *Korea and Her Neighbors.* New York: Fleming H. Revell

Brinton, Mary. 1993. *Women and the Economic Miracle: Gender and Work in Postwar Japan.* Berkeley: University of California Press.

Bumiller, Elisabeth. 1990. *May You Be the Mother of a Hundred Sons: A Journey Among the Women of India.* New York: Fawcett Columbine.

————. 1995. *The Secrets of Mariko: A Year in the Life of a Japanese Woman and Her Family.* New York: Vintage Books.

Campbell, D'Ann. 1990. The regimented women of World War Two. In *Women, Militarism, and War: Essays in History, Politics, and Social Theory.* Jean B. Elshtain and Sheila Tobias, eds. Savage, Md.: Rowman and Littlefield Publishers.

Cho Pong-jin, and Sŏng-t'ae Hong, eds. 1995. *Hoesagamyŏn chungnŭnda: Kyŏngchejuŭi damnonŭi pip'anŭl wihan pildstŏdi* (If you join a company, you're dead: A field study to criticize economistic discourse). Seoul: Hyŏnsilmunhwayŏn'gu.

Cho, Sŏng-lyul. 1996. Chaehaksaeng ibyŏng (sochip) yŏngichedoŭi pyŏnch'ŏn kwajŏng (A process of change in the students' enlistment postponement system). *Pyŏngmu* 32(winter):84–87.

Choi, Kwang-p'yo. 1997. Nambukhan pyŏngmuinsajedowa t'ongil Han'gukkun (Military service personnel systems in south and north Koreas and the unified Korean military). *Hankukkunsa* (South Korean military affairs) 5(7):91–110.

Chŏng, Hwan-sik. 1995. Pyŏngnyŏkdongwŏn hullyŏnsojipjedo pyŏnch'ŏnmit ch'ujinbanghyang (Change and a direction in the military manpower mobilization enlistment system). *Pyŏngmu* 31(fall):26–29.

Chŏng, Tong-jun. 1994. Kongik kŭnmu yowŏn sojipchedo (Public interests agents recruitment system).

Connell, Robert. 1987. *Gender and Power: Society, the Person, and Sexual Politics.* Stanford, Calif.: Stanford University Press.

————. 1995. *Masculinities.* Berkeley: University of California Press.

Devin, Delia. 1987. Gender and population in the People's Republic of China. In *Women, State, and Ideology: Studies from Africa and Asia.* Haleh Afshar, ed. Albany, N.Y.: SUNY Press.

Ehrenreich, Barbara. 1995. The decline of patriarchy. In *Constructing Masculinity*. Maurice Berger, Brian Wallis, and Simon Watson, eds. New York: Routledge.

————. 1997. *Blood Rites: Origins and History of the Passion of War*. New York: Henry Holt & Co.

Elshtain, Jean B. 1981. *Public Man, Private Woman: Women in Social and Political Thought*. Princeton, N.J.: Princeton University Press.

Folbre, Nancy. 1991. The unproductive housewife: Her evolution in nineteenth-century economic thought. *Signs: Journal of Women in Culture and Society* 16(3):463–484.

Gilmartin, Christina K. 1994. Gender, political culture, and women's mobilization in the Chinese nationalist revolution, 1924–1927. In *Engendering China: Women, Culture, and the State*. Christina K. Gilmartin, Gail Hershatter, Lisa Rofel, and Tyrene White, eds. Cambridge, Mass.: Harvard University Press.

Golan, Galia. 1997. Militarization and gender: The Israeli experience. *Women's Studies International Forum* 20(5/6):581–586.

Gramsci, Antonio. 1997. *Selections from the Prison Notebooks*. New York: International Publishers.

Han Kyŏng-hye. 1997. Abŏjisangŭi pyŏnhwa (Change in the image of father). In *Namsŏngkwa Han'guksahoe* (Men and Korean society). Yŏsŏnghan'guksahoeyŏn'guhoe (Women Korean Society Studies Association), ed. Seoul: Sahoemunhwayŏn'guso.

Han, Sang-tae. 1993. *Hyŏnyŏkpŏng ipyŏngjedoŭi pyŏnch'ŏn* (Change in the enlistment system for resident military service). *Pyŏngmu* 31 (fall):20–22.

Han'guk sanŏpsahoe yŏn'guhoe (Korea Industrial Society Research Association), ed. 1991. *Han'guksahoe'wa chibae ideologi* (Korean society and ruling ideologies). Seoul: Nokdu.

Hartmann, Betsy. 1995. *Reproductive Rights and Wrongs: The Global Politics of Population Control*. rev. ed. Boston: South End Press.

Hobsbawm, Eric, and Terence Ranger, eds. 1983. *The Invention of Tradition*. Cambridge: Cambridge University Press.

Hsiung, Ping-Chun. 1996. *Living Rooms as Factories: Class, Gender, and the Satellite Factory System in Taiwan*. Philadelphia: Temple University Press.

Institute for Defense Analysis. 1992. *Kungmin anboŭisikmit kungmin kukpanggwangye yŏronchosa yŏn'gu* (A study of public opinions concerning national security consciousness and national defense). Seoul.

————. 1995. *Pyŏngyŏkjedo kaesŏnbanghyang yŏn'gu* (A study of the direction to reform the military service system). Seoul.

Isaksson, Eva. ed. 1988. *Women and the Military System*. Proceedings of a symposium arranged by the International Peace Bureau and Peace Union of Finland. London: Harvester Wheatsheaf.

Janelli, Roger L. with Dawnhee Yim. 1993. *Making Capitalism: The Social and Cultural Construction of a South Korean Conglomerate.* Stanford, Calif.: Stanford University Press.

Jones, George Heber. 1896. The Status of Women in Korea. *Korea Repository* 3:223–229.

Jones, Kathleen. 1990. Dividing the ranks: Women and the draft. In *Women, Militarism, and War: Essays in History, Politics and Social Theory.* Jean B. Elshtain and Sheila Tobias, eds. pp. 125–136. Savage, Md.: Rowman and Littlefield Publishers.

Kang Chun-man. 1998. *Kamelleonkwa haiena: Han'guk ŏnllon 115 nyŏnsa, 1883–1998* (Chameleon and hyena: A history of 115 years of Korean mass media). Seoul: Inmulkwasasangsa.

Kang Kyŏng-hwan. 1996. Pyŏngyŏkpŏmnyŏngŭi chejŏnggwa chuyo gaejŏngnaeyong (The establishment of conscription law and its revisions). *Pyŏngmu* 32(winter):68–70.

Kendall, Laurel. 1996. *Getting Married in Korea: Of Gender, Morality, and Modernity.* Berkeley: University of California Press.

Kerber, Linda K. 1990. May all our citizens be soldiers and all our soldiers citizens. In *Women, Militarism, and War: Essays in History, Politics, and Social Theory.* Jean B. Elshtain and Sheila Tobias, eds. pp. 89–103. Savage, Md.: Rowman and Littlefield.

Ki Yong-ju. 1995. Pyŏngmuhaengjŏng soaesinŏdikkaji wannŭnga? (How far has the military service administration reform come?). *Pyŏngmu* 31(fall):30–33.

Kim Chae-il. 1996. Hyangt'oyebigun ŏpmu pyŏnch'ŏn (Change in the homeland reserve force's task). *Pyŏngmu* 32(winter):80–83.

Kim Chin-dae. 1996. Tokcha poch'ungyŏk chedoŭi pyŏnch'ŏn (Change in the system of assigning only sons to supplementary service). *Pyŏngmu* 32(winter):74–76.

Kim Chin-kyun. 1988. Han'guknongminch'ŭnge daehan kyegŭmnonjok chŏpgŭn (A class approach to the stratum of Korean peasants). In *Sahoegwahakkwa minjokhyŏnsil* (Social sciences and national reality), Seoul: Hangilsa.

Kim Chin-kyun, and Sŭnghŭi Hong. 1991. Han'guksahoeŭi kyoyukkwa chibaeideologi (Education and ruling ideologies in Korean society). In *Han'guksahoe'wa chibae ideologi* (Korean society and ruling ideologies). Han'guksanŏpsahoe yon'guhoe, ed. Seoul: Noktu. pp. 227–257.

Kim Chŏng-hyŏn. 1996. *Abŏji* (Father). Seoul: Munidang.

Kim Chong-il. 1995. Nugurŭl wihan kyŏngyŏnghyŏksininga? (For whom is management innovation?). In *Hoesagamyŏn chungnŭnda.* Cho Pong-jin and Hong Sŏng-tae, eds. Seoul: Hyŏsilmunwha yŏn'gu pp. 59–67.

Kim Chu-su. 1973. Hyŏnhaeng kayokpŏpsangŭi namnyŏ ch'abyŏl (Sexual discrimination in the current family law). Yŏsŏng 91(May):5–10.

————. 1990. Kaejŏng kajobŏbŭi kaejŏng kyŏngwiwa kwaje (Issues in the revised family law). In Kaejong gajobŏbkwa Han'guksahoe (The revised family law and Korean society). Seoul: KWDI/Korean Family Law Studies Association.

Kim Chu-suk. 1990. Nongŏpsaengsan kujoŭi pyŏnhwawa kajok (Change in the structure of agricultural production and the family). In Han'guk kajŏngnon (Studies of Korean families). Yŏsŏng Han'guk Sahoe yŏn'guhoe (Women Korean Society Studies Association), ed. Seoul.

Kim, Elaine H. 1998. Men's talk: A Korean American view of south Korean constructions of women, gender, and masculinity. In Dangerous Women: Gender and Korean Nationalism, Elaine H. Kim and Chungmoo Choi, eds. pp. 67–117 New York: Routledge.

Kim Hwan-t'ae. 1993. Yuktup'um soryŏngŭi kundaeiyagi, sang; ha (A sixth tup'um major's military story) vol. 1 and 2. Seoul: Chaenggi.

Kim Mi-suk. 1990. Chungsodosi pinmingajogŭi sahoegyŏngjejok sŏnggyŏk (Socioeconomic characteristics of poor families in medium and small cities). In Han'guk kajŏngnon. (studies of Korean families) Yŏsŏng Han'guk sahoe yŏn'guhoe (Women's Studies Association), ed. Seoul.

Kim Pong-jin. 1995a. Kyegŭppyŏl kajokkwa yŏsŏng (Families and women by class). In Yŏsŏngkwa hanguksahoe (Women and Korean society).Yŏsŏng Han'guksahoe Yŏnguhoe (Women Korean Society Studies Association). ed. Seoul: Sahoe munhwayŏn'guso.

————. 1995b. Namjaga ihonŭl kyŏlsimhalttae (When men decide to divorce). Seoul: Saemunan.

Kim, Seung-Kyung. 1997. Class Struggle or Family Struggle? The Lives of Women Factory Workers in South Korea. Cambridge: Cambridge University Press.

Kim T'ae-hong. 1998. Kunbongmu kyŏngnyŏk injŏngchŏngch'aekŭi hyokwawa kaep'yŏnbangan (The effects of the policy to recognize military service as work experience and its reform direction). Emergency discussion meeting organized by the Korean Women's Associations United, the Korean Council of Women's Association, the Economic Justice Practice United, and the Participation United, and sponsored by the Special Council for Women. 16 September. Seoul.

Kim Tŏk-han. 1996 Sinsedaenŭn ŏtŏke kuninŭro mandŭrŏjina (How is the new generation transformed into soldiers?). Wŏlgan Chosŏn 196(July):402–415.

The Korea Herald. 27 February 1999.

KWDI (Korean Women's Development Institute). 1985. Yŏsŏng paeksŏ (Whitepaper on women). Seoul.

————. 1991 Yŏsŏng paeksŏ (Whitepaper on women). Seoul.

————. 1995. *Yŏsŏng t'onggye yŏnbo* (Statistical yearbook on women). Seoul.

————. 1999. *Yŏsŏng t'ongye yŏnbo* (Statistical yearbook on women). Seoul.

Koyama, Ikumi. 1996. Kunbongmu kyŏnghŏmi Han'guk namsŏngŭi ŭisike mich'in yŏnghyang yŏn'gu (A study of the influence of military service experience on Korean men's consciousness). Master's thesis. Yonsei University, Seoul.

Lee, On-juk. 1982. Han'guk yŏsŏngnodongjaŭi kyŏrhon'gwan'gwa chigŏpkwan (Korean women workers' views on marriage and occupation). *Aseayŏsŏngyŏn'gu* 21:181–223.

Lee, Sang-wuk. 1985. Yŏsŏngŭi pŏpjŏk chiwiwa kajokpŏp kaejŏng'non (Woman's legal status and an argument for the revision of family law). *Yŏsŏng Munje Yŏngu* 343–359.

Lieblich, Amia, and Meir Perlow. 1988. Transition to Adulthood during Military Service. *The Jerusalem Quarterly* 47(summer):40–76.

Lorber, Judith. 1994. *Paradoxes of Gender*. New Haven: Yale University Press.

Mani, Lata. 1987. Contentious traditions: The debates on SATI in colonial India. *Cultural Critique* (fall):119–56.

Mann, Michael, and Rosemary Crompton, eds. 1986. *Gender and Stratification*. Cambridge: Polity Press.

Mies, Maria. 1986. *Patriarchy and Accumulation on a World Scale: Women in the International Division of Labor*. London: Zed Books.

Moghadam, Valentine. 1996. *Patriarchy and Economic Development: Women's Positions at the End the Twentieth Century*. New York: Clarendon Press.

Moon, Seungsook. 1998. Begetting the nation: The androcentric discourse of national history and tradition in south Korea. In *Dangerous Women: Gender and Korean Nationalism*. Elaine H. Kim and Chungmoo Choi, eds. New York: Routledge.

————. 2000. Overcome by globalization: The rise of a women's policy in south Korea. In *Korea's Globalization*. Samuel S. Kim, ed. Cambridge: Cambridge University Press.

Nyusmeikŏ. 1997. Abŏji! kundaegagi sirŏyo: Pyŏngyŏkŭn sisŏnghan ŭimuga anira tonŏpko ppaekŏpnŭn sŏminŭi chiminga? (Father! I don't want to go to the military: Is military service not a sacred duty but burden of the poor and ill-connected?). vol. 235 (14 August):28–37.

Nyuspŭlŏs. 1997. Ilgŭrŏjin kukpanggwan pyŏngyŏk, ŭimuinga sŏnt'aekinga? (A distorted view of national defense is military service a duty or a choice?). vol. 96 (14 August):14–20.

O Kyŏng-hŭi. 1995. Hoesaŭi kkot, chohwawa puchohwa (A company's flower, harmony and disharmony). In *Hoesagamyŏn chungnŭnda: Kyŏngcjejuŭi damnonŭi pip'anŭl wihan pild stŏdi* (If you join a company, you're dead: A field study to criticize economistic discourse). Hyŏnsuilmunhw yŏn'gu.

O Yŏng-hwan. 1997. Chŏnjaengnamyŏn tomangganda? Ch'ŏngsonyŏndŭlŭi hansimhan hogukkwan. Anbogwan (If war breaks out, will I run away? The youth's deplorable views of national protection and national security). *Wŏlgandonghwa* 10(8):120–125.

Ortner, Sherry B. 1974. *Is Female to Male as Nature is to Culture? In Women, Culture and Society.* Michelle Zimbalist Rosaldo and Louise Lamphere, eds. pp. 67–87. Stanford, Calif.: Stanford University Press.

Pak, Kye-hyang. 1998. 21 segi chŏgye yŏgunŭi yoram yŏgunhakkyo (Women's Military Academy, cradle of elite women soldiers of the twenty-first century). *Kunsasegye* (April):32–34.

Pak Min-ja. 1995. Kajokkwa yŏsŏngŭi wich'i (The family and women's status). In *Yŏsŏng kwa Han'guksahoe* (Women and Korean society). Yŏsŏng Han'guksahoe Yŏn'guhoe, ed. Seoul: Sahoemunhwa yon'guso.

Pak Sang-wŏn. 1995. Chingpyŏnggŏmsa chedoŭi pyŏnch'ŏn (The change in the conscription test system). *Pyŏngmu* 31(fall):16–19.

Pyle, Jean. 1990. *The State and Women in the Economy: Lessons from Sex Discrimination in the Republic of Ireland.* Albany, N.Y.: SUNY Press.

Pyŏn Hwa-sun. 1991. Kukka chŏngch'aekkwa yŏsŏng: Ch'ulsan chŏngch'aekkwa sŏngbi pulkyunhyŏng hyŏnsangŭl chungsimŭro (The state's policy and women: Birth control policy and sex ratio imbalance). *Yŏsŏngyŏn'gu* 29:109–133.

Pyŏngmu. 1995. Pyŏngmuch'ŏng ch'angsŏl 25 nyŏn paljach'wui (A 25-year history of the office of military manpower). vol. 31 (fall):16–33.

———. 1998a. Pyŏngyŏkŭimu, kungmindŭrŭn irŏkke saenggakhagoitta (Military service, the people think this way). vol. 38:23–29.

———. 1998b. Pyŏngyŏkŭimu, kungmindŭrŭn irŏkke saenggakhagoitta (Military service, the people think this way). vol. 39:30–35.

Pyŏngdung. 1998. T'ŭkchip: IMF sidaeŭi yŏsŏngnodongja (Special report: Women workers in the IMF era). vol. 9 (Jan/Feb):20–29.

Ralston, David. 1990. *Importing the European Army: The Introduction of European Military Techniques and Institutions into the Extra-European World, 1600–1914.* Chicago: University of Chicago Press.

Ryu, Yŏn-kwŏn. 1989. Pyŏngyŏkp'ungt'o, ŏttŏke pyŏnch'ŏndoeŏ wanna? (Social perception of military service, how has it changed?). *Pyŏngmu* 12:18–22.

Scott, Joan W. 1986. Gender: A useful category of historical analysis. *American Historical Review* 91 (5):1053–1075.

Soh, Chung-Hee. 1991. *The Chosen Women in Korean Politics: An Anthropological Study.* New York: Praeger.

Tilly, Louse, and Joan Scott. 1978. *Women, Work and Family.* New York: Holt, Rinehart, and Winston.

Wŏlgan Chosŏn (Monthly Chosŏn). 1992. Kundaean'gan "nop'ŭn pundŭl" (The "higher-ups" who did not serve in the military). November.

Women's Army Corps. 1990. *Yŏgunyŏksa sajinjip* (A photo history of the women's army corps). Seoul.

Women's Military School. 1993. *Yŏgunsa* (A history of the women's army corps). Supplementary textbook. Seoul.

Yi Hyo-jae. 1997. Han'guksahoeŭi namsŏng ideologi (Masculine ideology in Korean society). In *Namsŏnggwa Han'guksahoe*.

Yi T'ae-ho. 1996. Saenggye kollanja pŏyngyŏk kammyŏnjedoŭi pyŏnchŏ'n kwajŏng (A process of change in the system of reducing military service for the indigent). *Pyŏngmu* 32(winter):63–67.

Yi Yŏ-song. 1996. Pangwuisojip chedoŭi pyŏnch'ŏn (Change in the defense corps system). *Pyŏngmu* 32(winter):77–79.

Yŏsŏng sinmun. 1996. Yŏsŏnggye siptae nyus (Ten biggest news stories in women's world). (December 27):7.

Yuval-Davis, Nira. 1987 Front and rear: The sexual division of labor in the Israeli army. In *Women, State and Ideology*. Haleh Afshar, ed. Albany, N.Y.: State University of New York Press.

5

GENDER CONSTRUCTION IN THE OFFICES OF A SOUTH KOREAN CONGLOMERATE

roger l. janelli and dawnhee yim

The capitalist industrialization of south Korea and its concomitant cultural transformations present anthropologists with abundant opportunities but formidable challenges. The recent emergence of diverse occupations, institutions, class fractions, and lifestyles provides a multitude of new research sites and topics for ethnographic inquiry, but this very diversity seems overwhelming. How can we comprehend the advent of new social and cultural phenomena as well as their mutation before our very eyes? How do the new social phenomena articulate with each other and with the world economy with which south Koreans have become increasingly involved?

Among the major institutions of modern south Korea that invite anthropological attention are the giant business conglomerates (*chaebŏl*). These very large organizations are often credited with (or blamed for) spearheading south Korea's capitalist industrialization during the past few decades. They continue to dominate south Korea's domestic economy, mediate much of its trade with other nations, and reshape practices and social roles.[1] As these conglomerates continue to expand, they draw more and more employees into their offices and factories, and larger numbers of persons come into contact with them and have experiences with their capitalist methods. These apparently successful entities are the topics of frequent articles in the economic dailies, popular magazines, and broadcast media; they are the subject of numerous studies in the field of business administration (e.g., Hattori 1986; Yi 1986; Chŏng 1987), and their practices have become models for emulation by many individuals who seek to attain their evident success. Even the recent restructuring demanded by the south Korean government and the I.M.F. have been aimed at financing these organizations rather than at their internal practices.

Among the least well-studied aspects of the south Korean conglomerates is the construction of gender in their offices.[2] Yet a need for such inquiries seems to be warranted by the special role that conglomerates have played in leading south Korea's capitalist transformation and by the rising importance of offices as workplaces in the south Korean political economy. According to south Korea's Economic Planning Board, over one million women were employed in office work (samujik) in 1992, comprising about 14.4 percent of all employed women in south Korea (Pak and Kang 1994, 239).[3]

This chapter explores the social and cultural construction of gender in the offices of the headquarters building of "Taesŏng," the pseudonym we have given to one of south Korea's four largest conglomerates and the site of Roger Janelli's fieldwork in 1986 and 1987 (Janelli with Yim 1993). We seek to understand how recruitment, job assignments, rewards, and attendant social activities expected of women and men were differentiated, and we attempt to grasp some of the ways in which that differentiation was accepted and reproduced or challenged and transformed.

Our chapter provides no more than an initial exploration of these issues, however. Gender construction was not among the principal topics of our ethnographic research, and conditions of fieldwork conspired to bias communication far more toward male than female workers. Women office workers were busy during working hours and could spare little time to engage in conversations with a visiting researcher; Roger Janelli's minor work activities for the company—translation and editing services granted in return for the opportunity to conduct fieldwork—seldom involved women, and his request to have Dawnhee Yim interview the women workers was one of the few that the company's managers denied. Moreover, the most revealing conversations, with men or women, turned out to have been conducted in small—ideally, dyadic—encounters, and a male fieldworker seeking to arrange such encounters with young unmarried women would have invited suspicion. Finally, we cannot go back to the offices of 1986–1987 and obtain additional information. Thus, much more remains to be done, but we hope our chapter will at least outline some of the general contours of our topic.

In attempting this initial account of gender construction in the offices of the conglomerates, we have divided the actors broadly into three major categories: the male bourgeoisie, the male "new middle class," and the female "new middle class." The major reason for this division is that the people in each of these categories possessed a very different constellation of political-economic interests, both in the wider society and in the organization at which they worked. Rather than treat each category of actors as autonomous, however, we seek to portray the interaction between them, for we view gender construction as a result of ongoing interaction, continued attempts at domination and efforts of resistance, and persistent struggles to advance or defend political-economic interests (Connell 1987).

We label both male and female office workers as "new middle class" because both confronted the labor market with more than raw labor power. Both had acquired skills and other forms of cultural and symbolic capital (Bourdieu 1984) that qualified them for positions more advantaged than those of factory workers. Yet assigning both genders to the same class label obscures the fact that their positions within the conglomerate and within south Korean society belonged to very different fractions of the new middle class. Different wage levels, working conditions, and chances for advancement significantly separated their interests.[4]

WIDER CONTEXTS

Although the offices of a south Korean conglomerate were the principal site of our research, gender construction in these settings was not independent of gender constructions elsewhere in the world. First-hand knowledge of gendering practices in the offices of other nations first entered Korea long ago. Large-scale, foreign-owned companies date back to the Japanese colonial period, and these enterprises introduced their already established practices during the critical years when capitalist commercial and manufacturing institutions were being created in Korea (McNamara 1989, 1990; Eckert 1991). Judging from the influence these institutions exerted in other areas of personnel management (Moskowitz n.d.), we surmise that their gendering practices also fostered understandings of gender differentiation in modern capitalist enterprises.

Long after the colonial period ended, knowledge of capitalist practices in Japan and the West, especially the United States, continued to inform choices and lend a measure of legitimacy to gendered inequality by contributing to the naturalization of such practices in contemporary commercial organizations. The field of business administration in south Korea, for example, historically has looked to Japanese and American firms for appropriate models.[5] Popular translations of western and Japanese writings on business and management have been widely available in south Korean bookstores (e.g., Suzuki 1988); south Korean economic dailies often contain accounts of foreign enterprises; and joint ventures with foreign firms also have spread knowledge of these practices among the south Korean population. The wearing of company uniforms by women office workers, for example, appears to have been derived from similar conventions in Japan. And the notion that typing is "women's work" did not originate in south Korea. Even at the two departments with which Roger Janelli is affiliated at his university in the United States, all but one of the secretaries have been women.

More recently, gender constructions have continued to enter south Korea in the form of popular guides to success or how to behave properly in an office setting. Many of these publications are either translations of Japanese works or popular guides authored by south Koreans who obtained overseas training. One such guidebook, for example, offers the following advice for women in the workplace:

29. How to Get Along with Male Workers

The best method for getting along with male coworkers is first of all to keep a measure of distance from them and always maintain a humble posture (*chŏ chase*) in front of them.

Secondly, you shouldn't confront male coworkers regarding work and don't try to outshine them.

Thirdly, as a woman worker, make an effort to understand male psychology, and let the men exercise leadership in work matters while you adopt a cooperative attitude (An 1986, 33).

In addition to the international context in which south Korean gender construction was enmeshed, myriad provisions of the south Korean state also contributed to gendering inequality in the offices of Taesŏng (e.g., Nam 1991). Of particular significance for our study have been the creation and maintenance of commercial high schools aimed primarily at women. In 1985, these educational institutions enrolled 28.4 percent of all women attending high school. The comparable figure for men was only 8.5 percent (*Statistical Yearbook on Women* 1994, 76–77). By 1990, the discrepancy had grown even greater: The percentage for women remained relatively unchanged (27.5 percent) but that of men had declined to 6.3 percent (ibid.).

Gender construction in the workplace also is related to gender construction in the family. The notion that women are primarily, if not exclusively, responsible for household maintenance and child rearing is often advanced, in the home as well as in the office, to legitimize both short-term employment for women (Myung-hye Kim 1992, 162; S. Kim 1992, 227–228) and a long working day for men.

Short-term rather than career employment for women prevails in white-collar work in south Korea. A survey of workers in finance, insurance, real estate, and business services, whose employees are comprised overwhelmingly of white-collar workers, revealed that although women outnumber men in the 15-to-24 age brackets, men far outnumber women at higher age levels (see Table 5.1).

THE BOURGEOISIE

Feminist critics of capitalism have already pointed to the ways in which the bourgeoisie gain from creating a dual labor market (Hartmann 1976), and much of their analysis seems relevant to contemporary south Korea. The principal owners and highest managers of Taesŏng comprised a kin group of males who profited from a gendered and unequal differentiation between positions and career paths. This was not only a strategy of divide and rule but also a device used to legitimize paying lower salaries for work needed by the enterprise. By using seniority as the primary criterion for justifying pay increases and encouraging or even requiring women to terminate employment after a few years of service, the bourgeoisie were able to reduce costs by paying lower wages and benefits for the work that women performed.

One of the most significant actions on the part of large capitalists was channeling women into lower-paying, dead-end jobs through the different hiring processes used to recruit workers. Male office workers at Taesŏng were hired through semiannual nationwide campaigns that were announced in front-page ads placed in south Korea's major newspapers. In fact, Taesŏng's published company history boasted that their conglomerate

Table 5.1 Employees in Finance, Insurance, Real Estate, and Business Services (1990)

| AGE | NUMBERS OF EMPLOYEES (THOUSANDS) | |
	MALE	FEMALE
15–19	13	45
20–24	27	106
25–29	108	52
30–34	94	36

Source: *Statistical Yearbook on Women 1994*, 132–133.

was among the first in south Korea to institute this process of "open hiring" (*kongch'ae*). Graduation from a four-year college, completion of (or exemption from) military service, and a maximum age of approximately 27 years were among the qualifications required of prospective male employees. For most male applicants, a written test and an interview were aimed at judging the prospective employee's intelligence, general knowledge, personality, and perhaps language abilities, but not his specific job skills. A smaller number of men, who had enrolled in R.O.T.C. and served their required period of military service as officers, were hired largely on the recommendation of their military commanders. Casual conversations with male workers who had been recruited through either means provided opportunities to listen to (or to try to comprehend) their dialects or to inquire about their regional origins. Information obtained in this way indicated that they were indeed recruited from throughout south Korea, though there was a noticeable underrepresentation of men from the Chŏlla provinces and an even more noticeable overrepresentation of men from the Kyŏngsang provinces. Regardless of their place of origin, university, major, or performance on the entrance exam, however, all male office workers entered the company at level 4 of the company's personnel ranking system. They could look forward to promotion to level 3 after three or four years of service and to levels 2 (section chief) and 1 (department head) after yet more years of service.[6] A few men who entered with M.B.A. degrees were granted two or three years of seniority and thereby qualified for promotion somewhat sooner than their cohorts.

Women office workers were hired through a very different process. In lieu of nationwide recruitment campaigns, women workers usually were hired on the recommendation of their high school officials during their last year. Most came from Seoul, as one woman explained when Roger Janelli happened to inquire about their lack of regional accents. After applicants satisfactorily passed a test of their secretarial skills and underwent an interview to assess their personalities, their dossiers were kept on file until there was an opening. Newly hired women entered the company at level 5, one level lower than the new male entrants, and could not look forward to any promotions.[7]

The different hiring processes generated major economic privileges for male workers. Women office workers were paid far less than men, even though the latter required extensive company training before they could become productive employees. Women needed (and were given) very little training by the company before or after taking their job assignments. According to a report in one of south Korea's major economic newspapers, among the five largest conglomerates in 1987 the starting salaries of new women workers with a high school degree were only 56 percent of the starting salaries of men with a college degree (*Maeil Kyŏngje Sinmun* 26 January 1987, 11). Since Taesŏng hired—with extremely few exceptions—only women without college degrees, the absence of this educational credential was used to lend an air of legitimacy not only to assigning them to level 5 but also to precluding them from later advancement to level 4 or higher, no matter how many years they worked or however meritorious their services.[8]

Because women were not promoted above level 5, they remained one level below the lowest male recruits and, according to company regulations, subject to their work demands. As a woman accumulated years of service, therefore, the age difference between her and the newest male entrants who outranked her disappeared. If a woman were to stay with the company for more than about six years, she would have been in the humiliating position of taking orders from men who were younger as well as far less knowledgeable about office procedures than herself. Difficult interpersonal relations between the youngest male workers and the more senior of the female workers sometimes arose because of this incongruity. In one instance, a woman worker was reassigned to another section as a consequence. If they had not already resigned at marriage, women workers usually quit before or shortly after they reached the age of the male entrants.

The different amounts of training given to men and women office workers also served to construct perceptions of gender. Newly hired male workers were provided with extensive information about the company's history, organization, products, and alleged contributions to national welfare. Shortly after being hired, male workers underwent a two-week conglomerate-organized training course and another two-week company-organized training course. After receiving an assignment to one of the conglomerate's several companies, a man then underwent further training in his respective division's, department's, and section's responsibilities before assuming full-time work. Women workers, by contrast, were given only a few days' training. The varying lengths of the respective training programs implicitly contributed to an expectation that men were somehow more "valuable" because they would be lifetime employees, whereas women's membership in the company was expected to be temporary.

The owner-managers had a variety of other devices for differentiating the roles of men and women in the company. Women were required to wear uniforms that were provided by the company, whereas men chose and paid for their own clothing; male and female office workers were also subject to different dress codes. And, until a few years before fieldwork began, women (but not men) had been required to sign pledges to resign at marriage.

A more indirect and perhaps unintended way in which the bourgeoisie contributed to the construction of gender was through their emphasis on "harmony," "teamwork," "cooperation," and other related concepts, such as portraying the company as a "family." Harmony, they never tired of pointing out, ought to be fostered not just for the sake of producing pleasant working conditions and boosting morale but also for generating a more efficient organization. Their public speeches and actions aimed at promoting this ideology ostensibly pertained to women as well as men. For example, the company's and the conglomerate's monthly magazine contained essays composed by female as well as male workers, women were assigned to various quality-control circles, and women were included at all conglomerate, company, and division-sponsored recreational events, in addition to the company's monthly meetings for all headquarters employees. At these monthly meetings, moreover, at which the highest managers of the company presided and various pep talks were presented, men and women were not assigned separate seats but sat wherever they chose. Ironically, as we shall see, this promotion of harmony, together with the dual track of employment patterns the bourgeoisie had instituted, ultimately encouraged male white-collar workers, especially young managers, to marginalize women from their respective units of the organization.

New Middle Class Male Workers

Among male workers, the owner-manager's stress on the importance of harmony was something akin to a self-fulfilling prophecy. Men knew that their chances for promotion depended on their ability to get along (or appear to get along) with others and, in some instances, to obtain the help and cooperation of their coworkers. In private conversations, however, some of the men revealed that they wondered whether all the effort expended to maintain social relations did not absorb time and energy that could have been better invested in more productive ways.

Male workers acknowledged that much of their apparent harmony was artificial in two senses: it was humanly fabricated, and personal conflicts and animosities were often hidden, not absent. In several conversations, men expressed the view that their overt cordiality was not a natural expression of social solidarity but rather a manufactured outcome attained through constant attention and effort. Male coworkers thus expressed a very agency-centered view of social relations, maintaining that daily and deliberate human actions created such relations and could also repair—or at least smooth over—fault lines and fractures. In the division to which Roger Janelli had been assigned, for example, both premanagerial white-collar workers (*sawŏn*) and young managers contended that despite their ostensible harmony, competition and "individualism" (*kaeinjuŭi*), a word with negative connotations in Korean, were especially rife.[9] And a few men confided that there was a big difference between how they felt inside and what they showed outside.

The reasons for this competition are not difficult to find. Unlike women, men were locked in a long-term contest for advancement. And since most promotions took the form of moving to a higher position within one's own office, a male worker's chief competitors were his male coworkers. Although advancement at the lower managerial levels closely matched years of service, the expectation of a perfect correlation informed perceptions of progress up the career ladder and even slight deviations were noticed by all. To be surpassed by another man who had entered at the same time or just a few months prior to oneself was described as a painful humiliation.

To foster more harmonious human relations among their respective sections and departments of Taesŏng, male managers at the lower levels (i.e., section chiefs and department heads) periodically were allotted funds, most of which they used to finance after-hours recreation. In both written statements by company workers that appeared in the company magazine and in the oral testimony of male informants, after-hours recreation offered opportunities to relieve stress, to build a sense of camaraderie, and to repair any social relationships that may have been injured, even inadvertently, during the hectic workday.

After-hours recreation thus had a pragmatic, and sometimes manipulative, character. At one weekly meeting of a division's young managers, for example, section chiefs were admonished by a higher manager for not "training" their white-collar subordinates properly. The manager then went on to add that Saturday mornings provided good opportunities for such "training" since the pace of work was a bit slower on those days and because the subordinates then could be taken out for recreation in the afternoon to repair any hard feelings that had arisen as a consequence of the "training." (Only a half-day's work was required on Saturdays.)

Another instance of the utilitarian quality of after-hours recreation occurred just before the new male recruits in one division were about to end their formal training program and begin actual work in their respective sections and departments. These young men and all of the women workers of the division were treated to an evening on the town. The event was intended, according to the manager who planned it, to make the women workers more willing to accept orders from the newly hired men.

Often, however, women were excluded from after-hours recreation. Sometimes this occurred because the events were created spontaneously, as the men were about to leave the office on a weekday, usually sometime after 7:30 or 8 P.M. Since women generally left between 6 and 7 P.M., their absence precluded their invitation. At other times the men chose an activity in which women would not or could not participate with them, such as visiting a public bath or sauna and then spending several hours gambling in a room provided by the establishment. On one occasion, when a manager proposed organizing an activity in which women and men could participate, another complained that including women workers would be "just a loss." Recounting another event, to which the women workers had not been invited, a manager acknowledged that the women of the unit ought to have been included in principle but that its male workers had wanted a kind of activity that women workers did not enjoy. When women were included, the second event of the evening was usually an activity for which they expressed a desire, such as bowling or dancing. The first event, usually comprised of eating and mild drinking, was for everyone; the third (and possibly fourth) event was devoted primarily to drinking.[10]

With the exception of the frequent exclusion of women, the frequency of after-hours events organized by men to produce harmony generally corresponded with the conglomerate's organization chart. Harmony was not expected to be distributed uniformly throughout the office, but rather varying degrees of gendered solidarity were supposed to correlate with the company's and the division's organization. Thus, more of a man's efforts were directed toward the other male workers of his own section than toward men of other sections in his department, and more efforts were directed toward men of his own department than toward men of other departments in his division. In light of frequent reassignments between sections and departments, however, much of the harmony that the managers and male office workers sought to create was implicitly temporary; and reformulations of social relationships that occurred after transfers of personnel even within the same office were often striking. A reassignment called for an immediate reorientation of a man's efforts, although not all their social ties were so transitory as to correlate exactly with the fortuities of job assignments.

The correlation between the company's formal organization and the frequency of after-hours socializing by men was not perfect, however.

While the after-hours events about which men openly spoke were composed of male (and sometimes female) coworkers who were expected to socialize together, many men also engaged in surreptitious after-hours gatherings that crosscut their organization chart. The participants at these latter events were often men who had formed close ties when they had been stationed in the same unit in prior years.[11] And some men occasionally chose to absent themselves from after-hours socializing with the other men of their unit, citing pressing obligations elsewhere. These absences were often viewed as signs of ill will or hard feelings, as in the case of a man who had recently been passed over for promotion. Managers spoke with apparent pride when they pointed out that everyone in their unit had attended one of these occasions.

The exclusion of women from many after-hours events organized by managers for their subordinates seems to have been motivated not only by the higher potential for conflict among male coworkers but also by the hiring practices of the conglomerate. These practices implicitly made the contributions of women less monetarily "valuable" and therefore less of a risk to the success of a unit. Though we could find no explicit sanction of this idea in the bourgeoisie's public exegeses of managerial ideology, statements of male office workers sometimes implied that women were more easily replaceable. In the section from which a woman had been reassigned because of difficult relations between her and a male worker, the section chief called together his male workers for some "training" and discussed a similar problem that had arisen between the same man and the new woman worker assigned to that section as well. According to one of the white-collar men who used this anecdote to criticize his superior, the section chief said that, if the problem were not resolved, they would get rid of the new woman just as they had gotten rid of her predecessor. In an attempt to improve the efficiency of his section, on which his own career depended, the young male manager evidently had concluded that his woman worker was more expendable than his male subordinate.

The gendering of harmony production according to the conglomerate's organization chart was evident not only in the after-hours recreation organized by the managers but in many other social activities as well. Male coworkers of the same section ate lunch together daily, either in the conglomerate's cafeteria, where all its headquarters' employees could obtain a free standard meal, or occasionally at the expense of their manager (or his expense account for such purposes). When they went to lunch together, moreover, they often ordered the same item from the menu. After one of the semiannual recruitment drives, for example, Roger Janelli had established good working relationships with two new recruits of different companies in the conglomerate and began the practice of having lunch with each of them about once every week or two. After a few months at the company, however, both men began to decline his invitations, explaining that they were expected to eat with their sections. Perhaps they had tired of his companionship, but the fact that both men offered the same reason as an adequate explanation for declining an invitation was nonetheless revealing.

Women workers, by contrast, were very seldom treated by their managers to lunch at a restaurant. They almost always ate the standard noontime meal provided by the conglomerate in its cafeteria. Women of the same division usually ate with each other without regard to section or department, just as they typically sat together at the company's monthly meeting. Each section normally had only one woman and several male workers, and a woman who ate with the other members of her section would have been isolated from other women at lunchtime.

In addition to daily eating arrangements, a number of other practices contributed toward differentiating what was expected of men and women at the office. When a male worker married, for example, the other men of his division each contributed a gift of cash, the men of each of the respective sections collecting their contributions together and presenting them in one envelope. (Men explained that they preferred to present their gifts in the office rather than at the wedding because parents often appropriated gifts given at the wedding and recorded in the gift register, alleging the funds were used for wedding expenses.) Women, whose salaries were far lower than those of men, were not included in this organized form of gift giving, implying that they were peripheral members of their respective sections and divisions. Similarly, when a wedding or family funeral of a male worker occurred in Seoul, the other men of his division actively participated in the event. In the case of a funeral, the section chiefs of a division formed a plan whereby each of their units took turns visiting the house in mourning to stay up (and gamble) through the night. In the case of weddings, which typically were celebrated on weekends, photocopied wedding invitations were circulated throughout the division and several of its men usually attended. At one male worker's wedding, most of the other men of his division but only a few of its women workers attended. At the Saturday afternoon wedding of a very recently resigned women worker, on the other hand, only one man other than the men of her own section and Roger Janelli appeared. Most of the women of her division, on the other hand, were present. And at the hundredth-day celebration of the birth of a male office worker's child, and at the celebration of the departure of a male office worker for a temporary overseas assignment, most of the men but only a few of the women of their division were present. Women workers had less money with which to buy gifts for such occasions and for the transportation costs to and from the home of the celebration. The principal events of these gatherings, moreover, consisted of a meal followed by gambling, and women workers had little money with which to gamble.

NEW MIDDLE CLASS FEMALE WORKERS

In the morning of Roger Janelli's first full day of fieldwork at Taesŏng, the deputy director of the division to which he had been assigned called a brief meeting of its two department heads and eight section chiefs to introduce him to these managers and to explain to them the nature of his research project. During this initial meeting, the deputy also instructed him on the terms of address used by office workers. Managers, he said, were addressed by their titles, and nonmanagerial male workers were addressed by their full names plus the suffix "ssi" (e.g., Hong Kiltong-ssi). Women workers, on the other hand, were addressed by the term "Miss" plus their last names. But the women workers recently had complained of this practice, he went on to explain. They viewed it as discriminatory and wanted to be addressed in the same way as the nonmanagerial male office workers.[12] "We are thinking about their request," he added. In another conversation that took place some weeks later, the same manager noted that relations between men and women in the office were sometimes difficult because the women were younger and less educated than the men but complained that any differentiation between them and the men was a form of gender discrimination.

Throughout the following months, Roger Janelli was able to observe several other examples of how women workers sought to reshape the ways in which they evidently were perceived and marginalized by their male coworkers. When the director of the division to which he was assigned asked him to teach English classes to the male workers, for example, the women workers initiated a request for classes of their own. The day after he agreed to this request, one of the women workers brought Roger Janelli a cup of coffee served in a ceramic cup, a cup normally reserved only for the highest managers and their guests. When asked the reason for such kind hospitality, the woman chose not to respond, but a section chief explained that it was because he had agreed to the women's request to teach them English. The male workers' response to their English class was strikingly different: Many if not most regarded it as an attempt by their manager to extract another hour of their time and thereby add to their already overly long workday. Not surprisingly, the classes for women workers were better attended and lasted far longer, although the managers rarely spoke of them as benefiting their division.

There were other instances of the women worker's response to gender discrimination that revealed their awareness and resentment of their marginality. At the conclusion of a weekend training session for both the men and woman workers of one division, the administrative section chief announced that a photograph of the gathering was about to be taken by the company's photographer and indicated the place to assemble for the picture taking. Thinking this would be a good opportunity to obtain a photo of the division, Roger Janelli took out his own camera, whereupon one of the women workers asked him to take a photo of her and her women coworkers. Unsure of whether or not their inclusion in the official photograph was intended, the woman workers refrained from moving to the place where it was to be taken until they were explicitly asked to join the male workers. On another occasion, a divisionwide party at which Roger Janelli lent his camera to a woman worker, the developed film revealed that the photos she had taken were mostly posed shots of each of the respective sections that included both men and women members. She evidently had asked each of them to assemble together. On yet another occasion, when the men and women workers of one department had participated in a picnic that included group games, a woman worker commented quietly to Roger Janelli that she had enjoyed the event. At most other such events, she added, the men just gambled and the women washed the dishes.

In response to their marginalization or exclusion by male workers, women workers organized some of their own social activities. If male coworkers went out drinking after work, women coworkers said they often went shopping together after work. The seventeen women workers of one division formed a club,[13] and with dues of about three dollars a month from each member, they organized small birthday parties for each other. On these occasions, they bought a birthday cake and enjoyed it together in one of their office's meeting rooms during the lunch hour, when the women were free and the room was otherwise unoccupied.[14]

Women's actions or comments about the more ostensibly material aspects of their working conditions were not absent entirely, but they were far less frequent. None ever complained at the disparity between their wages and those of the men. Yet women workers were aware of that disparity, since one of their tasks was to distribute uncovered pay slips to the men of their respective sections each month. Compared with factory workers, who led the fight for organized labor in the 1970s (S. Kim 1992, 228; Koo 1993, 140), the responses of the women office workers seem mild indeed.

Indignation at the lack of career opportunities available to women was another sentiment rarely expressed. When asked why they usually left the company after a few years of employment, most women cited the Korean family system, saying that their husbands or mothers-in-law would not like them to continue their employment after marriage. A few women said that they had little desire to continue such demanding employment for more than a few years. But the senior woman worker and apparent leader of the women workers in her division responded that women quit because "there are no positions into which we can be promoted."

Yet on the whole, the comments and actions of the women workers focused more sharply on their social marginalization from the units to which they were assigned and the construction of a gendered "otherness." For a monthly issue of the conglomerate's magazine that included employees' commentaries on the theme of harmony, one woman office worker wrote

Aren't we maintaining relationships between coworkers and between superiors and subordinates too coldheartedly?

We tend to let relationships between superiors and subordinates come to feel very self-interested and difficult. How about looking at them from a different perspective, however: as relationships between parents and children?

Parents never feign ignorance of their children's talents and abilities. [Instead,] they cultivate their children's abilities and strive to acknowledge their talents. Also, the children have complete trust and faith in their parents, and live with a respectful attitude toward them. In addition, the youngest daughter can be said to occupy a very important place as the darling (*usŭm kkot*) of the family.

Let's try grafting this atmosphere onto the office. The managers have warm human affection, like the parents' devotion, toward the *sawŏn* (employees), cultivate the knowledge and abilities of each individual, and guide their talents and abilities to evaluate [their own] work. The *sawŏn* too, like sons and daughters toward parents, have faith in and respect for them, and fulfill their own responsibilities. And how would it be if, like the youngest daughter who becomes the darling of the family, the female employees fulfilled the role of reducing friction in their departments and became the basic bridges between personnel [literally, the basic stepping stones of business]?

One can read this piece merely as an acquiescence to subordination; but when considered in the context of gender construction, the statement can also be seen as a challenge to the marginalization of women workers by arguing for the centrality of these workers in maintaining the social relations of their respective units. That the owner-managers included this essay in their conglomerate's monthly magazine suggests that the frequent exclusion of women from after-hours events aimed at promoting harmony may not have been intended by the owner-managers but was rather instigated largely by the new middle class male workers.

CONCLUSION

Several reasons can be advanced to account for the apparent acquiescence of women workers to the inequality of material rewards in the offices of the conglomerate's headquarters. As members of the new middle class, albeit one of the least advantaged fractions of it, women office workers did not have the same daily experiences as those of women factory workers. Moreover, they did not enjoy the same assistance from outside. Students, intellectuals, and religious activists concentrated their attempts to organize and forge a working class consciousness among factory workers rather than office workers (Koo 1993, 149–150). Indeed, one recent study of female office workers showed that their class consciousness was nearly identical to that of their male coworkers (Yu 1991).

Another reason why women office workers and factory workers held apparently different views can be found in the physical arrangements of their workplaces. Women office workers were greatly outnumbered in the headquarters building, and few worked side by side, as in a factory's assembly line. Instead, each woman normally worked in a section as its lone secretary—or occasionally as one of two secretaries—among a group of three to six men.[15] In fact, one of the higher managers of Taesŏng had revealed that women "troublemakers" (i.e., activists) in the regional offices and factories were sometimes reassigned to the headquarters building so they could be observed more easily. The companywide organization for women workers had been co-opted by the company, which set its agenda (e.g., charitable activities for the poor, flower arranging) and thereby precluded its operating as an effective vehicle for defending the women's material interests.

That women workers anticipated only temporary employment lowered their personal stakes in struggling to raise women's wages. In a study of women office workers conducted in the early 1980s, respondents to a questionnaire ranked obtaining social experience well ahead of earning money when asked to identify their motivation for holding a job (Cho 1982, 10, 12). Directing their energies toward more long-term personal benefits, such as enhancing symbolic and cultural capital rather than maximizing immediate economistic returns, was more congruent with their major motives for seeking employment.

Opting to direct their efforts primarily against their social marginalization, rather than at their low wages, may well have been viewed by these women as a preferred strategy for other reasons as well. Protests over the more ostensibly material remuneration for their labor probably would have provoked greater resistance. Until July of 1987, shortly before fieldwork ended, male office workers often expressed sympathy for the salaries of factory workers but were silent about the salaries of women office workers. And men did not complain about their own salaries, evidently because their perception of their own exploitation derived not from their salaries but from their long working hours, a condition from which women office workers were largely exempt. Thus, women might well have anticipated that complaints about salaries would have fallen on deaf male ears.

Perhaps too, some of the women considered the possibility of marriage to male office workers and thereby chose to represent themselves as social equals rather than risk being identified with women factory workers who explicitly demanded higher wages. Romantic attachments between male and female office workers were not matters of public discussion or even private rumors shared with Roger Janelli, but these kinds of alliances could not have been entirely absent. Intracompany marriages occurred often enough that office workers had a term (*sanae kyŏrhon*) to designate such unions. Explained one male manager, himself married to a former office worker, a measure of embarrassment surrounded such couples, for coworkers surmised that the pair had probably been intimate before marriage. Yet he enumerated four other men, or a total of about 8 percent of the men of his own division, who were married to his company's former office workers. Despite the parental opposition that male office workers might have expected for choosing a spouse who lacked a college degree, some bachelors expressed a preference for marrying someone who had worked in an office before marriage. Such a wife would probably understand their situation (i.e., have a greater appreciation of the difficulties they faced at the office).

Finally, some of the women's efforts to combat their marginalization were apparently successful, which may have further encouraged them to aim their energies in that direction. During the months of fieldwork, male workers and managers began addressing women workers with the same form used for premanagerial men. An essay in the conglomerate's magazine, published in November of 1990, detailed the terms of address to be used for various office personnel but made no mention of the term "Miss." Evidently, this trend away from the use of that word was aided by rising nationalism and the perception of "Mr." and "Miss" as foreign terms (e.g., *Chosŏn Ilbo* 3 July 1991, 10). The differential inclusion of men and women in after-hours socializing was also lessened in later years, although for unexpected reasons. Male workers began resisting invitations to these events because these occasions added yet more hours to workdays that men already considered too long (*Tonga Ilbo* 18 November 1989, 19). Perhaps the example set by women workers encouraged the men later to seek redress for one of their own grievances.[16]

POSTSCRIPT: OPTIMISM FOR THE FUTURE?

While the women workers hired at level 5 continued to be seriously disadvantaged, other developments within the conglomerate and elsewhere in south Korean society offered the possibility of reducing some of the gendered inequalities at Taesŏng. During the mid to late 1980s, a women's movement in south Korea aroused greater public indignation at inequalities in the workplace. The main owners of the largest south Korean conglomerates, sensitive about their public image in light of the problematic legitimacy of their huge enterprises and their personally privileged positions, began to hire women openly for managerial-track jobs. In the fall recruitment drive of 1986, Taesŏng and several of the other large conglomerates invited applications from women college graduates, announcing in their newspaper ads that positions for college graduates would be open to applicants of both genders.

The open solicitation of applications from women, rather than their actual hiring, represented a major departure from the practices of past years. A manager in Taesŏng's personnel department explained that a few women with college degrees had been hired in the past because they had majored in a field that enabled them to be put immediately to use. This had been done on the presumption that they would leave at marriage and thus the firm could expect no long-term benefits, he explained. By his account, about twenty-five of these women were already employed in the company in the fall of 1986. Although none had ever been promoted to managerial rank, the company was thinking about that possibility, he added. Another woman, who evidently had graduated from a junior college, worked as the conglomerate's librarian and was attached to one of the divisions at Taesŏng's headquarters. Except for the librarian, the other women with college degrees presumably worked in regional offices, research labs, or factories, for we never encountered any of them at the headquarters building.

Concern with public image was probably aided by other developments in the south Korean labor market which fostered a greater willingness to consider women for jobs designated as managerial-track. The ratio of male applicants for the total number of these positions had dwindled from 10 to 1 to about 4 to 1 in the previous few years, and a few of Taesŏng's managers expressed concern about the declining quality of the pool of prospective male employees. Whether repulsed by the long working hours and the top-down style of management that prevailed in the conglomerates or attracted to different employment for other reasons, many of the best male college graduates evidently were choosing alternative careers. This trend also may have encouraged personnel departments in the major conglomerates to consider more seriously the potential talents of women college graduates.

Yet another development that may have served, albeit inadvertently, to challenge the construction of gendered inequality at Taesŏng was the formation of a joint venture that involved the conglomerate and an American firm that had company regulations stipulating equal opportunities for men and women. The managers from Taesŏng who were assigned to this joint venture voiced numerous criticisms about the imposition of American business and other cultural practices (Janelli with Yim 1993, 188–189), but none ever complained about working with or extending employment opportunities to women.

None of these recent developments necessarily imply significantly improved employment conditions for women at Taesŏng. Despite the claims of the advertisements in 1986, few women were actually hired during that recruitment season, as several south Korean newspapers observed. Taesŏng in particular recruited about three hundred men and only four women. Like their predecessors, all four women had skills that could be put to immediate use. One had majored in business administration, another in chemistry, and two in computer science. Whatever gains women had made in gaining entry to managerial-track career employment in that year soon encountered unanticipated obstacles. In the mid-1990s, for example, a few male white-collar workers at one of Taesŏng's companies told us of an instance in which secretarial women office workers had objected to cleaning the desks of the recently hired managerial-track women. They maintained that since the latter were women, they should clean their own desks.

The economic downturn that began in late 1997 posed an even greater setback to women's white-collar career employment throughout south

Korea, as the structural reorganizations and downsizing of that year had a far greater impact on women than men. A newspaper devoted to women's affairs (*Yŏsŏng Sinmun* 18 December 1998, 7) reported that

> It is strikingly evident that women employees were the first to be let go among the financial institutions, where women [workers] are concentrated. The records of an official inspection of the Ministry of Labor last October showed that up to 93 percent of the honorary dismissals in the banking industry during the first half of the year were those of women bank employees.

For office workers in all industries, a report published by the Presidential Commission on Women's Affairs revealed that between July 1997 and July 1998 the total number of male office workers increased by 5.3 percent, whereas women office workers decreased by 18.4 percent (Cho Sun'gyŏng 1998, 10).

Looking at the gendering of unemployment across all occupations, the *Chosŏn Ilbo* (3 January 1999, 19) reported

> If one looks at last July's records of the National Statistical Office, there were 1,112,000 unemployed men and 539,000 unemployed women. The unemployment rate by gender [was] 8.5 percent for men and 6.3 percent for women. If one looks at jobs lost during the same period, however, compared with the 719,000 lost positions that had been held by men (5.7 percent of the male workforce), those that had been held by women shrank by 725 thousand (8.5 percent of the female workforce). This makes it apparent that the impact of the economic crisis was even harsher on women.

The current situation in the offices at Taesŏng and other specific companies is difficult to ascertain, in part because company officials have good reason not to publicize discrimination against their women employees. A number of published anecdotes about other organizations suggests that the dismissal of women office workers has not been random but targeted at those whose husbands also had employment or who did not have dependant families. Unfortunately, these reports usually omit information about whether the women had been hired as temporary or career-track employees. According to one account, for example

> When a large electronics company underwent a structural reorganization last March, it demanded the resignations of twenty-three women office workers. The majority of these were married women. In those cases in which resignations were not forthcoming, the company sent the persons for long-term

education and reassigned them. In those cases in which the worker could not be reassigned, the women were moved to a waiting list. The women office workers filed a petition with the Ministry of Labor stating that this was a clear case of sexual discrimination and [employed] other means of group resistance. The education in the provincial areas was cancelled, but as a result of this process thirteen women left the company (*Chosŏn Ilbo,* 3 January 1999, 19).

Commenting on such developments, the Korean-language Internet edition of the *Chosŏn Ilbo* observed that

> The Chinese-character expression *namjon yŏbi* [male privilege] has acquired a new meaning. It now refers to married women belonging to dual-income couples and unmarried women without dependant families, both of whom suffer dismissal from their jobs, and its new interpretation is that "men are left in place whereas women suffer the pain of dismissal" (http://www.chosun.com/w21data/html/news/199812/199812230083.html).

Though real gains may have been small and subsequently offset by the recent economic difficulties, the small opening created in the decade following 1986 may well have set significant precedents and altered men's and women's consciousness about the possibilities for alternative gender constructions in the workplace. The women hired by Taesŏng in 1986, for example, were put through the same rigorous conglomerate and company training programs as their male counterparts, including the physically demanding mountain-climbing exercise, apparently for the first time. One older male manager related that when all the new recruits were gathered and asked to give self-introductions, the men were surprised to hear the women hires say that they wished to be treated as colleagues rather than as women.[17] And although several published reports indicate that recent economic conditions in south Korea have made career employment for women all the more difficult, the very existence of the media attention given to these developments suggests a higher degree of popular awareness of gender discrimination in the workplace than had ever existed in the past.

NOTES

For helpful comments on an earlier version of this chapter we are indebted to Eun Mee Kim and Laurel Kendall.

1. For accounts of these conglomerates, see Y. Chung (1987); Steers, Shin, and Ungson (1989); Amsden (1989); Kang, Ch'oe, and Chang (1991); Woo (1991); Choong Soon Kim (1992); Janelli with Yim (1993); and Chung, Lee, and Jung (1997).

2. For accounts of women office workers in Japan, see Lo (1990, 35–50), Pharr (1984), and Ogasawara (1998).

3. For a recent review of the literature on women office workers in south Korea, see Kim Misuk (1994, 15–16).

4. For a discussion of the complexities involved in defining classes in contemporary south Korea, see Sǒ (1985), Koo (1993), and Abelmann (1997a, 1997b).

5. An interest in south Korean firms emerged in the late 1970s and early 1980s and has continued to grow. The first major work to examine the management of south Korean firms from the perspective of business administration was Sin Yugŭn (1984).

6. Levels and managerial rank did not correlate perfectly, but the exceptions were few and temporary.

7. Later reports indicated that many south Korean companies have also been using height and weight limitations and considering physical attractiveness when recruiting women workers, but we do not know if such practices prevailed at Taesŏng during the time of fieldwork.

8. According to Taesŏng company regulations distributed to newly hired male employees at the time of their initial company training, promotion from level 5 to level 4 was technically possible even without a college degree. Indeed, one senior manager even pointed to a 55-year-old male section chief who had entered the company as a blue-collar worker. Yet no promotions for women workers occurred.

9. Perhaps this was because the white-collar male workers in this office dealt directly with customers. We thank James L. Watson and Kim Kwang-Ok for suggesting that attempts to satisfy customers can compete with the desire to improve social relations among coworkers in Chinese enterprises.

10. Rarely did these late rounds involve professional hostesses. The per-capita cost of such services was too high to fit easily within the budget allocated for promoting harmony between lower-level office workers.

11. Only because of Roger Janelli's own involvement in some of these gatherings did he learn of them. We surmise there were many more of which he was unaware.

12. Seung-kyung Kim (1997) notes that women factory workers complained of the terms by which they were addressed and would have preferred to be called "Miss" followed by their last names.

13. A few more women, who worked in a nearby room and actually were assigned to another division, were also allowed to join because their own division had too few women to form a group of its own.

14. They also used a portion of the funds to buy a wedding gift, which they brought to the house of a new couple when they were invited.

15. Of the four divisions that Roger Janelli came to know well, there was only one exception: the administrative section of the division to which he had been formally assigned was composed of two men and seven women. Another woman, the director's secretary, was formally assigned to this section as well but occupied a desk by herself next to the entrance to the director's office.

16. The years immediately following the popular demonstrations of 1987 witnessed a major spurning of authoritarian rule in many sectors of south Korean society.

17. We do not know if any of these women were later promoted to a managerial level.

References

Abelmann, Nancy. 1997a. Women's class mobility and identities in south Korea: A gendered, transnational, narrative approach. *Journal of Asian Studies* 56:398–420.

———. 1997b. Narrating selfhood and personality in south Korea: Women and social mobility. *American Ethnologist* 24:786–812.

Amsden, Alice H. 1989. *Asia's Next Giant: South Korea and Late Industrialization.* New York: Oxford University Press.

An Yŏnghun. 1986. *Yŏja sawŏn ŭi chikchang saenghwal ŭi chihye* (A woman employee's wisdom for the workplace). Seoul: Myŏngji ch'ulp'ansa.

Bourdieu, Pierre. 1984. *Distinction: A Social Critique of the Judgment of Taste.* Richard Nice, trans. Cambridge, Mass.: Harvard University Press.

Cho Oakla (Cho Ongna). 1982. Samujik yŏsŏng (Women office workers). In *Han'guk ŭi tosi yŏsŏnggwa chigŏp* (Korea's urban women and employment). Cho Hyŏng, Cho Haejoang (Cho Hyejŏng), and Cho Ongna. eds. pp. 7–20. Seoul: Yunesk'o Han'guk wiwŏnhoe (Korean National Commission for Unesco).

Cho Sun'gyŏng. 1998. Kujo chojŏnggwa yŏsŏng koyong (Structural reorganization and women's employment). *Yŏsŏng t'ŭkpyŏl wiwŏnhoe sosik* (The presidential commission of women's affairs' news) 3:10–11.

Connell, Robert W. 1987. *Gender and Power: Society, the Person, and Sexual Politics.* Stanford, Calif.: Stanford University Press.

Chŏng, Kuhyŏn (Jung Ku Hyun). 1987. *Han'guk kiŏp ŭi sŏngjang chŏllyak kwa kyŏngyŏng kujo* (The growth strategy and managerial structure of Korean firms). Seoul: Taehan sanggong hoeiso (Korean chamber of commerce).

Chung, Young-Iob. 1987. Capital of *chaebŏl* in Korea during the early stages of economic development. *Journal of Modern Korean Studies* 3:11–41.

Chung, Kae H., Hak Chong Lee, and Ku Hyun Jung. 1997. *Korean Management: Global Strategy and Cultural Transformation.* Berlin and New York: Walter de Gruyter.

Eckert, Carter J. 1991. *The Koch'ang Kims and the Colonial Origins of Korean Capitalism, 1876–1945.* Seattle: University of Washington Press.

Hartmann, Heidi I. 1976. Capitalism, patriarchy, and job segregation by sex. *Signs: Journal of Women in Culture and Society* 1(no. 3, pt. 2):137–169.

Hattori Tamio. 1986. Han'guk kwa Ilbon ŭi taegiŏp kŭrup pigyo (A comparison of Korea's and Japan's large-enterprise groups). In *Han'guk kiŏp ŭi kujo wa chŏllyak* (The structure and strategy of Korean enterprises). Yi Hakchong (Lee Hak Chong), Chŏng Kuhyŏn (Jung Ku Hyun), et al., eds. pp. 149–203. Seoul: Pŏmmunsa.

Janelli, Roger L., with Dawnhee Yim. 1993. *Making Capitalism: The Social and Cultural Transformation of a South Korean Conglomerate.* Stanford, Calif.: Stanford University Press.

Kang Ch'ŏlgyu, Ch'oe Chŏngp'yo, and Chang Chisang. 1991. *Chaebŏl: Sŏngjang ŭi chuyŏk in'ga, t'amyok ŭi hwasin in'ga* (*Chaebŏl*: Driving force of growth or incarnations of greed?). Seoul: Pibong ch'ulp'ansa.

Kim, Choong Soon. 1992. *The Culture of Korean Industry: An Ethnography of Poongsan Company.* Tucson: University of Arizona Press.

Kim Misuk. 1994. Yŏsŏnghak yŏn'gu tonghyang: Yŏsŏng nodongŭl chungsim ŭro (Trends in women's studies: With a focus on women's labor). *Han'guk sahoehak p'yŏngnon* (Review essays in Korean sociology) 1:3–47.

Kim, Myung-hye. 1992. Late industrialization and women's work in urban south Korea: An ethnographic study of upper-middle-class families. *City & Society* 6(2):156–173.

Kim, Seung-kyung. 1992. Women workers and the labor movement in south Korea. In *Anthropology and the Global Factory.* Frances Abrahamer Rothstein and Michael L. Blim, eds. pp. 220–237. New York: Bergin & Garvey.

———. 1997. *Class Struggle or Family Struggle? The Lives of Women Factory Workers in South Korea.* Cambridge: Cambridge University Press.

Koo, Hagen. 1993. The state, *minjung*, and the working class in south Korea. In *State and Society in Contemporary Korea.* Hagen Koo, ed. pp. 131–162. Ithaca, N.Y.: Cornell University Press.

Lo, Jeannie. 1990. *Office Ladies/Factory Women: Life and Work at a Japanese Company.* Armonk, N.Y.: M. E. Sharpe.

McNamara, Dennis L. 1989. The Keishō and the Korean business elite. *Journal of Asian Studies* 48:310–323.

———. 1990. *The Colonial Origins of Korean Enterprise.* Cambridge: Cambridge University Press.

Moskowitz, Karl. n.d. Current assets: The employees of Japanese banks in colonial Korea. Unpublished manuscript.

Nam, Jeong-Lim. 1991. Income inequality between the sexes and the role of the state: South Korea, 1960–1990. Ph.D. diss., Department of Sociology, Indiana University.

Ogasawara, Yuko. 1998. *Office Ladies and Salaried Men: Power, Gender, and Work in Japanese Companies.* Berkeley: University of California.

Pak Kinam, and Kang Isu. 1994. Yŏsŏng kwa nodong (Women and labor). In *Yŏsŏnghak kangŭi: Han'guk yŏsŏng hyŏnsil ŭi ihae* (Lectures in women's studies: Understanding the reality of Korean women), rev. ed. Han'guk yŏsŏng yŏn'guhoe (Korean Women's Studies Association), ed. pp. 233–263. Seoul: Tosŏ ch'ulp'an tongnyŏk.

Pharr, Susan J. 1984. Status conflict: The rebellion of the tea pourers. In *Conflict in Japan.* Ellis S. Krauss, Thomas P. Rohlen, and Patricia G. Steinhoff, eds. pp. 214–240. Honolulu: University of Hawai'i Press.

Sin Yugŭn (Shin Yoo Keun). 1984. *Han'guk kiŏp ŭi t'ŭksŏng kwa kwaje* (The characteristics and issues of Korean enterprises). Seoul: Seoul National University Press.

Sŏ Kwanmo. 1985. Han'guk sahoe kyegŭp kusŏng ŭi t'ŭkching kwa chŏpkŭn pangbŏp (Special features of and methodological approaches to the class formation of Korean society). In *Han'guk chabonjuŭi wa sahoe kujo* (Korean capitalism and social structure). Pak Hyŏnch'ae, Yi Taegŭn, Ch'oe Changjip (Choi Jang Jip) et. al., eds. pp. 165–195. Seoul: Tosŏ ch'ulp'an hanul.

Statistical Yearbook on Women. 1994. Seoul: Korean Women's Development Institute.

Steers, Richard M., Shin Yoo Keun, and Gerardo R. Ungson. 1989. *The Chaebŏl: Korea's New Industrial Might.* Grand Rapids, Mich.: Harper and Row.

Suzuki, Kenji. 1988. *Sinip sawŏni haeduŏya hal il* (What a newly hired worker ought to do). Sŏk Ch'ŏn, trans. Seoul: Chŏnwŏn munhwasa.

Woo, Jung-en. 1991. *Race to the Swift: State and Finance in Korean Industrialization.* New York: Columbia University Press.

Yi Hakchong (Lee Hak Chong). 1986. Han'guk usu kiŏp ŭi t'ŭkching (Distinctive characteristics of superior Korean enterprises). In *Han'guk kiŏp ŭi kujo wa chŏllyak* (The structure and strategy of Korean enterprises). Lee Hak Chong, Jung Ku-Hyun (Chŏng Kuhyŏn), et al. pp. 87–109. Seoul: Pŏmmunsa.

Yu Hŭijŏng. 1991. Kyegŭp ŭi chŏngch'i wa sŏng ŭi chŏngch'i: Samujigŭl chungsim ŭro (Class politics and sexual politics: With a focus on office work). In *Sahoe kyegŭp: Iron kwa silche* (Social class: Theory and reality). Seoul taehakkyo sahoehak yŏn'guhoe, ed. pp. 421–443. Seoul: Tasan ch'ulp'ansa.

6

THE CONCEPT OF FEMALE SEXUALITY IN KOREAN POPULAR CULTURE

so-hee lee

The question I would like to pose is not, Why are we repressed? but rather, Why do we say, with so much passion and so much resentment against our most recent past, against our present, and against ourselves, that we are repressed? By what spiral did we come to affirm that sex is negated? What led us to show, ostentatiously, that sex is something we hide, to say it is something we silence?

(Foucault 1978, 101–102)

MARRIAGE IN CURRENT KOREAN POPULAR CULTURE

Contemporary Korean women struggle against their Confucian cultural heritage as they search for their own sexual subjectivity. My discussion of female sexuality in Korea since 1993 takes the form of a cultural criticism. It focuses on the sociohistorical discourse and textual analyses of three novels, two films, and one television drama that were written, for the most part, by women. First, let me begin with my own experience of the term "sexuality." I went to Britain for the first time in August 1986, as a British Council Study Fellow in the Faculty of English, Cambridge University. My topic was "Women Characters in Victorian Novels." During the lectures and seminars, I was acutely embarrassed by what I heard. Why was everyone talking about sexuality, masculinity, and femininity? What was the relationship between those terms and feminist literary criticism?

In those days, Koreans did not have exact counterpart terms for "sex," "sexuality," "sexual intercourse," and "gender." I was very confused as I struggled to determine the appropriate meanings. In Korean, one very general term (*sŏng*) could be used for these four concepts, its particular meaning dependent on the speaking and listening context. Korean society in the mid–1980s did not find it necessary to make sharp distinctions between these concepts. At the annual Korean Women's Studies Association Conference in 1989, the issue of sex language was raised and discussed. More recently, the Korean counterpart of the term "sexual intercourse" (*sŏnggyo*) has gained wide usage, accompanied by the frequent use of a Korean counterpart for the term "sexual violence" (*sŏngp'ongnyŏk*). In 1991, the Korea Sexual Violence Relief Center opened in Seoul, the first service of this kind. Sexual violence has now become a recognized issue in need of a discourse.

Korean concepts of sexuality have changed profoundly since the Democratic Revolution of 1987 (Howard 1995; Shin and Cho 1996), which transformed the authoritarian military political regime of the last thirty years into a citizens' democracy.[1] In 1995, the most popular topics among university students were sexuality, sexual identity, and other sexual subjects. There are many reasons for this. I examine one dimension of these changes from a feminist point of view, focusing on the emergent social discourse on female sexuality as it appears in stories of married women in the age range of 25 to 35. In Korea, there is still no broad popular social discourse on female sexuality outside of marriage. The works that I describe are artifacts of a moment when female sexuality is brought into consciousness in unprecedented ways. Precisely because this chapter is about the progressive act of defining a distinctively Korean female sexuality, I have chosen not to lard it with citations from a now-abundant Western literature on gender and sexuality. It is my firm belief that while thought-provoking, no Western theory can satisfactorily account for the social conditions that produce Korean women's sexuality.

In his book, *Understanding Popular Culture*, John Fiske writes of the political potential of popular culture that "Popular art is progressive, not revolutionary" (Fiske 1989, 161). Popular culture is not a mere representation of the workings of power in society but also the leading discourse through which current social institutions are subverted in the name of progressive social action. The works that I have selected for this discussion should be considered not only as illustrations of contemporary concerns but also as generating social discourse on female sexuality. Between 1993 and 1996, each publication and each media screening provoked intense discussions throughout Korea.

The novel *Marriage* (*Kyŏrhon*) by Kim Su-Hyŏn, a famous television drama writer and novelist in her fifties, was published in 1993 and made into a television drama in 1994. The novel has achieved a wide readership, and the television drama was even more successful. The main plot of *Marriage* concerns three sisters, Chi-Yŏng, age 34, Sŏ-Yŏng, age 32, and Ch'ae-Yŏng, age 25, and their respective marriages. The three sisters have very different perceptions of marriage, reflecting the different circumstances of their university years. Another novel, *Go Alone Like the Rhinoceros's Horn* (*Mussoŭi ppulchŏrŏm honjasŏ kara*)[2] by Kong Chi-Yŏng, a writer in her early thirties, was also published in 1993 and made the best-sellers list as soon as it appeared. It focuses on the marriages of three woman friends, Hye-Wan, Kyŏng-Hye, and Yŏng-Sŏn, all 31 years old. This novel also was produced as a play, performed for seven months in 1994, and released as a film in 1995. Both adaptations were successful. The film *Mommy Has a Lover* (*Ŏmmaege aeini saenggyŏssŏyŏ*), was released in May 1995 and was considered a financial success. This film, which focused on a woman's extramarital love affair, deals with the sexual lives of wives in their late twenties. It challenges the long history of female fidelity and chastity in Korea as enjoined by Confucianism. The novel *The Pornography in My Mind* (*Nae maŭmŭi p'ornogurap'i*), published about the same time as this film, was written by Kim Pyŏl-A while still in her mid-twenties. In this, her first novel, Kim bravely deals with a previously forbidden theme. The novel rebels against the sexual double standard, insisting on the existence of female sexual desire in contemporary Korea, where adultery is still illegal. In September and October 1996, two cultural products directly attacked established social institutions. The television drama *The Lover* (*Aein*), and the film *The Adventures of Mrs. Park* (*Pak Pong-Kon kach'ul sakkŏn*) were both commercially successful. These works raise the provocative topic of women's love affairs outside of marriage and the wife's abandonment of the home. By analyzing these novels, films, and television drama, all produced between 1993 and 1996, I explore Korean women's concepts of female sexuality as they are linked to the profound social transformation of Korean society in these same years.

ON THE BORDER LINE: INSIDE/OUTSIDE MARRIAGE

In order to understand the marriages of Korean women in their early thirties, it would be helpful to look at the social circumstances in which they were raised. The women were the first of the Korean baby boom generation, born between 1960 and 1965 when Korea had just launched its ambitious economic development plans.[3] Their childhoods coincided with the

April 19, 1960, Democratic Demonstration; the May 16, 1961, military coup; and the start of the Park regime's five-year economic plan, which played an important role in changing Koreans' lifestyle from that of an agricultural to that of an industrial economy (OECD 1996). They were also the first female generation to go to school en masse, side by side with their brothers. As Wonmo Dong (1988) argues, they learned democracy and its fundamental principles of liberty and equality as an academic subject, not as something to practice in everyday life.[4] From the beginning of their university days, around 1980, they were pushed into the whirl of extremely violent demonstrations to demand national political democratization. Although political protests had long been a part of Korean student life, there was something about the culture of protest that emerged in the 1980s that was different from what had gone before; student activism became an all-pervasive and all-defining experience.[5] In those days, various slogans and ideologies relating to the struggle for democracy were strongly imprinted on the consciousness of this generation as a metadiscourse. However, the students of the 1980s never examined these democratic values in the context of their own everyday lives.

Go Alone Like the Rhinoceros's Horn (*Mussŏŭi ppulchŏrŏm hon'jasŏ kara*) illustrates the bifurcation between theory and practice. Looking at their mothers' lives, Korean women in their early thirties believed that their marriages would be different. Because the Korean standard of living and patterns of material life changed very quickly, they believed that Korean ways of thinking had been transformed with the same speed. This is where their tragedy begins. As Hye-Wan in the novel says, mothers "teach daughters to live differently from themselves but teach sons to live like their fathers" (Kong 1993, 83–84). As a result, the daughters' generation experiences an enormous conflict between the real and the ideal.[6] During sixteen years of schooling, they have learned that equality is an important democratic value, but nowhere have they been taught that women experience the institution of marriage as a condition of inequality. Many married women of this generation have experienced a process of self-awakening similar to that of Yŏng-Sŏn, who early in the novel tries to kill herself. She says, "Where have I been during the last eight years of my marriage?" and concludes, "Though I don't want to accept it, I've been a sincere and faithful maid who must carry out his every request" (109). Korean wives in their thirties cannot envisage a real-life alternative to the self-sacrifices of their mothers' generation.

What, then, are their husbands' ideas about marriage? Kyŏng-Hye's husband thinks that after a woman has given birth, her body is unable to provide the pleasure he desires. He announces to Kyŏng-Hye, "Enjoy your sexual life.

I won't divorce you because that would damage the reputation of my family" (Kong 1993, 204). A medical doctor and university lecturer, his idea of marriage is the sexual pleasure he derives from the female body. He expects Kyŏng-Hye to play the role of "The Angel in the Home," like the epitome of nineteenth-century Victorian femininity. According to Kyŏng-Hye, he states his position simply and reasonably enough "to make her feel as if there is no problem, as long as she finds her proper sexual partner outside of marriage" (204). Kyŏng-Hye has gone back to her old boyfriend and has "seen how he feels after intercourse, even with the light turned on." When she sees that his response is different from her husband's, she is consoled because this confirms that she is still sexually attractive (205–206). Kyŏng-Hye's response is distinctly different from that of a woman of her mother's generation, who would have had an entirely different concept of female sexuality. Women of the mother's and grandmother's generations accepted the sexual double standard as a woman's fate and put their sexual energy into rearing children, identifying themselves as asexual, strong mother figures.[7] Korean women in Kyŏng-Hye's generation give priority to their identities as sexual beings, struggling to conceptualize a sense of individual selfhood while the mystified ideology of mothering and family obligation, which has repressed Korean women for so long, collapses (Cho in this volume).[8]

Kyŏng-Hye's friend Yŏng-Sŏn is a tragic victim of this confusion between older notions of female virtue and her own individual desire. Her advice to the third friend, Hye-Wan, reveals a notion of marriage akin to that of their mother's generation: "You must accept and bear. . . . Every woman has suffered and endured" (Kong 1993, 276). But why must only a woman suffer and endure?

This question leads Hye-Wan to take a stand outside of marriage. Hye-Wan's case is more complicated due to her son's death. Her son dies in a traffic accident while he is following Hye-Wan on the street. On that day, Kyŏng-Hwan, a part-time university lecturer, refuses to take care of their son, even though Hye-Wan must go to work. These circumstances deepen Hye-Wan's sense of guilt over her irresponsible behavior as a mother. After their son's death, Hye-Wan and Kyŏng-Hwan go to a party for friends from their university days. When they come back from the party, they quarrel and Kyŏng-Hwan rapes Hye-Wan. This incident lays bare the power structure of patriarchal marriage, where a husband legally possesses and dominates a wife's human rights through sexuality.

"Don't argue and analyze like that. Can't you understand? You're a married wife. Behave like other women! Like other wives! Why do you think you are an exception?" . . . Then, as soon as he entered the gate, he ripped off her clothes. After slapping her cheeks several times, he forced her to part her legs. It was not his violence itself that caused her to yield, but her recognition that it spelled "The End" for her marriage! "Maybe you don't want to see it. Your wife is still young, she's talking with her old friends, laughing and enjoying herself like old times when she was single. You don't want to see it. So, you need to confirm it. 'You are mine even if you act like a single woman.' To confirm it and feel it, nothing is better than sex. . . . I have never dreamt of being a Cinderella. If I wanted money or social fame, I would not have married him. But, this is not what I want. At least, this is not. No, not!" (82)

This scene is a clear example of "wife rape" in Korean society within the legality of marriage. A husband rapes a wife when he feels intellectually, financially, and socially inferior, because rape is the most effective way to exercise the masculine power which a patriarchal culture bestows on him. This very primitive idea, that a wife is one of her husband's possessions and not an independent human being, still exists among highly educated couples in modern Korean society.[9] In short, female sexuality, especially a wife's sexuality, appears as an object to be acquired, possessed, dominated, and conquered.[10] Even though Hye-Wan has been with Kyŏng-Hwan for a long time, and even though he has not had any mistresses or subjected her to routine violence in everyday life, the issue of sexual violence remains a problem and ultimately renders them complete strangers to each other. Is it really so difficult to communicate seriously about sexuality?

Another novel, *Marriage* (*Kyŏrhon*), deals with the relationship between female sexuality and money, also a prominent theme in many Victorian novels. This novel illustrates the extent to which a woman's lifestyle depends on the social circumstances of her teenage years in a rapidly changing Korea. Chi-Yŏng, the eldest daughter, succeeds in getting married after threatening suicide when her mother refuses to accept her boyfriend as a son-in-law because of his poor economic prospects. Chi-Yŏng's mother sees marriage as a way to achieve social advancement and material prosperity, as it was in the Victorian era.[11] These ambitions have come to the forefront in Korea since the 1970s, due to rapid economic development and consequent aspirations to class mobility and consolidation during the last thirty years. This novel is a good illustration of how, given the pace of change in Korea, everybody has a different point of view on marriage, depending on their gender, class, and generation. The issue of communication across generations has become a serious matter.[12] Generation is an important attribute of identity in Korea, like race in the United States.

As the novel develops, Chi-Yŏng's struggle results in profound mental anguish, especially when she discovers that her husband has had a mistress. She feels a deep sense of loss and betrayal. In her suicide note to Ch'ae-Yŏng, Chi-Yŏng confesses, "After almost one year of marriage, I could find it in my heart to say that I have constantly wished to die" (S. Kim 1993, II: 179). "When I had finally discovered his relationship with the other woman, five years after my wedding, I was close to death" (II: 180). Chi-Yŏng, who "loves nothing but her feeling of love" (II: 164), had tried to begin a new life with another married man. She grew even more desperate when she realized that all he had to offer her was abuse, while he protected his own marriage. Chi-Yŏng is too faithful, sincere, and naive to struggle with the violence of patriarchal social culture. Like Yŏng-Sŏn in *Go Alone Like the Rhinoceros's Horn*, Chi-Yŏng commits suicide as the most extreme form of resistance to the condition of being a woman.

The situation of the youngest sister, Ch'ae-Yŏng, is different. Because she desires the social protection that marriage provides and regards marriage as an economically practical contract, she is forced to remain within the institution of marriage. Even when she discovers, during her honeymoon, that her husband is in the bath with his mistress and that her marriage seems "like putting her head into a bag, filled with snakes" (S. Kim 1993, I: 153), she realizes that she is struggling "to find any clues or excuses to keep her marriage" (I, 205). Through this process, Ch'ae-Yŏng awakens her unconscious anxiety about standing alone outside of marriage. Ch'ae-Yŏng is a member of that youthful Korean age cohort whose vivid memories begin only with the material prosperity of 1980s Korea. Her sense of the world sets her apart from her elder sisters, who are already in their thirties. The sentiments she expresses indicate a remarkable change in Korean women's way of thinking, a striking contrast with views espoused by women who came of age only a few years previously.

> The eldest, Chi-Yŏng, lives for love and the second eldest, you, lives for an ideal. I don't want to live in such a poor marriage. Five years after my marriage, planning to buy a tiny apartment from scant, meager savings, having an almost empty refrigerator with only a kimchee jar. No, I am not sure whether I can manage that kind of poor life. (I: 21)

The marriage between Ch'ae-Yŏng, who sees matrimony as a financial proposition and considers love a fantasy, and Hyŏn-Sŏp, who must bow to his parents' hope of becoming the in-laws of a university professor, illustrates how the desire for money and class is activated within the social institution of marriage. This marriage is sustained by bribes, the BMW which Ch'ae-Yŏng receives as soon as she comes back from her disastrous honeymoon, and the sum of $380,000, which her mother-in-law gives her when Ch'ae-Yŏng discovers Hyŏn-Sŏp's illegitimate son. Because Hyŏn-Sŏp's family is not highly educated, although they are quite rich, the alliance with a university professor is important to them. Here, you must not simply apply American notions of the relative value of class, education, and money to the Korean context. What Hyŏn-Sŏp's family needs is a public acknowledgement of honor and respect, which they gain by matrimonial association. In the novel, Ch'ae-Yŏng's father has been a university professor of law (the most prestigious academic discipline in Korea) for almost thirty years, but he does not know how to make money. That is his wife's job. During the 1970s and early 1980s, middle class Korean wives, women in their fifties, frequently made more than their husbands' salaries through investments and real estate speculation. Ch'ae-Yŏng's mother is a novelistic representation of those Korean women who would, by whatever means, provide their family with a secure identity as "modern" and "middle class" (see Cho and Abelmann in this volume). The mother favored Ch'ae-Yŏng's marriage over those of her other daughters, because in this marriage alone she could exercise her motherly desires and maternal authority in the selection of a suitable son-in-law.

The way of thinking of the second eldest sister, Sŏ-Yŏng, is the exact opposite of Ch'ae-Yŏng's. She was deeply involved in the Democratization Movement during her university years in the 1980s. The following dialogue between the two sisters shows the tension between their two different points of view, conflicts that are articulated readily in contemporary Korean society regarding the relationship between money and female sexuality inside marriage.

"Whatever happens in your marriage, how can you complain? Remember, you did it for money! Isn't it a big deal if they give you sums so vast you can't spend them in a lifetime? I don't suppose you refuse it, do you?"

"Who says that I did it for the money? Am I out of my head, money-mad? Did I take nothing but money into account?"

"Stop yelling and be honest with yourself! You decided to marry him just because of money. If it wasn't for money, then what made you decide to marry? Tell me. What is there? Does it make sense that you decided to marry him right after the first meeting, without any hesitation? Why? For what? What made you sure? What deceived you? You didn't know anything about his character, his way of thinking, his future life plan, his sexual habits or history, I mean, whether he can be a proper partner for you, or not. You only knew that he was a healthy man and the heir to great wealth. What do you and the rest of us know about him? Tell me. How could you decide your marriage on such poor information and such short reflection? How could you go forward to marriage? How foolish, how selfish, how irrational can you be?" (S. Kim 1993, I: 170)

In this scene, Sŏ-Yŏng cruelly takes off the final mask which barely hides Ch'ae-Yŏng's great shame. Ch'ae-Yŏng, who has already made a lifelong deal "because she does not want to fail in her marriage" (S. Kim 1993, II: 16), carefully calculates the possible difficulties and disadvantages should she decide to leave her marriage. Even though she has graduated from a university, she is utterly unprepared for an independent life; she even lacks determination.

"Look . . . what do you think of my future if I divorce? I'm not interested in studying. Wasting time at home while becoming a family disgrace as a divorced daughter, then, marrying again? To whom? I don't want to have a job. I may not have so many opportunities to meet a nice man as when I was single. Then, imagine that I shall have to agree to another arranged marriage. This time, to whom? To what type of man? Not a bachelor, of course, but a widower or divorced man without any child. Can I even find a man who suits my taste? If my next marriage is going to be just like this one, then isn't it better to remain within this marriage? I could consider it as my second marriage, couldn't I?" (II: 71–72)

Ch'ae-Yŏng lacks the courage to confront any kind of harsh reality. On reflection, Sŏ-Yŏng concludes that Ch'ae-Yŏng is basically different from herself and accuses her, "You can keep your marriage, receiving stinking money and endless presents for your husband's dirty acts" (S. Kim 1993, II: 41). In fact, Sŏ-Yŏng and Ch'ae-Yŏng embody the most prominent differences between Korean women in their twenties and those in their thirties. The former have constructed their female identities during the period of rapid capitalist development and active opposition to the political regime; they are somewhat idealistic. The latter have known only abundant consumption in their everyday lives and are willing to compromise for the sake of their individual needs and desires.

THE MARRIAGE STORY OF THE "MISSY"

The new term "Missy," invented in 1994, now is used widely as an expression of the strong desire of young Korean wives in their late twenties for an alternative way of life. This term first was used in 1994 in the marketing advertisement of a grand department store in Seoul. As soon as it came out, it was adopted widely to indicate a particular kind of housewife, a married woman who still looks like a single woman. Even the copywriter was surprised at the speed with which this term took on social meaning and evoked specific images of women and femininity. "Missy" rapidly permeated the Korean language once the advertising industry recognized the consumerist implications of this target age group's flamboyant desires.

The essential condition of being a Missy is a preoccupation with being looked at. Kim Hoo-Ran (1996) describes the typical Missy as: "a woman walking through a shopping mall in a tight leather miniskirt and long boots and with her short hair flipped" (30). Film, as a visual medium, has provided the best representation of this kind of social desire, not confined to material possessions but inclusive of an active and blatant sexuality. While Kyŏng-Hye in *Go Alone Like the Rhinoceros's Horn* and Chi-Yŏng in *Marriage* decide to have lovers in reaction to their husbands' relationships with mistresses, the Missy jumps into affairs to satisfy her own needs and desires.

Another fundamental condition of membership in the Missy club is her professional job. The film *Mommy Has a Lover*, released in May 1995, addresses the extramarital love stories of two Missys. The main figure, Un-Chae, a freelance illustrator for a publisher of children's books, satisfies all the conditions of the Missy. After a seven-year marriage, she possesses a luxurious apartment, an able husband, a pretty daughter, and—as the most important condition—her own professional job. In spite of all this, she falls in love with Chin-U, a foreign exchange dealer, as she gradually discovers that he is gentle, generous, and sweet. Unlike Ch'ae-Yŏng, Un-Chae does not consider his financial situation at all. Un-Chae only considers what she wants to do.

Until very recently, it was common in Korean public discourse to portray women's reluctance and shame when they intentionally or unintentionally had a lover outside of marriage. Un-Chae, however, never expresses those feelings. For the Missy, the sexual double standard in contemporary Korean society seems to be completely ignored. The advertising copy for this film hypes the sexuality of young Korean wives: "What? Only once a month? One o'clock in the afternoon, why isn't she at home?" It reports a survey's findings that "64 percent of the Missys want to have their lovers!— But, the other 36 percent have already had lovers!" It sounds as if having a lover is the essential condition for being a Missy. Yun-Su, Un-Chae's friend, has gone one step further and is divorced. In the end, her lover becomes her second husband. Un-Chae goes back to her former life because Chin-U, after he is promoted, leaves with his wife for a foreign country.

The film is thus quite exceptional in presenting sexual liberation from the wife's point of view. No woman is punished for her fall, in contrast to the prior conventions of Korean films. The primary audience for this film was housewives in their thirties and forties, women somewhat older than the typical Missy. Considered a success, although not a great success, the film was seen by 100,000 people during a two-week run in Seoul (*Cine 21*, No. 8, May 1995, 18). The audience's response at the film's first showing was divided along gender lines. Men complained about the ending because it seemed to glorify a wife's affair, while women expressed absolutely no complaint about the story (Ahn 1995).

The development of a sexual identity among women now in their late twenties is described frankly in the first-person narrative of the recent novel *The Pornography in My Mind* (*Nae maŭmŭi p'ornogurap'i*). The novel employs the literary form of a fictional autobiography written by a 26-year-old wife. In the Afterword, in a firm yet modest tone, the author makes clear her purpose for writing this book:

> I only hope that this novel is at least able to console the girls with ballooning curiosity, the unmarried women full of conflict and a sense of guilt, and the married women paralyzed by the risk of loss from the exposed secret who resign themselves to the stereotypic duty of mothering. I think that they can be more honest than they are now (P. Kim 1995, 284–285).

Kim is writing a young woman's autobiographical experience of resistance to female fidelity and chastity as symbolized by the silver knife that Confucian culture would enjoin a woman to use to end her own life should her virtue be compromised. She believes that "There is no door in the world that is made for the purpose of not being opened, even if there are locked doors or doors with rusty hinges" (285).

This novel has played an important role in an emergent sexual politics by bringing the forbidden theme of female sexuality into the public sphere via television talk shows and other media events. However, this public discussion has been confined to the experiences of married women.[13]

In the novel, *I*, the first-person narrator, the second child of the Han family, has attempted to establish her own sexual identity. She has cultivated her female self since the late 1980s, when the dominant sociocultural discourse began to move in the direction of sexual topics. She resolved that never in her life would she give up her own desires for the sake of familial duty. Like her Missy peers, she gives first priority to her own individual self. This is what distinguishes her from older Korean women, even only slightly older Korean women in their thirties. I-Pun says, "I have realized that all the lessons of my parents' generation are no more than old-fashioned preaching, and they have been choking me for 19 years." She declares, "My being was filled with the fierce desire never to be a victim of self-sacrifice" (P. Kim 1995, 178–179). This sentiment is in striking contrast with anything we might expect to hear from Korean women over forty. In pursuit of this ideal, I-Pun has tried every kind of experimentation and taken an ambivalent stance, simultaneously naive and cunning, in her sexual relationships:

> Anyway, sexual relationships did not so much provide excitement, as satisfy my curiosity. I am a very skillful single woman and have known sexual pleasure without crossing the boundary of what is acceptable. I didn't realize that my skill could only be accepted by a gentle, polite partner (who would stay within the boundaries of what is acceptable). At that time, I was too brave to be afraid of anyone or anything, at all (186).

At the age of 24, when she has experimented with her anonymous partner in all of the world's secrets that had absorbed her curiosity for such a long time, she says that she feels absorbed in an ecstasy such as she has never before experienced (P. Kim 1995, 259). Later, she asks herself, "When can I enjoy sex in the same way that I enjoy playing computer games or bowling?" In the course of this process of sexual self-discovery, I-Pun examines her way of thinking and describes how, "The temptation toward deviation versus old-fashioned morality, these contradictory values are fighting each other in my mind" (256–257). In contrast with Korean men and women in their thirties who define their lives through a metadiscourse, she defines human life as a simple game of standing inside or outside of an accepted boundary (256).

Korean teenagers normally are not allowed much freedom to make any decisions of any kind because of the strong social and familial pressure on them to prepare for university admission. For I-Pun's generation, sexual relationships would provide the first opportunity to decide their own subjective positions on a specific issue. This is precisely the site of I-Pun's inner conflict:

> I have already experienced the tedium of a morally ethical life as well as the striking ecstasy of deviation. However, I have quite often surrendered my hands to the handcuffs, compromised, and been forced to follow what they

call morality. I feel that far less danger lies in the moral life because many people have chosen that way of life (P. Kim 1995, 257).

After her experiment with the anonymous partner, I-Pun accepts that she is "now standing outside the boundary" and recognizes that, "Until now, I have only wished to explore outside of the border line" (P. Kim 1995, 257). But her real conflict comes later, as soon as she begins to suspect that she is pregnant. Here her narration seems to regress, as she states "That deviation was too adventurous an experiment," and "Outside the boundary, I have awakened many things that I have never felt inside it" (263). When it becomes clear that her pregnancy was an imaginary and psychological symptom, she admits, "To me, the world is as wide as the range of my experience." From now on, she is not going to accuse anyone of being beyond the pale and she is going to be confident when she stands outside (267).

What I find most interesting in this novel is its illustration of the transformation of the Korean concept of female sexuality as articulated through one specific individual, speaking from a woman's position. Through I-Pun's first-person narrative, the reader can follow her search for a satisfactory female sexual identity subjectively as well as concretely. While most female characters in Korean novels worry about the consequences of sexual experience for their future marriage prospects, I-Pun announces, "Because I'm not his possession, I don't have any complex about being a broken vessel, not at all" (P. Kim 1995, 270). In short, she has her own definition of virginity:

> I don't think that I was soiled or broken. When I blushed with his first gentle kiss, I felt my virginity newly coming into bud. It is not that I am not a virgin, but that I can be a virgin always, whenever I stand in front of my true love. This is my own definition of virginity (271).

Perhaps by now you have noticed the wide gap between Ch'ae-Yŏng's and I-Pun's understanding of female sexuality, even though both characters are described as being in their twenties. While Ch'ae-Yŏng's story is told from the perspective of her mother's generation by an author who is in her mid-fifties, I-Pun's story is narrated from within the perspective of her own generation. The woman in her twenties fashions a sexual identity focused on individual desire; the woman in her fifties is more concerned with materialistic desires. For I-Pun, the first consideration for marriage is her own desires, not what she can gain materially. For I-Pun, her own experiences, mediated through her female body, are of prime significance; marriage means the embodied duty of bearing and rearing a man's baby in her womb (P. Kim 1995, 271). She hesitates because she is not sure whether she can keep her liberated way of life after marriage. In the end, she finally decides to settle down with her husband because she is confident that he has the special skill to heal all her wounds and not compound them.

In Korean culture, where an unmarried woman's sexual experience implies a big, dangerous burden, and every woman is educated to respond negatively to sex, a researcher claims that a young woman could have an invaluable chance to restructure her repressed notions of sex and sexuality through her own sexual experience (Y. Cho 1995, 94). I-Pun's transformation well illustrates how a woman could gain a subjective understanding of female sexuality through such a process of experientially constructing her own sexual identity. I-Pun's husband, by contrast, is described in the novel as an ambiguous and anonymous character, a conspicuous strategy in contemporary Korean women's writing to emphasize the female subject.

THE NEW SEXUAL MORALITY: THE CHALLENGE OF EXPERIMENTATION

In September 1996, a television drama, *The Lover* (*Aein*), stirred Korean society with the extramarital love story of two highly successful professionals in their mid-thirties. It reached a 36.3 percent second audience rating in October 1996 (K. Kim 1996). It even was discussed in the National Assembly because of the social implications of its theme, a challenging portrayal of a married woman's sexuality. This response reveals how powerful the television media is in subverting the traditional ideology of female sexuality. The heroine, Yŏ-Kyŏng, is a married career woman working at an advertising agency. She has a nine-year-old daughter who attends elementary school. Her husband, U-Hyŏk, is a typical "company man," socialized during Korea's peak decades of industrial activity. He has been devoted to the company as a route to the professional promotion that will satisfy his social ambition. He is almost incapable of communicating with Yŏ-Kyŏng. This circumstance provides the impetus for Yŏ-Kyŏng to fall in love with Un-O. He is a professionally successful businessman in his late thirties. Like Chin-U in *Mommy Has a Lover*, Un-O has a soft, gentle, and sweet personality, reflecting the new masculinity of 1990s Korea. He also has the perfect wife and two boys. There is no substantive reason for him to fly from his family. However, like the Missy's love story, *The Lover* explores the adventurous and forbidden theme of an extramarital affair, this time through the medium of television. But an extramarital love story of people in their thirties must confront the issue of familial duties.

Many married men in their forties and fifties called the broadcasting company to protest this drama, demanding "What is it trying to say?" On the other hand, a feminist scholar evaluates it highly, saying, "This drama gives serious consideration to an important issue rather than reducing it to simple human interest" (So 1996, 104). For Western readers, the extramarital love story is such a familiar theme that there is nothing exceptional about it. In the Korean cultural context, it has been usually labeled as immoral and a wife's extramarital affair is seen as particularly, even fatally, damaging to the family. Even though the Missy's extramarital love story in *Mommy Has a Lover* is regarded as a new cultural phenomena in 1990s Korea, it has not been sufficiently influential to shake the dominant social discourse by challenging the patriarchal ideology on female sexuality. *The Lover* is different.

There are, I think, two reasons for this. One has to do with the particular impact of television, the other with the generational difference between the two heroines. As a popular medium, television is much more conservative, and, because of the wide range of its audience, it exerts a much greater influence through its representation of everyday realities. It can even penetrate the small private space of a tiny room. In addition, when an extramarital love story concerns people in their thirties, the issue of familial obligations assumes greater weight. Therefore, it highlights the conflict between Korean familism and female sexuality.

Comparing the American film *Falling in Love* (1984) and the Korean television drama *The Lover* (1996), Yŏm Ch'an-Hŭi (1996) argues that the implication of the ending, in which Un-O and Yŏ-Kyŏng separate and return to their original homes, can be read as equivalent to the ending of *Falling in Love*, in which each character separates from and divorces their former spouse. In *The Lover*, as in the American film, the final sequence of episodes seems to be artificially orchestrated toward an inevitable outcome (59).[14] This artificiality is mainly motivated by the conservatism of the Korean audience.[15]

Nonetheless, I see this television drama as having accomplished a great deal in bringing into public discourse the issue of a middle-aged wife's sexuality. Until recently, the wife's subjective sexuality has been elided by the web of obligations spun by the husband's family or by the terms of a wife's subordination to her husband, as in Hye-Wan's case in *Go Alone Like the Rhinoceros's Horn*. However, in the mid 1990s, as the wife's subjective sexuality emerged through the weakening of Korean familism, a sympathetic rapport between a man and a woman became more important than the functional enactment of role obligations between a husband and wife, or of a father and mother to their children.

In September 1996, in the same moment that television audiences were watching *The Lover*, a new film portrayed a middle-aged wife's even more radical story. *The Adventures of Mrs. Park* (Pak Pong-Kon kach'ulsakkŏn) searched for a new morality that recognizes a wife's subjective sexuality and individuality. The film employed the romantic comedy genre but it was far from typical of the comedies that had been ubiquitous in the Korean commercial film industry since the 1980s. I call it an alternative romantic comedy because it gives a slight twist to the conservatism of the genre. Most Korean romantic comedies end with a happy marriage, the patriarchal ideology intact. This film, however, ends with Pong-Kon's second marriage, thus subverting a traditional morality that expects the runaway wife to come back home to restore everyone's happiness and familial security.

The film begins with an eight-year-old boy's schoolroom narration of why he has two fathers. According to the boy, his mother, Pong-Kon, has absconded because she could not endure the patriarchal aura of her husband, Hŭi-Chae, a company baseball team director. Their inability to communicate is illustrated in the first scene, where we see them eating together at the dining table. After Pong-Kon leaves, Hŭi-Chae employs a private detective, X, to find her. Through the process of looking for Pong-Kon, X falls in love with her and finally marries her.

This film presents a wife whose lifestyle and class orientation are very different from the Missy's. Pong-Kon has a humble dream. She wants to become a singer, and this motivates her to run away. She comes from a definitely lower class than Un-Chae in *Mommy Has a Lover* and Yŏ-Kyŏng in *The Lover*. Middle-aged, lower class wives usually have been represented in Korean popular films as submissive to their very patriarchal husbands due to their economic dependence. But in this film, once she has run away, Pong-Kon is able to make money on her own and takes the private voice lessons that will bring her dream into reality. The film poster hints that Pong-Kon is in possession of two men simultaneously. She is depicted as embracing them both and bursting into laughter while Hŭi-Chae and X stare fiercely at each other.

In fact, the film director was worried about how a conservative audience might respond to this uncommon story and its unexpected ending.[16] The film suggests that Korean wives in the middle and lower classes today are subjectively searching for their individuality and sexuality, influenced by the Korean women's movement since the 1980s, which has delivered a message of self-actualization to young women. This feminist assertion now is articulated widely, not only by middle class wives, but by lower class wives as well. One research survey, carried out in the same month as the film's release, relates that 59 percent of Korean married women have felt the urge to run away, feeling resentful when husbands undermined their pride (Kwak 1996a, 169).

This film was a great commercial success, presumably because it addressed their feelings. Approximately 170,000 people saw it during the first three weeks of its Seoul release.[17] However, the film critics' responses were divided. A woman critic praised the new director's successful experimentation, transforming what would, in real life, be a serious event into a cheerful tale of elopement (M. Lee 1996, 64). She commended the director's cinematic imagination and his techniques of representation. Another woman critic faulted the director on this same point, arguing that the film glosses over its most substantial issue, why a housewife would run away from home. The wife's flight becomes a mere plot device facilitating the story of a pleasurable escapade (Kwak 1996b, 254).

I agree with Kwak, in part, but I would like to underscore the social message implicit in the film's cheerful ending: Pong-Kon emerges victorious in her search for subjective selfhood. Such an ending is possible only because the director chose to deal with this story in the romantic comedy genre, using a witty and humorous touch. If he had opted for more somber realism, he could not have arrived at that destination. How one chooses to represent the story is as important as the story itself.

As with *The Lover*, the potential and limitations of different media are crucial to determining how a certain story develops and gives its radical message a broad hearing in society. Feminist aesthetics and politics must be negotiated through prior conventions of cultural production. These two stories, *The Lover* and *The Adventures of Mrs. Park*, exemplify necessary compromises in producing works that challenge feminist ideology. Lee Chang-Soon (1996), the director of *The Lover*, emphasizes that his intention is to expose the contemporary moment as "The Age of Hypocrisy," where expressed morality, the product of Confucian culture, persists despite its incompatibility with contemporary social reality. He insists that "It is high time we formulated a new morality through a social consensus arrived at through diverse kinds of discussion" (105).

Both stories have experimented with the possibility of recognizing a new morality governing middle-aged wives' subjective sexuality and individuality.[18] The social discourse around these two stories has shown that female sexuality in modern Korea is no longer symbolized by the silver knife or dominated by Confucian notions of fidelity and chastity. Rather, a woman's sexuality has become the barometer of her own subjectivity.

THE PROSPECTS FOR THE SOCIAL CONCEPT OF SEXUALITY IN TWENTY-FIRST-CENTURY KOREA

My reading of the concept of female sexuality in Korean popular culture might suggest that Korean society is now at a stage of development comparable to America in the 1970s, when every kind of women's issue appeared in the realistic novel form. My argument may recall such works as Erica Jong's *Fear of Flying* (1973), Rita Mae Brown's *Rubyfruit Jungle* (1973), and Marilyn French's *The Woman's Room* (1978). If this parallel holds, then what kind of story is unfolding in twenty-first-century Korea? It is not difficult to imagine that a viable revolution against sexual repression might take place. Many young Korean women novelists have confessed that it is in marriage that they have begun to recognize their repression as women for the very first time. Novelist Oh Su-Yǒn (Oh, Shin, and Song 1995) describes this process in an interview with other young woman novelists in their mid-twenties:

> When I went into the real world after my university graduation, everything was different from what I had heard at school. Everything was a lie. That's how I feel. They must teach us about real situations, not just talk (in abstractions) about the inequality between men and women. While I was adapting myself to the social structure, I began to think about my life as a woman. I found that the problem was that I have never before thought of myself as a woman. Both marriage and the family system have intensified my repression to a very high degree. I think the most important fact of my life is that I am living a woman's life, not that I am repressed because of being a woman. . . . For me, being honest with myself means the realization that I am a woman and I am living as a woman. So, naturally, my writing incorporates this awakening and now I'm in the middle of struggling with how to do it well (165–166).

Writers in this younger generation have a clear idea of their sexual identity. They would like to create the image of a new woman who has already passed through the process of self-struggle and appears as a "subjective" woman. Shin I-Hyǒn, another participant in that interview, offered similar comments (Oh, Shin, and Song 1995, 166). The three novelists are beacons for the future direction of Korean women's writing as well as for a more liberated social discourse on female sexuality.

But while this discussion of the changing process of female sexuality in popular culture from 1993 to 1996 gives the impression that Korean women now are marching to demand their sexual subjectivity, in reality, most Korean women are marching only as the passive consumers of the sorts of cultural products described previously, not as their active cultural producers. When women are able to intervene in the process of cultural production as subjective consumers with a feminist point of view, the Korean concept of female sexuality can be transformed more rapidly than before.

A survey of 300 married women in Seoul, conducted in December 1996, just after the success of *The Lover* and *The Adventures of Mrs. Park*, found that the majority of Korean married women are not yet inclined to experience sexuality outside of marriage or to take sexual initiatives within marriage, even if they are now strongly influenced by a social discourse of sexual liberation. According to this survey, 55 percent of the women interviewed consider sex with one's husband as the wife's duty. Only 22 percent prioritize desire, and another 22 percent define the purpose of sexual intercourse as the confirmation of their love. On the other hand, 93.7 percent of the respondents claim that they never have considered divorce on the basis of sexual dissatisfaction. Only 6.3 percent have considered divorce for this reason. While 35.4 percent have been tempted by an extramarital love affair out of discontentment with their husbands, like Yŏ-Kyŏng in *The Lover*, only 27.7 percent admitted being tempted owing to their own sexual instinct (*Talk about Women* 1996).

If we are to form a new sexual subjectivity and morality, what we urgently need is a flourishing of more diverse discourses derived from various aspects of women's sexual experience. Cho Haejoang (1996) emphasizes the fundamental importance of this experiential process for forming and nurturing a new subjectivity, especially in non-Western, postcolonial societies like Korea, which have never struggled to achieve suffrage and therefore lost a critical lesson in how to organize women for an institutional reformation.

The recent social discourse on homosexuality is a precise example of this new wave of awareness coming from more diverse experiential discussions. Since January 1995, books, films, and television dramas have begun to deal with homosexuality as a theme, although none of the main characters in any best-selling novel has been a manifest homosexual yet.[19] It is still noteworthy that some minor characters in women's fiction have been portrayed as homosexuals. Meanwhile, on the university campuses a political movement for homosexual rights has gone into action. Homosexual student unions have organized and published a monthly newspaper. The Korean lesbian community, *kkirikkiri*, organized with just six members on November 27, 1995, has grown to 200 members in one year's time (*Kkirikkiri* 1996).

Looking at Korean culture with a certain detachment, I can imagine that the years 1995 and 1996 will be remembered as a critical period for the emergence of a social discourse on sexuality, especially female sexuality. The year 1995 was particularly remarkable in that housewives began, on their own initiative, to speak in public about wives' subjective sexuality. Apart from the novel *The Pornography in My Mind*, Lee Chae-Kyŏng and Kim Yŏng-Mi published *Sex Talk Written by Housewives*. The two writers have confessed that they were able to write the book because they are *ajumma* (married women), who can freely talk about sex as privileged by their own sexual experiences. In 1997, the annual Korean Women's Studies Association Conference chose as its theme "The Feminist Approach to Sex Culture and Education in Korea."

It is an interesting coincidence that the *May OECD Economic Surveys* (1996) describes 1995 as the year in which the level of per capita income in Korea reached almost $10,000, predicting a doubling to $20,000 by 2001 (13). The national economy has had an overwhelming influence on all other areas of daily life for all Koreans, and nobody can ignore the radical changes in lifestyle that a society experiences as it attains new levels of capitalist development and a rising level of GNP. Even with the economic downturn since November 1997, this tide is still in motion.

There can be no return to a sexually inarticulate past. Korea is now entering into a new stage with respect to women's issues. As is true of the women's movements of western Europe and North America, we can begin to confront the politics of daily life in the private domain where each individual struggles with intimate issues, including the issue of female sexuality. I can state with fair certainty that discourses of female sexuality will continue to gain ground within Korean society, accelerating in both volume and diversity. We will find Korean women's sexual subjectivity in that particular borderland of the global village between Korea's Confucian cultural heritage and Western views of sexual pleasure and desire.

NOTES

An earlier version of this chapter was delivered at the East Asian Studies Seminar on January 24, 1996, at the University of Durham, and at the

Gender Studies Seminar on January 30, 1996, at the University of Hull, United Kingdom.

1. This is one of the main reasons why Kim Hak-Sun, then in her late sixties, became the first former Korean military sexual slave of the Japan empire who felt empowered to come forward to tell her story at a church group's office in Seoul on August 14, 1990.

2. "Musso" is the Korean name for the animal *rhinoceros unicornis*. The novel draws on its most characteristic feature, its solitary horn. While the unicorn only existed in Western mythology, the rhinoceros lived in South Asia and Africa in historic times. The rhinoceros's horn in the title emphasizes independence and subjectivity in real social circumstances.

3. Korea's rapid economic development began in 1961. Korea is considered one of the few countries that have managed the transition from a rural, underdeveloped society to a modern economy in just one generation. Since 1963, economic growth has averaged 8 percent a year, bringing a twelve-fold increase in output while per capita income has risen seven-fold during the same period (OECD 1996, 124).

4. Wonmo Dong (1988) argues that one of the most serious contradictions of Korean education in the 1970s and 1980s was the school curriculum's unrealistic emphasis on the virtue of liberal democracy, a philosophy that was incongruous with the reality of military-controlled authoritarianism in Korea.

5. Although the student movement in Korea has a historical tradition, dating back as early as the fifteenth century, it failed to receive scholarly attention until the 1980s when student demonstrations became a daily ritual. For the characteristics of the Korean student movement in the 1980s, see Dong (1987) and Lew (1993).

6. The serious differences in gender-role expectations among students have been documented. In 1994, the Korean Association for Democracy and Sisterhood (Yŏsŏng Minuhoe) surveyed 214 primary and middle school students, asking whether they would like to be a woman like mother (to girls) or a man like father (to boys). In the case of girls, 52.3 percent answered no and 42.3 percent answered yes. In the case of boys, 69 percent answered yes and 24.5 percent answered no (KBS-TV, *Morning Ground*, "I don't want to live like my mother," 14 June 1995).

7. In the Confucian gender structure, the woman's position was clearly subordinate to the man's. However, a woman as mother could exert lasting influence on her child's intellectual and emotional development, thus acquiring limited authority.

8. Martina Deuchler (1992, 258) argues that the pattern of Confucian behavior for women demanded the rigidity of a stereotype, which did not allow for individual variations. In other words, Confucian society historically acclaimed particular women not for their individuality, but for the degree of perfection with which they were able to mimic the stereotype.

9. In Korea, "wife rape" is not officially considered a crime of sexual violence under the criminal code. Shim Young-Hee (1992, 253–254) argues, based on her research in 1990, that 67.3 percent of Korean married women have experienced "wife rape" but only 35.5 percent of these women recognized it as an act of sexual violence.

10. For instance, the term "washing board" was used to describe a wife's passive and subordinate sexuality in the 1992 Korean film *A Story of Marriage*. Since then, "the washing board" has gained wide circulation among young Korean women as a metaphor for current perceptions of female sexuality.

11. For a description of contemporary Korean matchmaking practices, where these concerns are aired, see Kendall (1996).

12. The generational factor is one of the most important explanatory variables for the attitudinal and behavioral patterns of contemporary Koreans. Wonmo Dong (1993, 2) insists that no other country in the world has been beset with as serious a problem of generational alienation and disaffection as the Republic of Korea in recent decades.

13. KBS-TV, *Morning Ground*, "Wives' sexuality: Is it time to talk, now?" 21 June 1995.

14. Un-O's wife faints during an acquaintance's wedding ceremony and is carried to a hospital, where her third pregnancy is discovered. This incident prevents Un-O and Yŏ-Kyŏng from flying to America, where they had planned to start a new life. After a business failure, U-Hyok, Yŏ-Kyŏng's husband, begins to regret abandoning his family for the sake of a professional promotion. Through this artificial-seeming plot contrivance, Un-O and Yŏ-Kyŏng separate and return to their respective homes. In the last scene, one year after they have parted, they meet by chance in a crowded department store at a shopping mall.

15. The woman scriptwriter included a sexual encounter in an early episode, but after many viewers called the broadcasting company with objections to this scene, the writer refrained from portraying sexual desire in subsequent episodes.

16. His interview is quoted from *Cine 21*, No. 71, 24 September–1 October 1996, 24.

17. This was announced in *Cine 21*, No. 74, 15–22 October 1996, 26.

18. Park Hye-Ran (1996) argues that Korean married women over forty are also very interested in searching for their identity as sexual subjects through extramarital relationships because the priority of their desires now is moving from materialistic prosperity and familial security to subjective individuality. However, in her diagnoses, most of these women are standing on the borderline between fantasy and reality.

19. The last scene in Ch'oe Yun's "The Last of Hanak'o" (1997) hints at the heroine's possible lesbian identity, describing her relationship with her friend as

"sometimes colleagues, sometimes partners." In *If Mozart Is Alive* (1995) by Kim Mi-Jin and in *The Thought on the Knife* (1995) by Kim I-So, minor characters are described as homosexuals. Song Kyŏng-A directly deals with the lesbian issue in "Trout and Sweetfish" (1994), although she has chosen to represent this issue in an imaginary space of her own creation.

REFERENCES

Ahn, Jung-Sook. 1995. Review: *Mommy Has a Lover. Hankyoreh (Sinmun)* (May 19):15.

Cho, Haejoang. 1996. Feminist intervention in the rise of "Asian" discourse. Paper delivered at the 1996 Asian Women's Studies Conference, The Rise of Feminist Consciousness Aganist the Asian Patriarchy. Ewha Woman's University, May 10.

Cho, Yoon-Jung. 1995. A study on the formation of woman's sexual identity: Consciousness formation through sexual experience. Master's thesis. Department of Sociology, Yonsei University.

Ch'oe Yun. 1997. "The Last of Hanak'o." In *Wayfarer: New Fiction by Korean Women.* Bruce Fulton and Ju-Chan Fulton, eds. and trans. Seattle: Women in Translation 11–41.

Deuchler, Martina. 1992. *The Confucian Transformation of Korea.* Cambridge, Mass.: Council on East Asian Studies, Harvard University.

Dong, Wonmo. 1987. University students in south Korean politics: Patterns of radicalization in the 1980s. *Journal of International Affairs* vol. 40(2), winter/spring.

———. 1988. Why radical students in south Korea are rebelling. *The Chronicle of Higher Education* (July 20)34:45.

———. 1993. Generational differences and political development in south Korea. *Korean Studies* 17:1–16.

Fiske, John. 1989. *Understanding Popular Culture.* Boston: Unwin Hyman.

Foucault, Michel. 1978. *The History of Sexuality. Vol. I An Introduction.* Robert Hurley, trans. New York: Random House.

Howard, Keith, ed. 1995. *True Stories of the Korean Comfort Women.* London: Cassell.

Kendall, Laurel. 1996. *Getting Married in Korea: Of Gender, Morality, and Modernity.* Berkeley: University of California Press.

Kim, Hoo-Ran. 1996. "Missy" looks become common. *Newsreview.* (January 20):30–31.

Kim Kap-Sik. 1996. "The Lover" has flown, leaving the "Beautiful Immorality" topic. *Donga Ilbo* (October 27):30.

Kim Pyŏl-A. 1995. *Nae маймйи p'ornogurap'i* (The pornography in my mind). Seoul: Tapgae Publishing Co.

Kim Su-Hyŏn. 1993. *Kyŏrhon* (Marriage). vol. I, II. Seoul: Yeowon Publishing Co.

Kkirikkiri (Lesbian community). 1996. *Tto tarun sesang* (The alternative world). no. 3. Seoul.

Kong Chi-Yŏng. 1993. *Mussoŭi ppulch'ŏrŏm hon'jasŏ kara* (Go alone like the rhinoceros's horn). Seoul: Munye madang.

Kwak Shin-Ae. 1996a. Park Pong-Kon's abscondance. *Kino* (September) 18:168–169.

————. 1996b. Review: *The Adventures of Mrs. Park*. *Kino* (November)20:252–254.

Lee, Chae-Kyŏng and Kim Yŏng-Mi. 1995. *Sex Talk Written by Housewives*. Seoul: Ji-Sung Sa.

Lee, Chang-Soon. 1996. Interview: I want to suggest the new morality. *Sisa Journal* (October 17)354:105.

Lee, Myung-In. 1996. The point where the desire and the desire separate. *Cine 21* (October 15–22)74:64–65.

Lew, Seok-Choon. 1993. Student movement in Korea: Structure and functions. *Korea Journal* (spring)33(1).

OECD (Organisation for Economic Cooperation and Development). 1996. *May OECD Economic Surveys: 1995–1996, Korea*. Paris: OECD.

Oh, Su-Hyŏn, Shin I-Hyŏn, and Song Kyong-A. 1995. Interview: Young women novelists think like this. *Sangsang Quarterly Journal on Cultural Studies* (summer)8:156–171.

Park Hye-Ran. 1996. Desire standing on the borderline between 'already' and 'yet'. In *The Feminist Writings on Marriage*. Vol. 1 *Inside (marriage)*. The Alternative Culture Group, ed. pp. 281–295. Seoul: Alternative Culture.

Shim Young-Hee. 1992. *Women's Social Participation and Sexual Violence*. Seoul: Nanam.

Shin, Yong-Sook, and Cho Hye-Ran. 1996. On the characteristics and special nature of the Korean "military comfort women" under Japanese rule. *Korea Journal* 36(1):50–78.

So, Sung-Moon. 1996. The sweetbitten ending taste of the extramarital love story. *Sisa Journal* (October 17)364:104–106.

Yŏm, Ch'an-Hŭi. 1996. Where is beautiful nature? *Cine 21* (November 5–12)77:58–59.

Films, Television Dramas, and Talk Shows

Mommy Has a Lover. May 1995.

The Lover (Aein). MBC (Munhwa Broadcasting Company) Television. September–October, 1996.

The Adventures of Mrs. Park (Pak Pong-Kon kach'ulsakkŏn). September 1996.

Talk About Women. MBC Television. 28 December 1996.

7

LIVING WITH CONFLICTING SUBJECTIVITIES: MOTHER, MOTHERLY WIFE, AND SEXY WOMAN IN THE TRANSITION FROM COLONIAL-MODERN TO POSTMODERN KOREA

cho haejoang

You probably are familiar with the celebrated story of south Korea's miraculous economic transformation. You may not have heard the terrible story of its cultural transformation—a story about regressive changes in the roles and images of women in late twentieth-century south Korean society.

When I came to the United States to do my graduate study in 1971, I was shocked by certain forms of women's behavior. During my first semester at a Midwestern state university, I lived in a dormitory for female graduate students. On Friday nights at the dorm, inevitably one saw students looking as depressed as if they were at a funeral. They were the "leftover" girls who did not have dates. One of those girls, who considered herself unattractive and shy, told me, "I envy you because you can marry by parental arrangement!" Her comment puzzled me because I had been teased recently by a "sexy" undergraduate female student, " How barbarian you Koreans are! I've heard that you people marry someone with whom you are not in love."

I felt uncomfortable seeing a nice girl so depressed just because she did not have a date, and another girl who behaved so arrogantly, as if she could do whatever she wanted, just because she was sexy. I was annoyed by young women who tried so hard to present themselves as sex objects. The sight of older women who struggled desperately to look young and sexy depressed me. The American rule that one should never ask a woman's age puzzled me. A male American classmate told me repeatedly, with anguish on his face, that I must realize what was in the heads of American people: "Their minds are filled with sex, Haejoang—you'd better realize that."

In my opinion, the United States was a terrible place for women. Of course, in south Korea there were also girls who wanted to be sexy and who thought of romantic love all the time, but they were the minority. Most south Korean girls cared much more about their female friends than about boyfriends. I remember thinking to myself, "You are lucky to be a Korean woman. You do not have to adopt a self-conscious pose to attract other people's attention, men's in particular. You say whatever you want to say without worrying about losing your femininity, and you are not preoccupied with your external appearance."

It took me a long time to realize that I came from a homo-social culture, a culture that values same-sex friendship and social interaction over heterosexual relationships and romance. Through anthropological studies, I learned that traditional culture is not an unchanging essence and that cultural particularity cannot be understood ahistorically. I came to see that my image of women was a product of an agrarian cultural tradition and, at the same time, of the particular style of south Korea's (colonial) modernization. In spite of my pride in the powerful individual Korean women who surrounded me in my youth, I came to realize that these women were not collectively empowered. That is, in spite of the homo-social circumstances that appeared so laudable to me, south Korean women's power was not institutionalized and consequently was limited to their immediate social relationships.

This realization leads me to the first question that I raise in this chapter. Why could south Korean women appear to be so powerful when they are structurally so powerless? My second question is intimately related to the first; that is, why do women appear to be more "modern" than men in south Korea? This question begs other issues: how "modernity" was constructed in south Korean history, how the formation of the middle class was tied to that construction, and what colonialism had to do with it.

I have an image of my society as a grand conspiracy that is reproduced by conservative, inflexible, and extremely self-defensive men and their super-adaptive women. The image is a reflection of modern Korean history, an informal backstage version of history, the history that has been hidden behind official history without which no one can properly comprehend how modern Korean society came to be. I believe that feudalistic authoritarianism (*ponggŏnjŏk kwŏnwijuŭi*) in East Asia is not just a phenomenon of culture lag. Rather, authoritarianism has been actively reinforced and reproduced within and through the experience of colonialism. Guha calls this "aborted" modernity: "the historic failure of the nation to come into its own, a failure that is due to the inadequacy of the bourgeoisie, as well as of the working class, to lead it into a decisive victory over colonialism through a bourgeoise revolution of either the classic nineteenth century type or a more modern type" (Guha 1985, 7).

It must be difficult for the patriarchs of "aborted" modernity to maintain flexibility and a sense of reality. It must have been and must still be difficult for the Korean male ego to recall its defeat in modern history. Over the past century's experience of colonial modernization, the image of the enormously strong and eternally self-sacrificing mother took on a particular cast in the expectation that invincible women should compensate for men's weakness, for their "emasculation" under colonialism.[1] Women were expected to have boundless fortitude in the face of men's shortcomings. The weakened agency of the Korean male subject forged a peculiar gender relationship: an over-protective mother and her feeble but noble son.

If Korean men in leadership positions failed to maintain their own autonomy and thus were fiercely defensive and self-conscious,[2] women also struggled to make their own space amid the frustrations of modern history. What did they get? They produced three generations of daughters who flatly refuse to live like their mothers. With this refusal, women also deny the wisdom transmitted from the mother's generation. Women of the daughter's generation have no ideal role models, only conflicting roles and images against which to measure themselves: that of mother, motherly wife, and sexy girl. Interestingly, women do not seem to feel conflict while going through such contradictory transformations. Does living with conflict become the rule, not the exception? Or are these women all schizophrenics?

This chapter describes the process of "housewifization," the transition from a mother-centered to a wife-centered patriarchy during the period of economic takeoff in south Korea beginning in 1960. Housewifization is a nearly universal phenomenon that accompanies modernization. As Lipman-Blumen (1976, 31) has phrased it, women as housewives, confined to individual households, are systematically excluded from the "male homo-social world" of territoriality, exclusivity, dominance, and resource accumulation. Women have had to utilize their capacity for sexuality, motherhood, and service to be allowed to share in the men's world. At this stage of modernization, a woman is represented more as the wife of one man than as the mother of another. Within half a century in Korea, the dyad of sexual partners and marital couples has gained precedence over that of mother and son.

The first transition of postcolonial south Korea from traditional patriarchy to modern patriarchy began in the 1960s and extended through the 1980s. Although the history of modernization in south Korea is much longer than that, the most visible transition from the extended family and from the rural collective family enterprise to the urban nuclear family occurred during these years. As the principal managers of the nuclear family in urban industrial settings, most Korean women now occupied the newly created "modern" domestic/private domain, while men occupied a vastly expanded public domain. The rise of consumer society marks the second transition. Korean women's vision and subjectivity have been greatly transformed by Korea's economic success and through their own related experience of a global culture united by capitalism. A drastic shift occurred between the 1980s and the 1990s, sweeping middle class housewives into consumerist postmodernity in their desire to be "charming" and "sexy." I use the term "postmodern" to emphasize the difference and discontinuity between the earlier stage of modernization, with its strong emphasis on economic production, and this late stage in which consumerism becomes the central focus of sociocultural production.

I have lived through these two stages of cultural transformations in late twentieth-century and early twenty-first-century south Korea. These circumstances made for confusing and conflicting experiences for most women; they were particularly baffling and distressing for feminists like myself. The recent changes make one wonder if women in the future will be no more than the postmodern world's floating signifiers. Because these cultural transformations have occurred in such a compressed time span, feminists who would advance feminist projects that are relevant to Korean women must first grasp the historical experiences of women of different generations. That is what I attempt in this chapter. My data is drawn from popular culture; from novels, television dramas, and movies; from participant observation of everyday life over many long years; from intensive interviews in various settings including feminist circles, housewives' health clubs, high school alumni lunch meetings, traditional dance classes for elderly women, and all manner of everyday encounters; and from students' homework assignments produced in 1993 and 1994.

I must emphasize that the picture I present is based on major trends or ideal types in the Weberian sense, not on any statistically verifiable reality. In truth, class position, temperament, and educational background have produced deviations in the roles and subjective experiences of women within each generation. Also, I look primarily at the women of the middle class who define themselves as "housewives" (chubu) or, in the case of the "new generation," who see themselves as prospective housewives. Given the extreme emphasis on uniformity and class mobility in south Korean society, these are the women who have established cultural distinctions in Bourdieu's (1984) sense by being actively engaged in "modernity projects," shedding their countrified ways and creating new lifestyles to match new class identities. While media idealizations of a modern, urban lifestyle accord closely with the lived reality of the middle and upper-middle classes, they have also constituted cultural models and ideologies that are pervasive throughout the whole of Korean society.

THREE GENERATIONS: A PATH FROM COLONIAL-MODERN TO POSTMODERN

In this chapter, I describe the lives of three generations of middle class south Korean women—"grandmother's generation," "mother's generation," and "daughter's generation," terms I employ loosely and symbolically. A middle class woman of the grandmother's generation who might now be 75 years old would have been born in 1920, come of age during the Japanese colonial era, and reared her family after the Liberation (1945). She might have had young children during the Korean War (1950–1953). Women of her generation are described as motherly women, the stronghold of the disrupted society. Her daughter would now be in her mid- to late fifties. She would have been born around 1940, acquired her most vivid memories after the Liberation, and experienced the Korean War as a child. She would have reared her family during the period of Korea's sudden economic growth, working as hard as her husband in the maelstrom of the Korean economic "miracle" (see Abelmann and June Lee in this volume). I characterize women of this generation as aggressive modern wives, the backstage managers of rapid industrialization.

Now imagine a 30-year-old woman, the daughter and granddaughter of the two women just described. She would have been born in 1965, come of age under the military regime in the period of economic development, and started her family in the late 1980s. Hers is the first generation to enjoy the fruit of the economic miracle without the effort of sowing and harvest, although many women of her generation are well aware of their parents' past hardship. At the same time, she was exposed to student activism in her college years when she would have experienced first-hand the prodemocracy and feminist movements of 1980s Korea. Her participation in or sympathy with a highly moralistic student activism would have prevented or at least postponed her full acquiescence to consumer capitalism. As a woman, she is thus caught between her mother's materialist ambitions and her own self-realization. The women of this generation are divided into two groups: working women and housewives. This femininity is encapsulated in the word "Missy," women who look like *agassi*, like independent "unmarried young women." Younger sisters, women who were born in the1970s, are now in their late twenties and early thirties. Critics of popular culture frequently refer to them as *sinsedae* (new generation) because they are the children of an absolute consumer society.

The Grandmother's Generation:Motherly Women, the Refuge of a Disrupted Society

Traditional Korean society often is described as an extreme form of Confucian patriarchy. Women held no public positions and were forced to obey men who were structurally central figures in families, lineages, and the larger society. There were, however, aspects of Confucian patriarchy that supported women's rights. Confucian familism was founded on values of filial piety and gender codependent models of social harmony symbolized by yin-yang dynamics (Park Yong-ok 1985; Kim Yong-ok 1986; Choi Jae-sok 1983; Yoon 1973; Lee Hyon-hee 1979; Yim Dawnhee 1986).

A popular Confucian idiom reads, "A man can be a true public leader only after he cultivates himself and regulates his family in harmony" (*Susin chega; chiguk pyŏngchŏnha*). Because this was a family-centered social order, women, through their maternal identity and role, could receive considerable respect not only in the family but also in the larger kinship groups and among the neighbors. If a son succeeded as a high official, his mother also was given an official title (Chŏng Yang-wan 1985; Chŏng Yo-sŏb 1973). Filial piety applied to both sexes indiscriminately. The strict division of gender roles within the household made women indispensable. Moreover, separated from the men's domain, women maintained their own social space and spiritual life (Kendall and Peterson 1983; Kendall 1985). Korean women who metamorphosed from powerless daughters-in-law to formidable mothers-in-law developed a sense of strength and fortitude, personal resources that would be demanded of them during the vicissitudes of modern Korean history.[3]

During the Japanese colonial era, many families were pulled apart when men emigrated as voluntary or involuntary laborers, or joined independence movements. Women assumed heavier responsibilities as family heads in their absence. The Korean War again separated many men from their homes. With family survival at stake, women assumed the burden of feeding and housing their families. In this context, assertive, aggressive mothers were accepted, appreciated, and even socially encouraged. The women of the grandmother generation spent their active years in a time and place where most of the population was rural. Radio and newspapers were the major channels of mass communication. Many women of this generation received some modern education, some up to middle school or high school (if they were both lucky and privileged). In school they were exposed to notions of history as a progress toward modernity. Although they lived with poverty and socioeconomic instability, they firmly believed that they would secure a bright future by sending their children to school. Those with middle class aspirations struggled to send their children to the university. Hope and deferred gratification sustained their miserable lives. If a woman was greedy in the pursuit of material resources, no one could blame her, because it was for the survival of her family in destitute times. In this generation, it was a lucky and an enviable woman who could live on her husband's income. Women were expected to be wise, hardworking, and competent in taking care of the extended family and orchestrating communal living, but their self-sacrificing was recognized and appreciated. In their social universe, the old patriarch was a distant figurehead; the mother was at the center of the family, taking care of everything from supporting the family to educating her children, all while preserving her husband's face.[4] The patrilineal principle was faithfully maintained as a cultural ideal, providing an ideological center of stability amid a reality of social disintegration.

Lee Sun's (1981) novel, *Our Children* (*Uri dŭl ŭi aidŭl*), describes the ideal family of these times as a tightly knit survival group. The image of a wise and competent grandmother who managed a large extended family, its fortunes in decline, is one of the most cherished and powerful images held by south Koreans, even today. The grandmother as earthly goddess remains a popular image among novelists and literary critics, both male and female. Such well-known novels as *Tŏji* (*The Land*) by Park Kyŏng-ri (1973), *Honbul* (Spirit fire) by Choi Myŏng-hee (1983), or *Surado* by Kim Chŏng-han (1988) have as central characters dignified grandmothers of immense insight, ability, and devotion. In a book review, Choi Won-sik (1995) commends a short story for its "typical portrait of 'our mother,'" a story that begins at the woman's deathbed:

> An old lady from the countryside who had raised seven children with no help from her totally incompetent husband, a life-long peddler who would walk eight kilometers in the early morning with the heavy load of vegetables she had picked even earlier in the morning to sell at the Pohang market, a mother who, despite her sons' attempts to keep her from working, would not stop peddling until she fell sick and was put to bed, this woman is not special but merely average, all too average a portrait of "our mother" (Choi Won-sik 1995).

The picture a woman from this generation most cherishes is that of her sixtieth or seventieth birthday, when all her offspring are gathered together to express their gratitude for her lifelong motherly endurance and nurturing. Her feminine identity is as a mother. Women of this generation think of themselves as mothers and organize their recollected life experiences around this identity. A woman who had assumed rough, assertive, "masculine" (namsŏngjŏk) behavior in the defense of her family's interests was not stigmatized. She was, simultaneously and without contradiction, a "womanly woman"(yŏja daun yŏja), so defined by her familial, caring, and managerial roles as the female head of an extended household.

Mother's Generation: Aggressive Modern Wives, Backstage Managers of Hustling Industrialization

Women of this generation were born in the 1940s and grew up in the 1950s and 1960s. They came of age with the slogan, "Economic growth first by all means!" In this period, rapid urbanization brought a third of the population to the cities within twenty years.[5] The women of this generation experienced Park Chung-hee's 5.16 (May 16, 1961) coup d'état in their youth and subsequently lived most of their young and active years under an authoritarian military dictatorship. Driven by statist economic planning and favorable international market conditions, the south Korean economy suddenly expanded. Both blue-collar and white-collar men labored through one of the world's longest working days, and, as Korean enterprises expanded, they began to work overseas, first in Vietnam, then in Saudi Arabia, then all over the world.

Living in urban settings, women of this generation had more education[6] and were exposed to Western culture through movies and television dramas. The women of this generation idealized a happy married life with a successful husband and two children, a life they glimpsed in countless Hollywood movies. Although many women in this generation dreaded the idea of an arranged marriage, most of them married by arrangement in the end. Although they might never experience a real romance or realize a love marriage, they could dance with Clark Gable's Rhett Butler privately, in their dreams.

Once married, many of them moved into the newly built apartment complexes where they began nuclear families. Although women of this generation grew up in relative poverty, they could raise their children in relative affluence. A wide informal economic space opened up for women whose ability to manage and invest family income made it possible to buy a better apartment, educate the children, and arrange advantageous marriages for their daughters and sons. In sum, they could do all of the things that would provide their family with a secure identity as modern and middle class. These modern wives pushed their children to play the piano and engaged in various other activities appropriate to their lifestyle (as described by Abelmann in this volume).

The nuclearization of the family and the women's own related housewifization are the two most visible changes experienced by this generation. Of course, ideological support for housewifization is not a totally new phenomenon in Korea. Early modernists of the colonial period offered a new narrative on the role and status of woman as the domestic partner of a man who worked in the newly created modern public sphere. Their most explicit model can be found in the "good wife, wise mother" of Meiji Japan, constructed through explicit national policies as the appropriate helpmate of the new modern man, who devoted himself to nation building (Nolte and Hastings 1991; Smith 1983).[7] Women's magazines from 1930s Korea include essays and articles on the ideal wife that parrot the Meiji ideal. The ideal wife was the woman who took care of all the domestic chores, economized on the family budget, kept the house clean at all times, knew her husband's every thought, and when conversing with her husband, maintained a smiling face like a blossoming flower.

Although Korea had possessed an ideological narrative for women as "good wives" (*yangch'ŏ*) from the 1930s, it was not until the 1960s that large numbers of women began to define themselves as wives who orchestrated nuclear households rather than as mothers who were embedded in a larger family collective. With economic growth and rapid urbanization, large numbers of young men finally could pursue secure and well-paying jobs in the modern sector that would sustain young wives who busily set about managing their husbands' income and orchestrating their children's education. Many terms were coined to describe the new wives of the newly emerging middle class. They are "frugal housewives" (*alttul chubu*) who negotiate to save pennies while shopping, avid participants in informal rotating credit associations (*kyekkun*). "The swish of a skirt" (*chimaparam*) describes housewives who try to influence people in the public sphere through the power of informal relationships. "Mrs. Realtor" (*pokpuin*) engages in buying and selling houses and land for pure speculative investment, "big hand" (*k'ŭnson*) deals large sums of money in the informal sector, and "Madame Procuress" Madam Ttu, makes a large sum of money by professionally arranging marriages for the rich and well connected. The era conjured images of wives who exhibited naked ambition and greed: women who bribed teachers to have their sons elected as class representative, forced their husbands to make money by any means, or, in their later years, abused those daughters-in-law who failed to bring extravagant dowries.[8]

Women who managed homes of their own in the city were transformed into "modern wives." Even in the countryside, some courageous women began to talk back to their mothers-in-law. On average, the women of this generation had been educated through middle or high school and also had experienced city living before they got married. Many did not show respect for their uneducated, rural-identified mothers-in-law. Some even refused to live with the "ignorant" mother-in-law on the grounds that her presence would be detrimental to the children's education. Concern for the children's well being was a weapon that these modern women frequently wielded. In the 1970s, "super modern" mothers began to read Dr. Spock's guide to child care and, on the basis of his professional authority, rejected the mother-in-law's old-style practices. In the 1980s, one of the major battlegrounds between the mother-in-law and the daughter-in-law in middle class homes was whether to lay the baby on its stomach or on its back. The young wife wanted to have the baby laid on its stomach so that its skull would not be flattened. The skull would remain more round and Western in appearance, a new mark of beauty and distinction in Bourdieu's (1984) sense, in contrast with a flatter physiognomy, now associated with the backward social practices of uneducated people. The mother-in-law worried that the baby could suffocate in a facedown position and would feel very uncomfortable.

Young husbands began to think that their first loyalty as household heads was to their nuclear family. As the nuclear family system became established firmly in this rapidly urbanizing society, wifely power gained a foothold over motherly power. The husbands of this generation appreciated their wives for their hard work and began to take the wife's side in domestic conflicts. Young husbands suffered for their divided loyalties and called themselves the "sandwich generation" because they were torn between mother and wife. Even so, a modern man knew that it was his wife, not his mother, who would manage his life. He credited her accordingly, yet he often felt deserted by a wife who focused her attention on her children. A man told me that the best part of the fish was no longer his share; once his son turned three or four, it went onto his son's plate.

The family was still as tightly united as ever, but it was increasingly nuclearized and smaller, an attribute explicitly linked to "modernity" in the rhetoric of the successful family planning campaigns of these years (Kim Eun-Shil 1993; Moon 1994). The women of this generation had insisted repeatedly that they would not live their mothers' lives, but they did. They made their own identities through their children and distanced their husbands by accepting the distinction between the public and domestic domain. Women thus continued to perceive the family as matrifocal, or "uterine," composed exclusively of mothers and children (following Wolf 1972). Marriage was just a fact of life. In their hard work and aggressive devotion to their families, and in their lack of intimacy with their husbands, they were the faithful daughters of their mother's generation. The husbands worked hard and played hard after their work outside the home. The drinking and sex industry expanded during those years to cater to their needs, fostered by the social expectations of the white-collar world and sustained, to some degree, by feelings of alienation at home (Janelli with Yim 1993; Elaine Kim 1998; June Lee in this volume).

The mass media, women's magazines in particular, revived the 1930s image of the modern housewife but for a vastly expanded new audience. *Yŏwŏn*, the forerunner of women's magazines in the 1970s and 1980s, promoted the slogan "Beloved Wife, Successful Husband." The journal implanted "wife-consciousness" among women, instructing them in how to behave as modern wives. These modern middle class wives were given every encouragement by the media to be "Mrs. Realtor" and "aggressive education mamas" so as not to be left behind. They worried about their husbands' extramarital affairs while grabbing after opportunities to marry their daughters into prosperous families. These middle class wives built a highly competitive and status-conscious culture that was as hastily and coarsely constructed as the Korean economy that made their maneuvering possible.

The eminent female novelist Pak Wan-sŏ has written several novels and short stories about the housewives of this newly emerging middle class. In her 1985 short story, "The Identical Rooms" (*Talmŭn pangdŭl*), Pak Wan-sŏ depicts typical middle class wives competing against one another for the purchase of commercial products in same-sized apartments in a grand apartment complex:

> How frugal and in what good taste she was running her household! It was just like a room in a fairy tale. . . . I tried so hard to make my room fancier than hers but ended up with nothing so special. The color of the curtain and the placement of the furniture all turned out to be just the same. . . . I wore the pretty apron and cooked rice and delicious dishes. . . . I asked about neurosis. She did not ask about my symptoms but said that she was suffering from neurosis and then listed all the names of other wives whom she knew to be receiving treatment for neurosis. . . . Just as my apartment resembled

Cholhee's, all the other apartments in our neighborhood, on the left and the right and up and down were alike. Of course, there were some differences in that some families had the washing machines that others did not have, and some had the pianos that others did not have. However, their self-satisfaction would not last long. Soon others would buy them and imitate the others. I was so sick and tired of this sameness, but I saved money to buy the washing machine which Cholhee's mother had. I cooked only with bean sprouts, bill fish, and artificial flavoring as Cholhee's mother had taught me to do (1985, 350–351).[9]

Pak Wan-sŏ is highly critical of the vulgarity of middle class housewives' culture as it took shape during this period of rapid economic growth. In her writing, the housewives' culture is characterized by sheer materialistic competition and conspicuous consumption. In Pak's short story, the middle class wives of this period are represented as full of selfish desires and competitive spirit. In fact, Korean wives were notorious for aggressively advancing their children and their husbands, with little concern for the larger community. Unlike middle class wives in Western societies or in Japan, Korean women have little interest in charitable works or community welfare programs (Tinker 1980, 4). They invest their time solely in immediate family matters or for their individual pleasure. By the 1980s, classes in aerobics and swimming were fully registered and expensive restaurants were mostly booked by housewives for weekday lunches, but few would participate in a more general communal gathering, regarding it as a waste of time. This lack of public consciousness in middle class housewives' culture is, in a sense, a symbolic representation of the anomaly of Korean modernity of the 1960s and 1970s, a consequence of women's hard work and constant, endless sense of relative depravation as they lived through the years of the rough and bustling economic boom.

I regard women of this generation as the main source of the Korean economic transformation's vitality. With such a strong yearning for modernity, refusing to live like their own mothers who struggled for mere survival, disregarding their incompetent fathers and husbands, they have transformed their society as well as themselves. As Nancy Abelmann describes them (in this volume), it was women's endless motivation for achievement, their yoksim[10] and competency (nŭngryŏk) that made a family succeed economically, the impulses that led to successful matches for their daughters. Abelmann highlights the yoksim of these women as a driving force in the formation of this new middle class through their desire or pursuit of upward mobility. They are now addressed as samonim, a word liter-

ally meaning "the honored wife of a teacher," but now broadened to connote any woman who has money and taste. The term is opportunistically
employed by realtors (mostly men) and other shrewd sales persons to distinguish the middle class woman, who has buying power, from the poor
ajumma (an ordinary married woman). *Ajumma* thus has come to connote
not young, unsophisticated, and not rich women.

The media and mainstream male culture often have criticized the *yoksim* of the wives, leveling disapprobation at wifely power. Social critics
blamed women for the many vulgarities of Korean modernization. Mothers
could be valorized, with sentimental hindsight, for their strength and determination, but the assertiveness of wives was not so positively valued. Men
in their fifties express ambivalence toward wifely power and often viewed
their wives as utterly materialistic, vulgar, and selfish. In the work of such
prominent poets as Hwang Ji-u or Kim Chi-ha, the wife is described as a
limited woman, constantly calculating or indulging in vulgar snobbery.

These formidable women create grim jokes about their husbands,
asserting with tongue in cheek that the luckiest woman is the woman who
is widowed in her fifties. More explicitly, there is the one about the widow
who asked the coffin carrier to carry her husband's coffin gently so that he
would not awaken, or the one about the widow who whispered joyfully
near the coffin, "You are the dearest charming person." This black humor
may be understood as a measure of the degree to which aging women find
their old husbands burdensome. These women have dutifully lived their
married lives by running asset-type families, families structured around
their common material and social assets. Now that their children are grown,
the women want to retire. In their fifties, they express this openly.

In 1995, there appeared a series of jokes regarding the old man "who
has an 'enlarged liver'" (*kank'ŭn namja*, equivalent to the English 'gutsy
man'). The man with an enlarged liver is the husband who dares to ask his
wife how she spent her money, where she spent her day, and what she talked
about over the telephone. He is the man who asks her to prepare dinner for
him when he comes home late. This humor was so much in vogue that the
popular singer Kim Heyon wrote a song on this theme.

Like women of the grandmother generation, the women of this generation did not worry about femininity as long as they were successfully
performing the roles assigned to them. It is difficult to imagine a woman
with *yoksim* and *nŭngryŏk* as feminine in the Western sense of gentle and
sexy. Although the women of this generation were able to use their new
economic resources to advance family interests and to strengthen a distinctively matrifocal family culture, the subculture they made was not in serious

conflict with modern Korean patriarchy, whose values they reproduce by ultimately identifying themselves, like the women of the grandmother generation, as the mothers of sons. Their daughters discover that the modern mother and the conservative mother-in-law are often two faces of the same woman. The daughters are, like the third world women of Mohanty's account (Mohanty 1991, 10), caught between the simultaneous oppression imposed by colonial modern, modern, and postmodern.

The Daughter's Generation: Women Caught between Mother's Yoksim and Self-Realization

Women of the daughter's generation were born in the 1960s and grew up in the 1970s under a strong military state and the equally strong influence of the mass media, particularly the television. A majority of these girls lived in urban settings and grew up in nuclear families. Their childhood memories are not of hunger but of going to piano lessons and martial arts classes. They had to struggle through an intense university examination war, more competitive for their generation than in the past, while endlessly exposed to the enticements of consumer capitalism.

On average, the men of this generation received 11.78 years of education, while women received 10.37 years (Kang 1996, 594). Daughters of the middle class went to college where, in the 1980s, many of them joined or sympathized with student activists, sometimes under the banner of the Nationalist–Democratic Movement (*Minjok minjung undong*). A new image of women emerged: They became the brave partners of patriotic men engaged in student activism. Korea's women's liberation movement was also launched at this time. Undergraduate and graduate programs in women's studies were set up in several women's universities and the Association of Women's Studies was founded. Women's studies courses became the most popular courses for both female and male students on university campuses. Various women's groups were formed to deal with such feminist issues as women's labor, feminist literature, domestic violence, and sexual harassment in the work place. The movement spoke in many voices, from Marxist feminist to socialist to liberal feminist. Liberal feminism gained great popularity as the mass media disseminated the idea of women's rights. Liberal feminists received attention because their agenda was appealing but also because they sounded less radical and threatening than the Democratic Movement activists. Although feminism was largely confined to an elite circle of activists and intellectuals, their demands became loud and persistent, and some of their goals were achieved: The demand for equal pay for equal work led, in 1988, to the passing of a legal guarantee of equal rights in employment. A special law prohibiting sexual violence also was chartered. An art film based on an actual rape incident, *Just Because You Are a Woman* (*Tanji kŭdaega yŏjaranŭn iyu manŭro*), attracted much attention and even succeeded commercially.

The image of independent and self-sufficient women was propagated widely. Women began to talk about "self-realization," asserting that they wanted to be defined not by familial relations but as individuals. In 1984, 76.7 percent of all female college students responded to a survey by indicating that they wanted to have a job after graduation (Lee, Kim, and Kim 1995, 195). The number of women in the labor market had steadily increased. Many young women worked in the public sphere, and while most quit work upon marriage, the number of career women who remained in their jobs, regardless of marital status, also increased. A slogan, "pro is beautiful" attracted the mass media. The buzzword, "self realization" (*cha-a silhyŏn*) was so loudly proclaimed that housewives felt depressed and frustrated. They felt overshadowed by working women, who were portrayed as enjoying social recognition and economic rewards. Subtle conflicts between housewives and working women surfaced.

The desire for self-fulfillment was high among the women of this generation, but society was not opening sufficient space to satisfy their desire. In this second generation of "modern wives," those women who gave up their careers usually did so because there was little support for child care. Not only did they lack institutional support, these women also lacked the support from other women that the previous generation had enjoyed, support from mothers, mothers-in-law, or domestic help. Women of the grandmother's generation had fully supported their professional daughters' "self realization." As dedicated mothers, they identified with their daughters and, where daughters had determined to work outside the home, their mothers had supported them by taking care of grandchildren and managing their daughters' households. Housewives of the mother's generation were reluctant to take this on, and domestic help had become prohibitively expensive. While mothers wanted to see their university-graduate daughters become successful career women, they also wanted their daughters to be suitable brides for upper-middle class families. These conflicting demands often confused their daughters when they were growing up, and, once the daughters were grown, their mothers were unwilling to provide the support they needed to sustain careers.

Women in their fifties, saying that they had already worked too hard, now wanted to relax and travel freely. Those women who had stayed in the domestic domain expressed their desire to make full use of their last opportunities for self-realization and personal enjoyment. In alumni meetings, one often heard women in their fifties say, "Children are no use!" Mothers of this generation had no intention of supporting their daughters so that their daughters could continue to work outside the home. Many daughters felt betrayed by their mothers and, at the same time, said that it was perfectly understandable. Since they wanted to assert their own individuality, they recognized that their mothers had the same right to do so.

Here we see the emergence of a third generation of "modern wives," women forced to give up a career because there was no support system for child care. *Go Alone Like the Rhinoceros' Horn* (*Musso ŭi ppulchŏrŏm honjasŏ kara*), a popular feminist novel by Kong Chi-yŏng (1993), tells the story of three college graduates who failed to become self-realized women because of the problem of child care and their egoistic husbands (So-Hee Lee in this volume). Unlike wives of the mother's generation, most college graduates of the daughter's generation seriously considered careers but were forced to be housewives. These young modern housewives are inclined to be individuals first and are determined to live a life free from the constraints of traditional patriarchy. Many women of this new generation, of course, have been raised by intensely achievement-motivated mothers with unlimited aspirations. The newly transformed social climate in which they were raised and their own mothers, who were the most active agents of this transformation, forced them to be independent on the one hand, and spoiled and perpetually dependent on the other. Living in nuclear families in urban settings, the young daughters had some measure of private space and individual voice. Interactions in this confined family setting, with its emphasis on individuality and self-reliance, tended to cause more direct intergenerational conflict. The daughters did not see themselves as owing filial respect to their mothers. They did not want their mothers to interfere with their lives, and planned to leave home as soon as possible. They sought their own private time and space and took their peer culture as a primary referent.

In this context, heterosexual relations came to the forefront as boyfriends and husbands became more intimate partners than mothers or female friends. Just as they did not turn to their mothers for child care support, many women of this generation did not turn to their mothers and female friends for emotional support. In Korea today, homo-social space is receding while heterosexual concerns are gaining in intensity. In this climate, young wives have begun to talk about postpartum syndrome. Postpartum syndrome is not just an imported western construct that sophisticated and sensitive wives have begun to emulate. A woman who gives birth in a maternity ward does not feel overjoyed just because she has become a mother, the experience of her mother's generation. New mothers today endlessly desire their husbands' personal attention and support, and demand that their own "private feelings" be satisfied by their heterosexual partners.

In spite of their strong rejection of their mothers' lives, women in their late twenties and early thirties share their mother's desperate desire to conceive sons. These modern young women once regarded the idea of son-preference as absurd but became seriously concerned about the baby's gender once they got pregnant. Many women exert tremendous efforts before conception and during pregnancy in order to bear a son. Significant numbers have even aborted female fetuses (Kim Eun-Shil 1993).

Their contradictory attitudes reflect a trend toward neoconservatism as Korea's economic growth slows down and the society becomes more stable. The feminist vision of enlightenment lost its vitality as the utopian movements of the 1980s died down. Neoconservatism is regaining popularity, while a sophisticated consumerism rapidly expands. Many young and educated women who once had progressive ideas seemed to change their minds: They now seem to think that it is wiser to adapt to the existing system than to resist it. These women realize that money derived from a husband's income is crucial and that a son is the source of power in the male-centered family structure. The hegemony of patriarchy is reinforced through compulsory motherhood.

Women of this second generation of modern housewives feel most empowered when they can monopolize child rearing, emotional resources, and services to husbands. "Beloved Wife, Successful Husband," once a motto propagated in a women's magazine in the 1970s, has become a reality. Men have finally recovered their lost sense of empowerment after long years of marginalization in modern Korean history. Young men who, in their college years, wanted to overturn the feudalistic patriarchy of their fathers, which oppressed both women and the young, have claimed the confidence of the moment and assumed primacy of place in both society and the household. Women now find their major source of empowerment as the wives of these successful men, not as mothers. The victory of wifehood over motherhood, ambiguous in the previous generation, is now fully realized. The modernization project that began with rapid economic growth in the 1960s has run its course.

The women of this generation glided into the consumer world, making themselves into attractive objects to be gazed at and purchased by desirable men (Kendall 1996, ch. 4). Young housewives, whose main playground is the department store, were particularly vulnerable to the carefully orchestrated consumer system and have been trapped by the desires it creates. South Korea became a genuine consumer society where the force of advertisements in the mass media accelerated. In the name of individuality and self-expression, the image of the feminine as embodied in a lovely and sexy woman was being constructed. Women bought the image, partly out of a desperate striving to escape their mothers' hold, to fashion themselves in their own style as promised by the new opportunities for consumption. Ironically, these newly feminine daughters were manufactured by the ambitious women of the previous generation, who encouraged them to undergo cosmetic surgery on their eyes and noses, believing that an improved appearance would change their daughters' life chances in marriage and employment. Mothers were the ones who raised these young girls to be coquettish, forced them to play the piano, and gave them a taste for luxury. Mother power still lingered on.

Choi, a sociology graduate student, used her own self-reflection to analyze why her generation cared so much about external appearances:

> I refuse to eat when my mother tries to dominate me. My mother has identified herself with food. Refusing to eat means utterly rejecting her entire being. It is so symbolic and powerful. In a way, I may be playing a game with my mother. I put on heavy makeup to tell her that my face belongs to me. Subconsciously, I want to tell her that my face is my own private matter.

Choi fasts and puts on heavy makeup because these are the only spaces she controls. She dreams of living alone, but, because she is economically dependent, she feels powerless most of the time. For young women like her, having sex with a man is also a declaration of independence and self-affirmation, at least to themselves, since they dare not disclose their secrets to their mothers.

The streets of Seoul are now filled with girlish women. Some look fragile, as if calling for protection. Women of this generation say that they want to be protected rather than to protect. Young girls who used to favor gentle "mama's boys" now turn their backs on them. They are anxious to fall in love with "tough guys" who look strong and even violent, like Choi Min-su and Lee Chong-jae, who played tough gangsters in the explosively popular 1995 television drama *Sand Clock* (*More sigye*) (*Han'guk Ilbo* 11 March 1995, B-1). Besides having a "tough guy" as a boyfriend, the women of this emerging generation want a pet. A pretty and coquettish girl, with a tiny, cute dog, beside a tough guy is part of this emergent new image.

The increased interaction between men and women, and the images propagated through the mass media, are producing young women who have a constant yearning to be sexy and attractive. The change is most noticable on university campuses. The mood that coed students create today is radically different from that of the 1980s. In the 1980s, the dominant female image was of a patriotic and intellectual woman. By the mid-1990s, campuses had filled with fashionable girls who imitated the styles of *Vogue* models or Sharon Stone in the movie *Basic Instinct*. Discovering their subjectivity away from their mothers and the weight of history, young women literally remade their faces with heavy makeup, plastic surgery, and sessions in private beauty schools. Campuses and streets became filled with model-like women with bright red lips and high heels. Some were hunting for handsome men but many claimed they were just looking for self-satisfaction.

This is the advent of narcissism. The phenomenon is noteworthy for the suddenness with which nearly every young woman has become extremely self-conscious about her looks. I may be overreacting, but I cannot but be surprised when young women spend their time and energy scrutinizing their faces and bodies, making a language out of them. Consider these student reports on the theme, "my opinion of my appearance," a topic assigned in women's studies classes:[11]

My forehead is too narrow and there is too much fat around my eyes. My nose is too flat and my cheeks are too wide. I have big hands and thick fingers. My legs are fat and not straight, my hips are like a duck's. Women became more pressured about their physical appearances as heterosexual interactions increased.

I went through an identity crisis when I gained weight. When I went shopping and found that the clothes I tried on did not fit me, I felt depressed and said to myself, "you are a fat girl." Buying clothes became a stressful event for me. I did not feel like going to meet boys. I lost my self-confidence and built a very negative self-image.

I have a bad habit that I don't approve of. Whether I walk on the street or study in the classroom, I look around and compare myself with other girls. Sometimes I feel that I am better than they are, and other times, I feel that I am less attractive than they are. More often I feel bad about myself and do not want to even look in the mirror. It is really painful for me to be on this campus which is full of pretty, sexy women.

My mother always tells me one thing, to diet so that she can take me out on the marriage market. She says that if I am fat, I will not have commercial value. So I diet every vacation.

It is not just college students, but also housewives who pay so much attention to their physical appearance. Consider this interview with a 32-year-old housewife:

> Stroll around the street and you will see all the girls who look like fancy fashion models. Think about my husband who strolls around these streets and comes home. Will he think I am a woman? If I have money and time, I want to take body fitness classes. Even if I don't have money, I want to take care of my skin, at least. If you don't have wrinkles and have good skin, any clothes will look good and makeup is also easy. Some people ask why I want to do such stupid things, but they do so out of jealousy. Give them money. . . . Nine out of ten would do exactly the same things I do. When married women (*ajumma*) like me try to attend physical fitness classes and tend to their beauty, we do so thinking that if we just made an effort, we could look as attractive as the young girls in the street.

Young wives are intensely interested in their appearance for at least two reasons: to attract their husbands' attention, and to not look like (*ajumma*), like middle-aged married women. They also know that money makes beauty. Their preoccupation with external appearances is not just a consequence of increased heterosexual interactions. Women describe social pressures from peer groups, mothers, or bosses. Among university students, a core group of women are determined to be successful professional women, but they, too, are pressured to look good. The following quotations are from interview conversations with two work-oriented women:

> When I was a sophomore, I was on a serious diet. I was not fat, but not that slender either. When I heard that competent seniors failed in their job interviews, it didn't sound like some other person's business. If you do not look reasonably good, you dare not ask for a recommendation letter from the teachers (23-year-old working woman).
>
> I have to diet. I am round like a plum and my boss keeps telling me to lose weight. They say it influences sales (24-year-old saleswoman).

Desire for an attractive appearance is a rational reaction on the part of women who know that good looks are one of the most crucial criteria for hiring women. This preference is not limited to specific jobs but applies to any regular office work for high school graduates or even college graduates. In the early 1990s, the employment document of major enterprises that was sent to women's commercial high schools specifically requested that applicants be at least 160 centimeters tall. This ignited a protest by school teachers and women's groups. School teachers were particularly upset because students were not concentrating on job training but on improving their external appearance through cosmetic surgery and crash dieting. Parents felt terrible, assuming that their own genetic make-up was responsible for their daughters' unemployment. Representatives of the personnel departments who made these requests, on the other hand, felt that this policy was reasonable insofar as attractive young women were good for the company's image and improved the atmosphere of the workplace. Many men considered this policy merely a "matter of taste" or even joked about it, saying that it was a fair policy because attractive women with no brains could have jobs too.[12]

These attitudes are pervasive. Young men joke that "a woman with a past can be forgiven but an ugly woman cannot be forgiven." Women of this generation sense that changes in the social structure leave them less and less social space. Only young and attractive girls can have power, so women find new ways to be powerful. Of course, the clothing industry also has a role here in making women more concerned about their looks. A 25-year-old working wife said this: "There are no clothes which really fit me. They must at least be right for my body, mustn't they? I just can't find them. All the stores seem to carry clothes in the recent fashion. They are made for young girls who are confident in their bodies. All the skirts are as short as four inches above the knee." Once a woman goes shopping for clothes, she feels that she has to diet. It is usual for a high school graduate to receive a cosmetic gift from female relatives and to be encouraged to do "beauty care." Following the television commercials, women believe that shiny skin is crucial to being popular and successful.

I discussed my analysis of the newly emerging generation with one of my feminist friends, Elaine, who is a Korean-American. Elaine Kim agreed with me by telling me her story. She visited Seoul about twenty years ago as a college student. At the university, all the young women tried so hard to behave like innocent ladies. Moreover, the ladies' space was severely limited. Elaine was naturally attracted to *ajumma*, who were free and powerful. She looked forward to going back when she became an *ajumma*. Elaine finally visited Korea in 1991 and found that the whole system had been changed. *Ajumma* were no longer so powerful. It was now the era of the attractive, sexy, unmarried young woman. We laughed when she said, "I missed it both times."

In this climate, the "Missy," (*misi-jŏk*) housewives, who look like young misses, has gained explosive popularity. This new image of femininity was produced by the consumer industry from its reading of the psychology of middle class housewives anxious to live active and independent lives

(So-Hee Lee in this volume). The story behind the Missy-driven marketing campaign is that a copywriter had an image of "a young housewife who
is somewhat independent, reasonable, and who knows how to make herself
look like a college girl, not a middle-aged *ajumma*." A washing-machine
commercial based on this image was a big hit (So Chung-sin, *Chung-ang
Ilbo* 14 October 1994). In the commercial, the behavioral principles for the
Missy were specified as follows:

> 1) Never give off the air of an *ajumma*. 2) My husband and the children are
> important, but I invest in myself. 3) I am a professional at housekeeping. 4) I
> know how to save money by shopping during the sale season.

Since the early twentieth century, the image of the diligent wife who
puts on makeup neatly competed with the image of the frugal wife who
would not spend money on decorating herself. Now wives are asked to be
both attractive and budget minded. The *ajumma* who does not take care of
her appearance and does not spend money on herself is condemned. The
new patriarchy of consumer capitalism and postmodern culture finds these
women a nuisance and demands that women try to be ever young and
attractive *agassi*. Why don't we see a similar shift in the men's world?
Chong'gak, the term for unmarried young men, has never been favored over
ajŏssi, a term for married men.

The Missy syndrome is here to stay, having been adopted by the media
and then perpetuated by the housewives themselves to indicate both home-
makers who manage to look like misses and housewives who lead active
and independent lives.

Despite young women's expressed enthusiasm for careers, do we now
have a new group of full-time housewives who accept the position of wife
and mother as naturally as their grandmothers did? What will be the social
implications of this change? What of the daughters of Missy housewives
who will be raised from childhood to be fundamentally concerned with
external appearances and who will grow accustomed to being "gazed"
objects as a matter of course?

DISCUSSION: GENDER, CLASS, AND GENERATION

The image of the powerful Korean woman is the product of an aborted and
colonized modernity. This image could be applied properly to the grandmother's and mother's generations but not to the daughter's generation.

When the family unit was the most crucial social unit and women, as mothers and wives, were central to its survival and advancement, women were powerful. But the image of the powerful woman is changing rapidly as south Korean society embraces consumer capitalism. To most women of the daughter's generation, the image of the powerful woman belongs to the age of their struggling mothers and grandmothers who lived through Korea's unfortunate modern history. It is not an attractive model.

The image of modern women needs to be assessed in relation to the image of defensive/nationalistic men. As private persons, middle class housewives could transform themselves into modern women while doing the work of status reproduction. In the public domain, men maintained face while the white-collar workplace bred conformity and conservatism. At the same time, women in the private domain of domesticity and informal economic transactions transformed themselves out of necessity in their struggles to be included in the new middle class.

As middle class women become the major target of the mass media, while men remain at the economy-driven work place, the cultural and emotional distance between the modern woman and the feudal man will continue to grow. Transformations of women's role and image have taken place swiftly as Korean society has regained self-confidence with rapid economic growth over the last several decades. As old patriarchs have been replaced by new, modern ones, their female counterparts have had to change their clothes twice, once from motherly clothes to wifely ones, and then again to those of attractive, sexy young girls.

The transformation from mother to wife signified that the transition from feudal/rural society to industrial/urban society had been completed, at least in form. The second transition appeared much more suddenly as the women of the mother's generation were perceived to be too aggressive, oppressive to both men's and daughters' individuality. At the same time, the job market has not expanded to meet young women's high aspirations for employment, a situation compounded by the financial crisis of 1997. In such a gloomy situation, young women attempt to secure their own space and new resources for power. They are back in the domestic realm but they have discovered the power of their female bodies. Women of the new generation no longer identify themselves as mothers and wives but as individuals. They try to make the family home a site of self-realization through consumption.

In this age of advertising, it seems normal that competency in the presentation of self is crucial for both men's and women's social success. However, it is women who have jumped, full force, into image management. Young women, who are desperate to be different from their mother's generation, have finally found an outlet in images. Young women now want to be psychocultural beings, not hardworking laborers like their mothers. As in John Berger's description, Korean society is approaching the point where "men act and women appear" (1977, 47).

POSSIBLE SITES FOR FEMINIST INTERVENTION IN THE ERA OF POSTMODERN FEMININITY

What does this recent change mean for a feminist? Throughout the 1980s, feminists had been making gradual progress in the family and in the workplace, but in recent years we find ourselves at a loss. However different they might appear, the women of the three generations discussed in this chapter know that the world they inhabit is male-centered, and most of them believe that it will be so for quite a long time to come. The roles and images of women were transformed in the bustle of modernization without any accompanying change in the deep structure of gender relations: Women exist for men's everyday living and to cater to the male ego. Modernity, understood as the birth of the individual, is for the male gender, while modernity, expressed in status and materialistic display, is for the female gender. Moreover, the homo-social world of Korean women is rapidly disintegrating.

I do not fantasize about an era in which motherly women of the grandmother's generation struggled for survival. While I do not like the image of aggressive, managerial mothers, I cherish the homosocial world of the *ajumma*, the ordinary married woman. The distinctively materialistic and instrumental culture animated by the middle class women of the mother's generation has been, in fact, oppressive to women of other classes and to their daughter's generation. The image of Missy wives is just another variation on the *samonim* culture, causing many other women to suffer in relative deprivation. While the patriarchs are busy restoring the nation's glory after long years of foreign domination, women are divided along several lines: housewives and professional women, *samonim* and *ajumma*, Missy wives and professional singles, and aggressive *samonim* and their passive daughters. The antagonism among them is rising. While the women's liberation movement produced a group of independent and able women active in the public sphere, this seems only to have compounded the frustration of housewives and to be irrelevant to the confused, sexy young women who appeared on the streets of 1990s Korea. It is in this context that feminists need to find a new means of intervention.

There are several areas where south Korean feminists must be attentive. First, motherhood requires a critical reexamination. Feminists need to be engaged in an intensive discussion about compulsory or institutionalized motherhood. Modernization, with only minimum change in the domestic-public dichotomy, has resulted in a large number of able women who instrumentalize their children, deploying them in competitive status games. Motherhood, as an institution of caring and communication, is superseded by instrumentality which, in turn, reinforces the materialism and instrumentality of society in general.

Modern patriarchy's ability to reinforce itself by maintaining the woman's identity as child bearer is an area that demands critical examination. Unless this fundamental definition can be changed, feminists' attempts to make any changes will fail. Why is south Korean society such a difficult place for unmarried women to live confidently? How long does a housewife without a son have to tolerate harassment from relatives and neighbors? In order to achieve the minimum space for a Korean woman to live on her own, one must understand the cultural and political technology of compulsory motherhood. It is not enough to change the family law; we must also change patriarchal life patterns, learn to accommodate ritualistic visits to both sets of parents equally for *chesa* (ancestor veneration) and at other ceremonious occasions. Secondly, feminists need to pay more attention to generational differences in experiences among Korean women. We all know that there is no one fixed space from which all women speak in a sovereign voice. Women have stood in "a variety of generational and class positions which have been discursively articulated in history"(Rofel 1994, 248). The three generations of women who experienced condensed modernization use totally different cultural premises and language to organize their lives.

While many women of the mother's generation in south Korea seemed to be aware of the gender contradictions in their lives, they tried to solve them not by confronting the patriarchal system but by merely climbing up the social ladder. Their efforts have contributed to the formation of a peculiar class structure in south Korea. Moreover, it is a tragedy that the shift of a woman's image from the industrious and resourceful *ajumma* to the indolent and private *agassi* has been accelerated in part by the desires of these domineering and pushy women of the mother's generation. Mothers' toil did not improve their daughter's lot.

Women of the younger generation find that they have more in common with Western women of their generation than with older women in south Korea. When I assigned Harriet Fraad's (1990) article, "Anorexia

Nervosa: The Female Body as a Site of Gender and Class Transition," female students responded with enthusiasm. They said that the paper dealt with their own experiences. The students seemed to be somewhat relieved to discover that many American women were obsessed with their bodily beauty for reasons similar to their own, and to recognize that they had been made to objectify their own bodies, to make them desirable to someone else (cf. Fraad 1990, 83).[13]

As global capitalism expands its pervasive power, there is a trend toward homogenizing women's status and images. Can discovering the body and sexuality be a new outlet for resistance? Will having a site for self-affirmation lead to a new naturalization of oppression? I ask this kind of question these days and try to come up with a postmodern solution for these postmodern girls. Fortunately, we realize "the experience of co-suffering," to use Ashis Nandy's (1987, 54) term, which has brought the modern world close together. In this space, women of the mass-media generation—both East and West—can work together. Here, I see the importance of generational politics, which must begin with a clear recognition of the experiential difference of each generation. Different issues and strategies need to be explored according to different generational experiences, which transcend national boundaries. I see now the increasing importance of media activism on a global scale.

AFTERWORD: AFTER THE FINANCIAL CRISIS OF 1997

As might be expected, young women who had found their jobs with such difficulty were the first to be laid off. As a consequence, the divide between family and profession that bisects the community of women has become even more acute. On one side of the division, women are even more deeply invested in marriage, while on the other, women are preoccupied with honing their skills and succeeding on the company entrance exam. Also, as opportunities for professional women have expanded with the transformation of the nation-state, competent and talented women aspire to work in the global sector. But when one looks at the dominant culture, one sees the gathering strength of a new conservatism under the banner of "Let's protect our fathers who have lost their vitality" or "Let's restore the authority of the family head." In opposition, new women's subcultures are stubbornly taking shape. At the heart of these developments is a new independent lifestyle that has emerged in response to a growing number of divorced and never-married women and the lifestyle of the younger generation. The emergence of diverse social groups, the rise of class polarization, and the feminization of poverty place marriage under siege, intensifying the polarization of the community of women. We must heed the direction of these trends as they unfold.

NOTES

I am grateful to Laurel Kendall and Nancy Abelmann, who read this chapter carefully and edited it. Once I was back in Seoul, it was painful to write a chapter in English. Without Laurel's patience and understanding, this chapter would be still in an utterly disorganized file box, ever incomplete. I told Laurel that this might be the last piece I write in English. My brain does not function properly when I think in a foreign language, I said. Korean studies needs to have excellent translators who are bilingual. I await them anxiously.

1. The image of Yi Sang, a patriotic poet in the 1920s, drunkenly weeping over the loss of his beloved nation, has been the archetypal image of Korean male intellectuals. Henry Em's an insightful reading of Yi Sang's "Wings" (1995) suggests that it can be read "as an allegory of how an entire generation of intellectuals sought to survive in a colonial setting by becoming entirely private, shielding themselves with self-deceptions until even that became impossible" (106). The narrator of the short story, according to Em, puts on an idiot-child mask (representing the emasculated intellectual), which allows him to exist within the pervasive and alien colonized culture without being assimilated by it. To Em, "Wings" should be read as a national allegory that is counter-hegemonic, that is, anticolonial and anticapitalist (109).

2. Recently, feminists have raised the issue of the Japanese Imperial Army's conscription of Korean women as "comfort women," gaining international attention through the United Nations. Most south Korean male leaders, both in politics and intellectual circles, simply want to put the problem away, saying, "It's shameful. Let's just not talk about it."

3. Here, I am reminded of an early Christian missionary's comment that a Korean woman of her acquaintance "was the real man in resourcefulness, energy, and ability to manage. Many Korean women do that, however, and they are quite used to it" (Underwood 1905, 222–223). Wolf (1972) describes how Chinese women forge "uterine families" as bastions of strength within the similarly Confucian Chinese family; her discussion has much in common with the dynamics of the Korean family.

4. Editor's note: For an account of a lower class woman, similarly resourceful in desperate times but bereft of family solidarity and resources, consider the mother's story in *The Life and Hard Times of a Korean Shaman* (Kendall 1988). Even the dream of a child's university education is remote from her experience.

5. The decline of the rural population was drastic. At the time of the Liberation, only 13 percent of the peninsula's population was living in settlements of over 50,000 persons, and approximately 80 percent were living in rural settlements of under 20,000 persons. The population in settlements of over 100,000 grew by 117 percent during the 1970s. In 1975, the urban population was 48.4 percent of the total population. By the middle of the 1980s, only 24 percent was rural (Cho Haejoang 1984, 195–196).

6. The average schooling of this generation (born between 1937 and 1946) is 8.52 years. For men, it is 9.88 years, for women 7.14 years (Kang 1996, 594).

7. Toward the end of the Meiji era, Baron Kikuchi, one-time Minister of Education and President of both Tokyo and Kyoto Universities, defined the goal of female education as follows (quoted in Smith 1983, 75):

> Our female education, then, is based on the assumption that women marry, and that its object is to fit girls to become "good wives and wise mothers." The question naturally arises what constitutes a good wife and wise mother, and the answer to the question requires a knowledge of the position of the wife and mother in the household and the standing of women in society and her status in the State.... [The] man goes outside to work to earn his living, to fulfill his duties to the State; it is the wife's part to help him, for the common interests of the house, and as her share of duty to the State, by sympathy and encouragement, by relieving him of anxieties at home, managing household affairs, looking after the household economy, and, above all, tending the old people and bringing up the children in a fit and proper manner.

8. Kendall's (1996) extensive study on modern south Korean practices of marriage and dowry describes various media treatments of extravagance. She notes that upper-middle class housewives, who orchestrate their childrens' weddings, are the common butt of criticism.

9. Editor's note: See Fulton and Fulton (1997, 139–160) for a translation of this story as "Identical Apartments."

10. Editor's note: *Yoksim* is usually translated as "greed", but implies a relentless appetite for wealth or recognition, an intense, driving craving.

11. These responses are from classes taught by Kim Eun-Shil and Yi Myong-son at Ewha Women's University in the spring of 1994.

12. Forty-four companies were accused of violating the equal opportunity employment law because of such hiring practices. In December 1994, the judge found eight companies guilty of this violation and asked them to pay a million wŏn (about US$1,300) in penalty. The rest of them were found not guilty because the competition was among members of the same sex with no comparable group from the other sex.

13. Fraad considers one of the cultural conditions contributing to anorexia to be a gender ideology that presents women as sex objects. She writes, "We learn what we look like rather than how to feel and know the sensations of our bodies. We are dependent upon external reinforcement for being attractive and sexy. Attractiveness is verified by those one attracts. Women's own sexuality, our own desire, is not cultivated as our own experience but the experience of being desirable to someone else" (1990, 83). The other condition Fraad discusses is a period of class and gender transition where the contraction of women's existence is dramatized by their being neither firmly situated in a male-supported household nor in emergent roles in both the household and the marketplace (1990, 82). Fraad concludes her paper thus:

> The seeming contractions in anorectic behavior express the conflict between current expectations of women and a past with which we are now breaking. For hundreds of years, women's primary labor has been socially defined as the production of household goods, services, and nurturance. Now, women are expected to maintain their roles as homemakers while succeeding at labor in the marketplace, all the while disciplining ourselves to fit media images of feminine attractiveness. Whereas formerly we had one master, the male head of the household, now we have three masters: men, bosses, and the media, all giving simultaneous contradictory directives. The radical break in ambitious, modern lives erupts in the form of eating disturbances expressing the rupture between generations of daughters and their mothers (Fraad 1990, 97–98).

REFERENCES

Berger, John. 1977. *Ways of Seeing*. New York: Penguin Books.

Bourdieu, Pierre. 1984. *Distinction: A Social Critique of the Judgement of Taste*. Cambridge, Mass.: Harvard University Press.

Cho Haejoang. 1984. Republic of Korea: Those left behind. In *Women in the Villages, Men in the Towns: Women in a World Perspective*. UNESCO, ed. pp. 187–246. Paris, France: Imprimérie de la Manutention.

Choi, Jae-sok. 1983. *Han'guk kajok chedo-sa yŏn'gu* (A historical study of Korean family institution). Seoul: Ilji-sa.

Choi Myŏng-hee. 1983. *Honbul* (Spirit Fire). Seoul: Tonga Ilbo-sa.

Choi, Won-sik. 1995. Book review. *Han'guk Ilbo*. February 9.

Chŏng Yang-wan. 1985. Kyubŏmryurŭl t'onghaebon Han'guk yŏsŏngŭi chŏnt'ongsange taehayŏ (The traditional image of Korean women based on norms), In *Han'guk Yŏsŏngŭi Chŏnt'ongsang*. Ha Hyŏn-gang, et. al., eds. pp. 49–71. Seoul: Minumsa.

Chŏng Yo-sŏb. 1973. Chosŏn wangjo sidae e issŏsŏ yŏsŏngŭi chiwi (Women's status in the Chosŏn period). *Asea yŏsŏng yŏn'gu* (Journal of Asian women's studies) 12:103–122.

Em, Henry H. 1995. "Wings" as colonial allegory: An anti-colonialist interpretation of Yi Sang's most widely read work. *Muae* 1:104–111.

Fraad, Harriet. 1990. Anorexia nervosa: The female body as a site of gender and class transition. *Rethinking Marxism* vol. 3 (3–4):79–99.

Fulton, Bruce, and Ju-Chan Fulton, eds. and trans. 1997. *Wayfarer: New Fiction by Korean Women*. Seattle: Women in Translation.

Guha, Ranajit. 1985. Some aspects of the historiography of colonial India. In *Subaltern Studies: Writings on South Asian History and Society*. pp. 37–44. Delhi: Oxford University Press.

Janelli, Roger L. with Dawnhee Yim. 1993. *Making Capitalism: The Social and Cultural Construction of a South Korean Conglomerate*. Stanford, Calif.: Stanford University Press.

Kang, In-sun. 1996. *The Challenged Generation: The Fifties in South Korea*. Sindonga, March. Tonga Ilbosa.

Kendall, Laurel. 1985. *Shamans, Housewives, and Other Restless Spirits: Women in Korean Ritual Life*. pp. 5–21. Honolulu: University of Hawai'i Press.

———. 1988. *The Life and Hard Times of a Korean Shaman: Of Tales and the Telling of Tales*. Honolulu: University of Hawai'i Press.

———. 1996. *Getting Married in Korea: Of Gender, Morality, and Modernity*. Berkeley: University of California Press.

Kendall, Laurel, and M. Peterson, eds. 1983. Introduction. In *Korean Women: View from the Inner Room*. pp. 5–21. New Haven: East Rock Press.

Kim Chŏng-han. 1988. *Surado. Kim Chong-han Sosŏl Sŏnjip* (Collection of short stories). pp 204–262. Seoul: Changjak kwa pop'yŏngsa.

Kim, Elaine. 1988. Men's talk: A Korean American view of south Korean constructions of women, gender, and masculinity. In *Dangerous Women: Gender and Korean Nationalism*. Elaine H. Kim and Chungmoo Choi, eds. pp. 67–107. New York: Routledge.

Kim, Eun-shil. 1993. The making of the modern female gender: The politics of gender in reproductive practices in Korea. Ph.D. dissertation. University of California, Berkeley.

Kim Yong-ok. 1986. *Yŏjaran muŏssinkka?* (What is a woman?) Seoul: T'ongnamu.

Kong Chi-yŏng. 1993. *Mussoŭi ppulchŏrŏm hon'jasŏ kara* (Go alone like the rhinoceros's horn). Seoul: Munye madang.

Lee Dong-won, Kim Mo-ran, and Kim Hyun-ju. 1995. Namyŏ taehaksaeng ŭi sŏngyŏkhal model-gwa chuyŏp mit kyŏrhon'gwan (Differences in the expectations of employment and marriage based on their sex role models: Comparing female and male university students.) *Han'guk Munwha Non Chong* (Journal of Korean cultural research institute) 66(2):192–212.

Lee Hyon-hee. 1979. *Han'guk kŭndae yosŏng kewha sa* (The history of enlightenment of Korean women). Seoul: Iwo publisher.

Lipman-Blumen, Jean. 1976. Toward a homo-social theory of sex roles: An explanation of the sex segregation of social institutions. *Signs: A Journal of Women in Culture and Society* 3:15–31.

Mohanty, Chandra. 1991. *Third World Women and the Politics of Feminism.* Bloomington: Indiana University Press.

Moon, Seungsook. 1994. Economic development and gender politics in south Korea (1963–1992). Ph.D. diss. Brandeis University.

Nolte, Sharon H. and Sally Ann Hastings. 1991. The Meiji state's policy toward women, 1890–1910. In *Recreating Japanese Women, 1600–1945.* Gail Lee Bernstein, ed. pp. 151–174. Berkeley: University of California Press.

Nandy, Ashis. 1987. *Tradition, Tyranny and Utopias: Essays in the Politics of Awareness.* Delhi: Oxford University Press.

Pak Wan-sŏ. 1985. Talmŭn pangdŭl (Identical rooms). In *Kŭ kaŭlŭi sahŭl tongan* (For the three days in that autumn). pp. 345–361. Seoul: Nanam Pub.

Park Kyong-ri. 1973. *Tŏji* (*The Land*). Seoul: Munhak Sasangsa.

Park Yong-ok. 1985. Yugyojŏk yosŏnggwanŭi chejomyŏng (Re-examination of Confucian thought on women). *Korean Women's Studies* vol. 1. Seoul: Korean Association of Women's Studies.

Rofel, Lisa. 1994. Liberation nostalgia and a yearning for modernity. In *Engendering China: Women, Culture, and the State.* Christina K. Gilmartin, et al., eds. pp. 345–361. Cambridge, Mass.: Harvard University Press.

Smith, R. J. 1983. Making village women into good wives and wise mothers in prewar Japan. *Journal of Family History* 8(1):70–84.

So Chung-sin. 1994. *Chungang Ilbo.* Women's Lives Section. October 14.

Sun Lee. 1981. *Uridŭlŭi aidŭl* (Our children). Seoul: Munhak kwa Chisŏng Sa.

Tinker, I. 1980. *Toward Equity for Women in Korea's Developmental Plans.* Report prepared for the World Bank, UNDP Korea Project ROK 78 002.

Underwood, Lilias Horton. 1984. *Ŏndŏwodu puinŭi Chosŏn saenghwal* (The life of Mrs. Underwood in Chosŏn a translation of fifteen years among the top-knots [first published 1905]). Seoul: Ppuri Kip'ŭn Namu.

Yim Dawnhee. 1986. Chŏng'gyo wa musok (Religion and shamanism.). In *Yŏsŏnghakŭi iron kwa silje* (Theory and reality of women's studies) pp. 137–143. Seoul: Tongguk University.

Yoon Hye-won. 1973. Kŭnse Han'guk yosŏngŭi sahoejŏk chiwi e kwanhan yŏn'gu (A study of the social position of Korean women in early modernity). *Asea Yŏsŏng Yŏn'gu,* vol. 12. Seoul: Sookmyung Women's University.

Wolf, Margery. 1972. *Women and the Family in Rural Taiwan.* Stanford, Calif.: Stanford University Press.

Contributors

Nancy Abelmann is the author of *Echoes of the Past, Epics of Dissent: A South Korean Social Movement* (University of California Press, 1996) and coauthor with John Lie of *Blue Dreams: Korean Americans and the Los Angeles Riots* (Harvard University Press, 1995). She also is the author of several recent articles on gender and social mobility. She holds a Ph.D. in anthropology from the University of California, Berkeley, and is currently an associate professor in anthropology and East Asian studies at the University of Illinois at Urbana-Champaign.

Cho Haejoang, a founding member of the Korean feminist Alternative Culture Group (Ttohanaŭi Munhwa), is the author of several works on gender and popular culture, including *Korean Women and Men* (Munhaggwa chisŏngsa, 1988) and the popular three-volume series, *Reading Texts, Reading Everyday Lives* (Alternative Culture, 1994), both in Korean. She holds a Ph.D. in anthropology from the University of California, Los Angeles, and is currently a professor in the Sociology Department at Yonsei University. She is also a director of the Center for Youth and Cultural Studies in Seoul.

Roger L. Janelli coauthored *Ancestor Worship and Korean Society* (Stanford University Press, 1982) and *Making Capitalism: The Social and Cultural Construction of a South Korean Conglomerate* (Stanford University Press, 1993). He also coedited *The Anthropology of Korea: East Asia Perspectives* (Japanese National Museum of Ethnology, 1998). Janelli holds a position as Professor of Folklore and East Asian Langauges and Cultures at Indiana University.

Laurel Kendall is the author of *Shamans, Housewives, and Other Restless Spirits: Women in Korean Ritual Life* (University of Hawai'i Press, 1985), *The Life and Hard Times of a Korean Shaman: Of Tales and the Telling of Tales* (University of Hawai'i Press, 1988), and *Getting Married in Korea: Of Gender, Morality, and Modernity* (University of California Press, 1996). She is also coeditor of volumes on Korean women, Korean ritual life, and religion and the modern nation states of east and southeast Asia. She holds a Ph.D. in anthropology from Columbia University. Kendall is Curator of Asian Ethnographic Collections at the American Museum of Natural History as well as Adjunct Professor in the Department of Anthropology at Columbia University.

June J. H. Lee received her Ph.D. from the Department of Anthropology at the University of Hawai'i in 1998. She has several publications on the gendered discourses surrounding health food consumption in contemporary Korea. She heads the International Organization for Migration, Seoul Office, where she works on issues involving migration and health.

So-Hee Lee was a British Council Research Fellow at Girton College, University of Cambridge in 1986-1987 and received her M.A. from the University of Hull in 1988. She holds two Ph.D.s in literature, one from Hanyang University (1996) and one from the University of Hull (1998). She is currently working on issues of postcolonialism, gender, and globalization. Her article "Nationality, Territoriality, and Communication: Korean Context/Canadian Test" will appear in *Feminisms on Edge: Politics, Discourses and National Identities*, edited by Gill Plain (Cardiff Academic Press, forthcoming). Lee is an Associate Professor in the English Department at Hanyang Women's College in Seoul, Korea, where she has taught since 1989; she also teaches at Hanyang University and Kyunghee University.

Seungsook Moon earned a Ph.D. in sociology from Brandeis University and is Assistant Professor of Sociology at Vassar College. Her most recent publication includes "Overcome by Globalization: The Rise of a Women's Policy in South Korea" in *Korea's Globalization*, edited by Samuel S. Kim (Cambridge University Press, 2000). She is currently working on a book examining the role of military service and the social organization of gender in South Korea.

Dawnhee Yim authored the Korean-language *Explorations in American Culture* (P'yŏngminsa, 1995) and coauthored *Ancestor Worship and Korean Society* (Stanford University Press, 1982) and *Making Capitalism: The Social and Cultural Construction of a South Korean Conglomerate* (Stanford University Press, 1993). A former president of the Korean Society for Cultural Anthropology, she holds a Ph.D. from the University of Pennsylvania and is Professor in the History Department of Dongguk University, Seoul.

Index